Docker on Windows

From 101 to production with Docker on Windows

Elton Stoneman

BIRMINGHAM - MUMBAI

Docker on Windows

First published: July 2017

Production reference: 1120717

Published by Packt Publishing Ltd.
Livery Place
35 Livery Street
Birmingham
B3 2PB, UK.

ISBN 978-1-78528-165-5

www.packtpub.com

Credits

Author
Elton Stoneman

Reviewer
Shashikant Bangera

Commissioning Editor
Kartikey Pandey

Acquisition Editor
Rahul Nair

Content Development Editor
Sharon Raj

Technical Editors
Mohit Hassija
Komal Karne

Copy Editor
Stuti Srivastava

Project Coordinator
Virginia Dias

Proofreader
Safis Editing

Indexer
Aishwarya Gangawane

Graphics
Kirk D'Penha

Production Coordinator
Aparna Bhagat

About the Author

Elton Stoneman has been a Microsoft MVP for 8 years and a Pluralsight author for 5 years, and now he works for Docker, Inc. Before joining Docker, he spent 15 years as a consultant, architecting and delivering very large and very successful solutions built on .NET and powered by Windows and Azure.

All the years he worked with Windows, Elton had a secret Linux server in his attic or garage, running core services for the home, such as music servers and file servers. When Docker started to take hold in the Linux world, Elton had early experience in a cross-platform project he worked on, got hooked, and started to focus on containers. He was made a Docker Captain, and for a time, was one of only two people in the world who were both a Microsoft MVP and a Docker Captain.

Elton blogs about Docker, tweets about Docker, and speaks about Docker all the time. He is a regular at local events and user groups; you will often see him at Docker London, London DevOps, and WinOps London. He's also had great fun speaking at fantastic conferences around the world, including DockerCon, NDC London, SDD, DevSum, and NDC Oslo.

You can't write a 300-page technical book without a lot of late nights, a lot of support, and a decent bean-to-cup coffee machine. Support is the most important of those, after the coffee machine. There are a lot of people I would like to thank. Everyone I work with at Docker, Inc. is exceptional, but Michael Friis and Brandon Royal are the pioneers of Docker on Windows and their work is driving this important technology forward. The Docker Captains are a fabulous group of people, and I have learned a great deal from Stefan Scherer and all his community contributions. And my friends and family are just all-out awesome, especially Nikki and Jackson.

About the Reviewer

Shashikant Bangera is a DevOps architect with 17 years of IT experience. He has vast experience of DevOps tools across the platform, with core expertise in CI, CD, and aPaaS. He has helped his customers adopt DevOps, and has architected and implemented Enterprise DevOps for various domains, such as banking, e-commerce, and retail. He has also contributed to many open sources platforms, such as DevOps Publication. He has designed an automated on-demand environment with a set of open source tools and also an environment booking tool, which is available on GitHub.

He has reviewed two Docker books for Packt: *Learning Docker* and *Docker High Performance*.

www.PacktPub.com

For support files and downloads related to your book, please visit www.PacktPub.com. Did you know that Packt offers eBook versions of every book published, with PDF and ePub files available? You can upgrade to the eBook version at www.PacktPub.com and as a print book customer, you are entitled to a discount on the eBook copy. Get in touch with us at service@packtpub.com for more details. At www.PacktPub.com, you can also read a collection of free technical articles, sign up for a range of free newsletters and receive exclusive discounts and offers on Packt books and eBooks.

https://www.packtpub.com/mapt

Get the most in-demand software skills with Mapt. Mapt gives you full access to all Packt books and video courses, as well as industry-leading tools to help you plan your personal development and advance your career.

Why subscribe?

- Fully searchable across every book published by Packt
- Copy and paste, print, and bookmark content
- On demand and accessible via a web browser

Customer Feedback

Thanks for purchasing this Packt book. At Packt, quality is at the heart of our editorial process. To help us improve, please leave us an honest review on this book's Amazon page at `http://www.amazon.in/dp/1785281658`. If you'd like to join our team of regular reviewers, you can email us at `customerreviews@packtpub.com`. We award our regular reviewers with free eBooks and videos in exchange for their valuable feedback. Help us be relentless in improving our products!

Table of Contents

Preface

Docker is a platform for running server applications in lightweight units called containers. You can run Docker on Windows Server 2016 and Windows 10, and run your existing apps in containers to get significant improvements in efficiency, security, and portability. This book teaches you all you need to know about Docker on Windows, from 101 to deploying highly available workloads in production.

What this book covers

Chapter 1, *Getting Started with Docker on Windows*, introduces the Docker runtime and walks through the options for running Docker on Windows, covering Docker Toolbox for older client versions, native Docker for Windows 10 and Windows Server 2016, and running Docker hosted on an Azure VM.

Chapter 2, *Packaging and Running Applications as Docker Containers*, focuses on the Docker image: a packaged application with all its dependencies that will run in the same way on any host that can run Docker. We'll see how to build Docker images with a Dockerfile for a simple website, and then run it on Windows.

Chapter 3, *Developing Dockerized .NET and .NET Core Applications*, shows how we can build applications with Microsoft technologies that can run on any operating system. .NET Core apps run equally on Windows (including Nano Server) and Linux, and they are ideally suited for packaging into a portable Docker container.

Chapter 4, *Pushing and Pulling Images from Docker Registries*, will look at publishing images we build in development and using automated builds, hooking Docker Hub into GitHub so new container image versions are built when code gets pushed. The chapter will also cover running your own private Docker registry for internal use.

Chapter 5, *Adopting Container-First Solution Design*, builds on the previous chapters, showing how the range of high-quality Docker images makes it straightforward to design distributed solutions, and mixing off-the-shelf images with custom ones. The Windows slant here is that you can run Windows hosts and manage them in the same way as other machines, but they could be running Linux software inside a Docker container.

Chapter 6, *Organizing Distributed Solutions with Docker Compose,* takes the ad hoc distributed solution from Chapter 5, *Adopting Container-First Solution Design* and builds it into a deployable package using Docker Compose--with a Docker Network so containers can communicate using hostnames. The chapter will also cover the structure of the Docker Compose YAML file and the runtime for Docker Compose.

Chapter 7, *Orchestrating Distributed Solutions with Docker Swarm,* covers production-ready clustering with Docker Swarm, briefly introducing the old Docker Swarm product for awareness, but focusing on the new Swarm Mode built into Docker from version 1.12. We'll set up a Swarm running on Windows in Azure, explore how the Routing Mesh works, and look at service discovery and reliability by deploying the solution from Chapter 6, *Organizing Distributed Solutions with Docker Compose* as Swarm services.

Chapter 8, *Administering and Monitoring Dockerized Solutions,* covers management of distributed Docker solutions. You'll see how to set up log shipping so container logs are sent to a central location, use both free and commercial tools to visualize the containers in a Swarm, and learn how to do rolling upgrades of a running service.

Chapter 9, *Understanding the Security Risks and Benefits of Docker,* covers the key aspects of Docker security: the risks of having multiple containers on one node, the potential for an attacker to compromise one container and access others, and how to mitigate that. We'll also look at how Docker improves security, with vulnerability scanning for images built into Docker Hub and Docker Trusted Registry and flagging security issues with the software inside images. Lastly, we'll cover built-in security between nodes in Docker Swarm.

Chapter 10, *Powering a Continuous Deployment Pipeline with Docker,* covers Docker in a DevOps workflow, where everything is automated. We'll build out a whole deployment pipeline using Docker, running GitLab for source control and builds, which will package a new Docker image when code is pushed, run automated tests, and deploy to a test environment.

Chapter 11, *Debugging and Instrumenting Application Containers,* looks at troubleshooting Docker containers during both build and run. We will cover how to structure the Dockerfile so that infrequently changing layers are preserved and containers are quicker to build, and see the best way to build up an image. For running containers, we'll cover viewing the logs, checking process performance, and connecting to the container for exploratory checks.

Chapter 12, *Containerize What You Know: Guidance for Implementing Docker,* will look at containerizing existing software stacks for non-production deployment, and also extracting a vertical slice from an application that can run in Docker, as a first move toward a microservice architecture.

What you need for this book

To execute the examples given in this book, you will need the following:

- Docker for Windows 17.06 or later
- Windows 10 or Windows Server 2016

Who this book is for

If you want to modernize an old monolithic application without rewriting it, smooth the deployment to production, or move to DevOps or the cloud, then Docker is the enabler for you. This book gives you a solid grounding in Docker so you can confidently approach all of these scenarios.

Conventions

In this book, you will find a number of text styles that distinguish between different kinds of information. Here are some examples of these styles and an explanation of their meaning. Code words in text, database table names, folder names, filenames, file extensions, pathnames, dummy URLs, user input, and Twitter handles are shown as follows: "If you run `docker container ls`, which lists all the active containers, you won't see this container."

A block of code is set as follows:

```
FROM microsoft/nanoserver
COPY scripts/print-env-details.ps1 c:\\print-env.ps1
CMD ["powershell.exe", "c:\\print-env.ps1"]
```

When we wish to draw your attention to a particular part of a code block, the relevant lines or items are set in bold:

```
FROM microsoft/nanoserver
COPY scripts/print-env-details.ps1 c:\\print-env.ps1
CMD ["powershell.exe", "c:\\print-env.ps1"]
```

Any command-line input or output is written as follows:

```
docker container run dockeronwindows/ch01-whale
```

New terms and **important words** are shown in bold. Words that you see on the screen, for example, in menus or dialog boxes, appear in the text like this: "In order to download new modules, we will go to **Files** | **Settings** | **Project Name** | **Project Interpreter**."

 Warnings or important notes appear like this.

 Tips and tricks appear like this.

Reader feedback

Feedback from our readers is always welcome. Let us know what you think about this book-what you liked or disliked. Reader feedback is important for us as it helps us develop titles that you will really get the most out of. To send us general feedback, simply e-mail feedback@packtpub.com, and mention the book's title in the subject of your message. If there is a topic that you have expertise in and you are interested in either writing or contributing to a book, see our author guide at www.packtpub.com/authors.

Customer support

Now that you are the proud owner of a Packt book, we have a number of things to help you to get the most from your purchase.

Downloading the example code

You can download the example code files for this book from your account at http://www.packtpub.com. If you purchased this book elsewhere, you can visit http://www.packtpub.com/support and register to have the files e-mailed directly to you. You can download the code files by following these steps:

1. Log in or register to our website using your e-mail address and password.
2. Hover the mouse pointer on the **SUPPORT** tab at the top.
3. Click on **Code Downloads & Errata**.

4. Enter the name of the book in the **Search** box.
5. Select the book for which you're looking to download the code files.
6. Choose from the drop-down menu where you purchased this book from.
7. Click on **Code Download**.

Once the file is downloaded, please make sure that you unzip or extract the folder using the latest version of:

- WinRAR / 7-Zip for Windows
- Zipeg / iZip / UnRarX for Mac
- 7-Zip / PeaZip for Linux

The code bundle for the book is also hosted on GitHub at `https://github.com/PacktPubl ishing/Docker-on-Windows`. We also have other code bundles from our rich catalog of books and videos available at `https://github.com/PacktPublishing/`. Check them out!

Downloading the color images of this book

We also provide you with a PDF file that has color images of the screenshots/diagrams used in this book. The color images will help you better understand the changes in the output. You can download this file from `https://www.packtpub.com/sites/default/files/downloads/DockeronWindows_ColorIma ges.pdf`.

Errata

Although we have taken every care to ensure the accuracy of our content, mistakes do happen. If you find a mistake in one of our books-maybe a mistake in the text or the code- we would be grateful if you could report this to us. By doing so, you can save other readers from frustration and help us improve subsequent versions of this book. If you find any errata, please report them by visiting `http://www.packtpub.com/submit-errata`, selecting your book, clicking on the **Errata Submission Form** link, and entering the details of your errata. Once your errata are verified, your submission will be accepted and the errata will be uploaded to our website or added to any list of existing errata under the Errata section of that title. To view the previously submitted errata, go to `https://www.packtpub.com/book s/content/support` and enter the name of the book in the search field. The required information will appear under the **Errata** section.

Piracy

Piracy of copyrighted material on the Internet is an ongoing problem across all media. At Packt, we take the protection of our copyright and licenses very seriously. If you come across any illegal copies of our works in any form on the Internet, please provide us with the location address or website name immediately so that we can pursue a remedy. Please contact us at copyright@packtpub.com with a link to the suspected pirated material. We appreciate your help in protecting our authors and our ability to bring you valuable content.

Questions

If you have a problem with any aspect of this book, you can contact us at questions@packtpub.com, and we will do our best to address the problem.

1

Getting Started with Docker on Windows

Docker is an application platform. It's a new way of running applications in isolated, lightweight units called **containers**. Containers are a very efficient way of running apps - they start in seconds, and the container doesn't add any overhead to the memory and compute requirements of the app. Docker is completely agnostic to the type of apps it can run. You can run a brand new .NET Core app in one container and a 10-year old ASP.NET 2.0 WebForms app in another container on the same server.

Containers are isolated units, but they can integrate with other components. Your WebForms container can access a REST API hosted in your .NET Core container. Your .NET Core container can access a SQL Server database running in a container or a SQL Server instance running on a separate machine. You can even set up a cluster with a mixture of Linux and Windows machines all running Docker, and have Windows containers transparently communicate with Linux containers.

Companies big and small are moving to Docker to take advantage of this flexibility and efficiency. The case studies from Docker, Inc. - the company behind the Docker platform - show that you can reduce your hardware requirements by 50% when you move to Docker, while still supporting high availability for your applications. These significant reductions apply equally to on-premises data centers and to the cloud.

Efficiency isn't the only gain. When you package your application to run in Docker, you get portability. You can run your app in a Docker container on your laptop, and it will behave in exactly the same way on a server in your data center and on a **virtual machine** (**VM**) in any cloud. This means your deployment process is simple and risk-free because you're deploying the exact same artifacts that you've tested, and you're also free to choose between hardware vendors and cloud providers.

The other big motivator is security. Containers add secure isolation between applications, so you can be confident that if one application is compromised, the attacker can't move on to compromise other apps on the same host. There are wider security benefits in the platform too. Docker can scan the contents of packaged applications and alert you to security vulnerabilities in your application stack. And you can digitally sign packages and configure Docker to run containers only from package authors that you trust.

Docker is built from open source components and is shipped as **Docker Community Edition (Docker CE)** and **Docker Enterprise Edition (Docker EE)**. Docker CE is free to use and has monthly releases. Docker EE is a paid subscription, it comes with extended features and support and has quarterly releases. Docker CE and Docker EE are available on Windows, and both versions use the same underlying platform, so you can run your apps in containers on Docker CE and EE in the same way.

Docker and Windows containers

Docker originally ran on Linux, taking advantage of core Linux features but making it simple and efficient to use containers for application workloads. Microsoft saw the potential and worked closely with the Docker engineering team to bring the same functionality to Windows. Windows Server 2016 and Windows 10 are the first versions of Windows that can run Docker containers. Right now, you can run only Windows containers on Windows, but Microsoft is adding support for Linux containers to run on Windows too.

There is no integration between containers and the Windows UI, though. Containers are only for server side applications - workloads like websites, APIs, databases, message queues, message handlers, and console applications. You can't use Docker to run a client app, like a .NET WinForms or WPF application, but you could use Docker to package and distribute the application, which would give you a consistent build and release process for all your apps.

There is also a distinction between how containers run on Windows Server 2016 and Windows 10. The user experience for working with Docker is the same, but the way containers are hosted is different. On Windows Server, the process that serves your application actually runs on the server, and there's no layer between the container and the host. In the container, you may see `w3wp.exe` running to serve a website, but that process is actually running on the server - if you had ten web containers running, you would see ten instances of `w3wp.exe` in task manager on the server.

Windows 10 doesn't have the same operating system kernel as Windows Server 2016, so in order to provide containers with the Windows Server kernel, Windows 10 runs each container in a very light VM. These are called **Hyper-V containers**, and if you run a web app in a container on Windows 10, you won't see `w3wp.exe` running on the host - it's actually running inside a dedicated Windows Server kernel in the Hyper-V container.

It's good to understand this distinction. You use the same Docker artifacts and the same Docker commands on Windows 10 and Windows Server 2016, so the processes are the same, but there is a slight performance hit in using Hyper-V containers on Windows 10. Later in this chapter, I'll show you the options for running Docker on Windows, and you can choose the best approach for you.

Windows licensing

Windows containers don't have the same licensing requirements as servers or VMs running Windows. Windows is licensed at the host level, not the container level. If you have 100 Windows containers running on one server, you only need a license for the server. There are considerable savings to be had if you currently use VMs to isolate application workloads. Removing the VM layer and running apps in containers directly on the server removes the licensing requirement for all the VMs.

Hyper-V containers have separate licensing. On Windows 10, you can run multiple containers, but not for production deployments. On Windows Server, you can also run containers in Hyper-V mode to get increased isolation. This can be useful in multi-tenant scenarios, where you need to expect and mitigate for hostile workloads. Hyper-V containers are separately licensed, but in a high-volume environment, you would use a Datacenter license run Hyper-V containers without individual licenses.

Microsoft and Docker, Inc. have partnered to provide Docker EE at no cost with Windows Server 2016. The price of the Windows Server license includes Docker EE Basic, which gives you support to run applications in containers. If you have problems with a container or with the Docker service, you can raise it with Microsoft and they can go on to escalate it to Docker engineers.

Understanding the key Docker concepts

Docker is a very powerful but very simple application platform. You can get started with running your existing apps in Docker in just a few days, and be ready to move to production in a few days more. This book will take you through lots of examples of .NET Framework and .NET Core applications, running in Docker. You'll learn how to build, ship, and run applications in Docker and move on to advanced topics like solution design, security, administration, instrumentation, and **continuous integration and continuous delivery (CI/CD)**.

To start with, you need to understand the core Docker concepts: images, registries, containers, and swarms—and understand how Docker actually runs.

The Docker service and Docker command–line

Docker runs as a background Windows service. This service manages all the running containers and exposes a REST API for consumers to work with containers and other Docker resources. The main consumer of that API is the Docker command-line tool, which is what I use for most of the code samples in this book.

The Docker REST API is public, and there are alternative management tools that are powered by the API, like Portainer (which is open source) and Docker **Universal Control Plane (UCP)** (which is a commercial product). The Docker CLI is very simple to use; you use commands like `docker container run` to run an application in a container and `docker container rm` to remove a container.

You can also configure the Docker API to be remotely accessible and configure your Docker CLI to connect to a remote service. This means you can manage a Docker host running in the cloud using Docker commands on your laptop. The setup to allow remote access should also include encryption, so your connection is secure—and in this chapter, I will show you an easy way to configure that.

When you have Docker running, you'll start by running containers from images.

Docker images

A Docker image is a complete application package. It contains one application and all of its dependencies, the language runtime, the application host, and the underlying operating system. Logically, the image is a single file, and it's a portable unit—you can share your application by pushing your image to a Docker registry. Anyone who has access can pull that image themselves and run your application in a container. It will behave in exactly the same way for them as it does for you.

Here's a concrete example. An ASP.NET WebForms app is going to run on **Internet Information Services (IIS)** in Windows Server. To package that application in Docker, you build an image that is based on Windows Server Core, add IIS, add ASP.NET, copy your application, and configure it as a website in IIS. You describe all these steps in a simple script called a **Dockerfile**, and you can use PowerShell or batch files for each step you need to perform.

You build the image by running `docker image build`. The input is the Dockerfile and any resources that need to be packaged into the image (like the web application content). The output is a Docker image. In this case, the image will have a logical size of about 11 GB, but 10 GB of that is the Windows Server Core image you're using as a base, and that image can be shared as the base across many other images (I will cover image layers and caching more in `Chapter 4`, *Pushing and Pulling Images from Docker Registries*).

The Docker image is like a snapshot of the filesystem for one version of your application. The image is static, and you distribute it using a registry.

Image registries

A registry is a storage server for Docker images. Registries can be public or private, and there are free public registries and commercial registry servers that allow fine-grained access control for images. Images are stored with a unique name within the registry. Anyone with access can upload an image by running `docker image push` and download an image by running `docker image pull`.

The most popular registries are the public ones hosted by Docker:

- Docker Hub is the original registry, which has become hugely popular for open source projects in the Linux ecosystem. It has over 600,000 images stored and has hosted over 12 billion image pulls.

- Docker Cloud is where you store images you build yourself, and you can configure images to be public or private. It's suitable for internal products, where you can limit access to the images. You can set up Docker Cloud to automatically build images from Dockerfiles stored in GitHub—currently, this is supported only for Linux-based images, but Windows support is coming soon.
- Docker Store is where you get commercial software, pre-packaged as Docker images. Vendors are increasingly supporting Docker as a platform for their own applications, and you will find software from Microsoft, Oracle, HPE, and more on Docker Store.

In a typical workflow, you might build images as part of a CI pipeline and push them to a registry if all the tests pass. The image is then available for other users to run your application in a container.

Docker containers

A container is an instance of an application created from an image. The image contains the whole application stack, and it also specifies the process to start the application, so Docker knows what to do when you run a container. You can run multiple containers from the same image, and you can run containers in different ways (I describe them all in the next chapter).

You start your application with `docker container run`, specifying the name of the image and your configuration options. Distribution is built into the Docker platform, so if you don't have a copy of the image on the host where you're trying to run the container, Docker will pull the image first. Then it starts the specified process, and your app is running in a container.

Containers don't need a fixed allocation of CPU or memory, and the processes for your application can use as much of the host's compute power as they need. You can run dozens of containers on modest hardware, and unless the applications all try and use a lot of CPU at the same time, they will happily run concurrently. You can also start containers with resource limits to restrict how much CPU and memory they have access to.

Docker provides the container runtime as well as image packaging and distribution. In a small environment and in development, you will manage individual containers on a single Docker host, which would be your laptop or a test server. When you move to production, you'll need high availability and the option to scale, and that comes with Docker swarm.

Docker swarm

Docker has the ability to run on a single machine or as one node in a cluster of machines all running Docker. This cluster is called a **swarm**, and you don't need to install anything extra to run in swarm mode. You install Docker on a set of machines, and on the first you run `docker swarm init` to initialize the swarm, and on the others you run `docker swarm join` to join the swarm.

I will cover swarm mode in depth in `Chapter 7`, *Orchestrating Distributed Solutions with Docker Swarm*, but it's important to know before you get much further that the Docker platform has high availability, scale, and resilience built in. Your Docker journey will hopefully lead you to production, where you'll need all these attributes.

In swarm mode Docker uses exactly the same artifacts, so you can run your app across 50 containers in a 20-node swarm, and the functionality will be the same as when you run it in a single container on your laptop. On the swarm, your app is more performant and tolerant of failure, and you'll be able to perform automated rolling updates to new versions.

Nodes in a swarm use secure encryption for all communication, using trusted certificates for each node. You can store application secrets as encrypted data in the swarm too, so database connection strings and API keys can be saved securely, and the swarm will deliver them only to containers that need them.

Docker is an established platform. It's new to Windows Server 2016, but it arrived on Windows after four years of releases on Linux. Docker is written in Go, which is a cross-platform language, and only a minority of code is specific to Windows. When you run Docker on Windows, you're running an application platform that has had years of successful production use.

Running Docker on Windows

It's easy to install Docker on Windows 10 and Windows Server 2016. On these operating systems, you can use the *Docker for Windows* installer, which sets up all the prerequisites, deploys the latest version of Docker CE, and gives you some useful options to manage image repositories and remote swarms with Docker Cloud.

In production, you should ideally use Windows Server 2016 Core, the installation with no UI. This reduces the attack surface and the amount of Windows updates your server will need. If you move all your apps to Docker, you won't need any other Windows features installed; you'll just have Docker EE running as a Windows service.

I'll walk through both these installation options and show you a third option using a VM in Azure, which is useful if you want to try Docker but don't have access to Windows 10 or Windows Server 2016.

 There is a fantastic online Docker playground at `https://dockr.ly/play -with-docker`. Windows support is currently in beta, and it's a great way to try Docker without having to make any investment - you just browse the site and get started.

Docker for Windows

Docker for Windows is available from Docker Store—navigate to `https://dockr.ly/docke r-for-windows`. You can choose between the Stable channel and the Edge channel. Both channels give you Docker CE, but the Edge channel follows the monthly release cycle, and you will get experimental features. The Stable channel follows the EE release cycle, with quarterly updates.

 You should use the Edge channel in development if you want to work with the latest features. In test and production, you will use Docker EE, so you need to be careful that you don't use features in development that are not yet available in EE.

Download and run the installer. The installer will verify that you can run Docker in your setup and will configure the Windows features needed to support Docker. When Docker is running, you will see a whale icon in the notification bar, which you can click on for options:

You need to select **Switch to Windows containers** before you do anything else. Docker for Windows can run Linux containers by running Docker inside a Linux VM on your machine. That's great to test out Linux apps to see how they run in containers, but this book is all about Windows containers - switch over, and Docker will remember that setting in future.

While Docker for Windows is running, you can open Command Prompt or a PowerShell session and start working with containers. First, verify that everything is working as expected by running `docker version`. You should see output similar to this:

```
> docker version

Client:
 Version: 17.06.0-ce
 API version: 1.30
 Go version: go1.8.3
 Git commit: 02c1d87
 Built: Fri Jun 23 21:30:30 2017
 OS/Arch: windows/amd64

Server:
 Version: 17.06.0-ce
 API version: 1.30 (minimum version 1.24)
 Go version: go1.8.3
 Git commit: 02c1d87
 Built: Fri Jun 23 22:19:00 2017
 OS/Arch: windows/amd64
```

```
Experimental: true
```

 The output tells you the version of the command-line client and the Docker service. The operating system field should read *Windows* for both; if not, then you may be in Linux mode, and you'll need to switch to Windows containers.

Now run a simple container:

```
docker container run dockeronwindows/ch01-whale
```

This uses a public image on Docker Cloud—one of the sample images for this book, which Docker will pull the first time you use it. If you don't have any other images, this will take few minutes, as it will also download the Microsoft Nano Server image that my image uses as a base. When the container runs, it shows some ASCII art and then exits. Run the same command again, and you will see that it executes much more quickly as the images are now cached locally.

That's all the setup you need. Docker for Windows also contains the Docker Compose tool I'll be using later in the book, so you're all set to follow along with the code samples.

Docker as a Windows Service

You can use Docker for Windows on Windows 10 and Windows Server 2016, and it's great for development and test environments. For production environments where you have a headless server with no UI, you can install Docker using a PowerShell module.

On a new installation of Windows Server 2016 core, use the `sconfig` tool to install all the latest Windows updates, and then run these PowerShell commands:

```
Install-Module -Name DockerMsftProvider -Repository PSGallery -Force
Install-Package -Name docker -ProviderName DockerMsftProvider
```

This will configure the server with the necessary Windows features, install Docker, and set it up to run as a Windows service. Depending on how many Windows updates were installed, you may need to reboot the server:

```
Restart-Computer -Force
```

When the server is online, check whether Docker is running with `docker version`, and then try to run a container from the sample image for this chapter:

```
docker container run dockeronwindows/ch01-whale
```

I use this configuration for some of my environments—running Windows Server 2016 Core in a lightweight VM, which has only Docker installed. You can use Docker on the server by connecting with Remote Desktop, or you can configure the Docker service to allow remote connections. This is a more advanced setup, but it does give you secure remote access.

It's best to set up the Docker service so that communication with the client is secured using TLS. Clients can connect only if they have the right TLS certificates to authenticate with the service. You can set this up by running these PowerShell commands inside the VM, supplying the VM's external IP address:

```
$ipAddress = '<vm-ip-address>'

mkdir -p C:\certs\client

docker container run --rm `
  --env SERVER_NAME=$(hostname) `
  --env IP_ADDRESSES=127.0.0.1,$vm-ip-address `
  --volume 'C:\ProgramData\docker:C:\ProgramData\docker' `
  --volume 'C:\certs\client:C:\Users\ContainerAdministrator\.docker' `
  stefanscherer/dockertls-windows

Restart-Service docker
```

Don't worry too much about what this command is doing. Over the next few chapters, you'll get a good understanding of all these Docker options. I'm using a Docker image from Stefan Scherer, who is a Microsoft MVP and Docker Captain. The image has a script that secures the Docker service with TLS certificates. You can read more details on Stefan's blog at https://stefanscherer.github.io.

When this command completes, it will have configured the Docker service to allow only secure remote connections and will also have created the certificates that the client needs to use to connect. Copy these certificates from `C:\certs\client` on the VM onto the machine where you want to use the Docker client.

On the client machine, you can set environment variables to point the Docker client to use a remote Docker service. These commands will set up a remote connection to the VM (assuming you have used the same path for the certificate files on the client):

```
$ipAddress = '<vm-ip-address>'

$env:DOCKER_HOST='tcp://$($ipAddress):2376'
$env:DOCKER_TLS_VERIFY='1'
$env:DOCKER_CERT_PATH='C:\certs\client'
```

You can use this approach to securely connect to any remote Docker service. If you don't have access to Windows 10 or Windows Server 2016, you can create a VM on the cloud and connect to it using the same commands.

Docker in an Azure VM

Microsoft makes it easy to run Docker in Azure. They provide a VM image with Docker installed and configured and with the base Windows images already pulled so you can get started quickly.

For testing and exploring, I always use DevTest labs in Azure. It's a great feature for non-production environments. By default, any VMs you create in a DevTest lab will be turned off every evening, so you don't end up with a big Azure bill from a VM you used for a few hours and forgot to turn off.

You can create a DevTest Lab through the Azure Portal and then create a VM from Microsoft's VM image **Windows Server 2016 Datacenter - with Containers**. As an alternative to the Azure Portal, you can use the `az` command-line to manage the DevTest lab. I've packaged `az` in a Docker image, which you can run in a Windows container:

```
docker run -it dockeronwindows/ch01-az
```

This runs an interactive Docker container that has the `az` command packaged and ready to use. Run `az login`, and you'll need to open a browser and authenticate the Azure CLI. Then, you can run this in the container to create a VM:

```
az lab vm create `
  --lab-name docker-on-win --resource-group docker-on-winRG236992 `
  --name dow-vm-01 `
  --image 'Windows Server 2016 Datacenter - with Containers' `
  --image-type gallery --size Standard_DS2 `
  --admin-username 'elton' --admin-password 'S3crett20!7'
```

The VM uses the full Windows Server 2016 installation with the UI, so you can connect to the machine with RDP, open a PowerShell cmdlet, and start using Docker right away. Just like the other options, you can check whether Docker is running with `docker version` and then run a container from the sample image for this chapter:

```
docker container run dockeronwindows/ch01-whale
```

If an Azure VM is your preferred option, you can follow the steps from the previous section to secure the Docker API for remote access. This way, you can run the Docker command-line on your laptop to manage containers on the cloud.

Learning Docker with this book

Every code listing in this book is accompanied by a full code sample on my GitHub repository at `https://github.com/sixeyed/docker-on-windows`. The source tree is organized into a folder for each chapter, and for each chapter there's a folder for each code sample. In this chapter, I've used two samples to create Docker images, which you'll find in `ch01\ch01-whale` and `ch01\ch01-az`.

The code listings in the book may be condensed for the page, but the full code is always in the GitHub repository.

I prefer to follow along with the code samples when I'm learning a new technology, but if you want to use working versions of the demo applications, every sample is also available as a public Docker image on Docker Cloud. Wherever you see a `docker container run` command, the image already exists on Docker Cloud, so you can use mine rather than building your own if you wish. All the images in the `dockeronwindows` organization, such as this chapter's `dockeronwindows/ch01-whale`—were built from the relevant Dockerfile in the GitHub repository.

My own development environment is based on Windows Server 2016, where I use Docker for Windows. My test environment is based on Windows Server 2016 Core, where I run Docker as a Windows Service. I've also verified all the code samples using Windows 10.

I'm using version 17.06 of Docker, which is the latest release at the time of writing. Some of the features I demonstrate need version 17.06 as a minimum—such as multi-stage builds and secrets. But Docker has always been backward-compatible, so if you're using a version later than 17.06, then the sample Dockerfiles and images should work in the same way.

My goal is for this to be a definitive book about Docker on Windows, so I've covered everything from the 101 on containers through modernizing .NET apps with Docker and the security implications of containers to CI/CD and administration in production. The book ends with a guide to moving forward with Docker in your own projects.

 If you want to discuss the book or your own Docker journey with me, feel free to ping me on Twitter at `@EltonStoneman`.

Summary

In this chapter I introduced Docker, an application platform that can run new and old apps in lightweight units of compute called **containers**. Companies are moving to Docker for efficiency, security, and portability. I covered:

- How Docker works on Windows and how containers are licensed
- The key Docker concepts: images, registries, containers, and swarms
- The options to run Docker on Windows 10, Windows Server 2016, and Azure

If you're planning to work along with the code samples in the rest of the book, you should have a working Docker environment by now. In Chapter 2, *Packaging and Running Applications as Docker Containers*, I'll move on to packaging more complex apps as Docker images and showing how to manage state in containers with Docker volumes.

2
Packaging and Running Applications as Docker Containers

Docker reduces the logical view of your infrastructure to three core components: hosts, containers, and images. Hosts run containers, which are isolated instances of an application. Containers are created from images, which are packaged applications. The Docker container image is conceptually very simple - it's a single unit that contains a complete, self-contained application. The image format is very efficient, and the integration between the image and the runtime is very smart, so mastering images is your first step to using Docker effectively.

You've already seen some images in Chapter 1, *Getting Started with Docker on Windows*, by running some basic containers to check your Docker installation was working correctly - but I didn't look very closely at the image or how Docker used it. In this chapter, you'll get a thorough understanding of Docker images: learning how they're structured, understanding how Docker uses them, and looking at how to package your own applications as Docker images.

The first thing to understand is the difference between an image and a container, which you can see very clearly by running different types of container from the same image.

In this chapter, you'll get a lot of experience of the Docker basics:

- Running containers from images
- Building images from Dockerfiles
- Packaging your own applications as Docker images

- Working with data in images and containers
- Packaging legacy ASP.NET web apps as Docker images

Running a container from an image

The `docker container run` command creates a container from an image and starts the application inside the container. It's actually equivalent to running two separate commands, `docker container create` and `docker container start`, which shows that containers can have different states. You can create a container without starting it, and you can pause, stop, and restart running containers. Containers can be in different states, and you can use them in different ways.

Doing one thing with a task container

The `dockeronwindows/ch02-powershell-env` image is an example of a packaged application that is meant to run in a container and perform a single task. The image is based on Microsoft Nano Server and is set up to run a simple PowerShell script when it starts, printing details about the current environment. Let's see what happens when I run a container directly from the image:

```
> docker container run dockeronwindows/ch02-powershell-env
Name                            Value
----                            -----
ALLUSERSPROFILE                 C:\ProgramData
APPDATA
C:\Users\ContainerAdministrator\AppData\Roaming
CommonProgramFiles              C:\Program Files\Common Files
CommonProgramFiles(x86)         C:\Program Files (x86)\Common Files
CommonProgramW6432              C:\Program Files\Common Files
COMPUTERNAME                    361CB712CB4B
. . .
```

Without any options, the container runs a PowerShell script that is built into the image, and the script prints out some basic information about the operating system environment. I call that a task container because the container performs one task and then exits. If you run `docker container ls`, which lists all the active containers, you won't see this container. But if you run `docker container ls --all`, which shows containers in all states, you'll see it in the `Exited` status:

```
> docker container ls --all
CONTAINER ID     IMAGE                                            COMMAND
```

```
CREATED          STATUS PORTS NAMES
361cb712cb4b     dockeronwindows/ch02-powershell-env     "powershell.exe
c:..."    30 seconds ago    Exited
```

Task containers are very useful in automating repetitive tasks - like running scripts to set up an environment, backing up data, or collecting log files. Your container image packages the script to run, along with the exact version of the engine that the script needs, so anyone with Docker installed can run that script without having to install the engine.

This is especially useful for PowerShell, where scripts can be dependent on several PowerShell modules. The modules may be publicly available, but your script is dependent on specific versions. Instead of sharing a script that requires users to install the correct version of many different modules, you build an image that has the modules already installed. Then, you only need Docker to run the script task.

Images are self-contained units, but you can also use them as a template. An image may be configured to do one thing, but you can run containers from the image in different ways to do different things.

Connecting to an interactive container

An interactive container is one that has an open connection to the Docker command line, so you work with the container as if you were connected to a remote machine. You can run an interactive container from that same Nano Server image by specifying the interactive options and a command to run when the container starts:

```
> docker container run --interactive --tty dockeronwindows/ch02-powershell-
env `
    powershell

Windows PowerShell
Copyright (C) 2016 Microsoft Corporation. All rights reserved.

PS C:\> Write-Output 'This is an interactive container'
This is an interactive container
PS C:\> exit
```

The `--interactive` option runs an interactive container, and the `--tty` flag attaches a dummy terminal connection to the container. The `powershell` statement after the name of the container image is the command to run when the container starts. By specifying a command, you replace the startup command that's been set up in the image. In this case, I start a PowerShell session, and that runs instead of the configured command, so the environment printout script doesn't run.

An interactive container keeps running as long as the command inside is running. While you're connected to PowerShell, running `docker container ls` on another window on the host will show the container is still running. When you type `exit` in the container, the PowerShell session ends, so there's no process running and the container exits too.

Interactive containers are useful when you're building your own container images, as you can work through the steps interactively first and verify that everything will work as you expect. They're good exploratory tools too. You'll see as you move further into this book that Docker can host complex distributed systems in a virtual network, with each component running in its own container. If you want to examine parts of the system, you can run an interactive container inside the network and check on individual components, without having to make the parts publicly accessible.

Keeping a process running in a background container

The last type of container is the one that you'll use most in production - the background container, which keeps a long-running process running in the background. It's a container that behaves like a Windows Service. In Docker terminology, it's called a **detached container**, and it's the Docker service that keeps it running in the background. Inside the container, the process runs in the foreground. The process might be a web server or a console application polling a message queue for work, but as long as the process keeps running, Docker will keep the container alive.

I can run a background container from the same image again, specifying the `detach` option and a command that runs for some minutes:

```
> docker container run --detach dockeronwindows/ch02-powershell-env `
    powershell Test-Connection 'localhost' -Count 100

ce7b2604f681871a8dcd2ffd8898257fad26b24edec7135e76aedd47cdcdc427
```

In this case, when the container has launched control returns to the terminal; the long random string is the ID of the new container. You can run `docker container ls` and see the container running, and the `docker container logs` command shows you the console output from the container. For commands operating on specific containers, you can reference them by the container name or by part of the container ID:

```
> docker container logs ce7

Source          Destination   IPV4Address   IPV6Address
------          -----------   -----------   -----------
CE7B2604F681    localhost
CE7B2604F681    localhost
```

The `--detach` flag detaches the container so it moves into the background, and the command in this case just pings `localhost` repeatedly one hundred times. After a few minutes, the PowerShell command completes so there's no process running and the container exits. That's a key thing to remember - if you want to keep a container running in the background, the process that Docker starts when it runs the container has to keep running.

Now you've seen that a container is created from an image, but it can run in different ways - so you can use the image exactly as it was prepared, or treat the image as a template, with a default startup mode built in. Next, I'll show you how to build that image.

Building a Docker image

Docker images are layered. The bottom layer is the operating system, which can be a full OS like Windows Server Core, or a minimal OS like Microsoft Nano Server. On top of that are layers for each change you make to the base OS when you build an image - by installing software, copying files, and running commands. Logically, Docker treats the image as a single unit, but physically, each layer is stored as a separate file in Docker's cache, so images with a lot of common features can share layers from the cache.

Images are built using a text file with the Dockerfile language - specifying the base OS image to start with, and all the steps to add on top. The language is very simple, and there are only a few commands you need to master in order to build production-grade images. I'll start by looking at the basic PowerShell image I've been using so far in this chapter.

Understanding the Dockerfile

The Dockerfile is the source code for an image. The complete code for the PowerShell image is just three lines:

```
FROM microsoft/nanoserver
COPY scripts/print-env-details.ps1 c:\\print-env.ps1
CMD ["powershell.exe", "c:\\print-env.ps1"]
```

It's pretty easy to guess what's happening even if you've never seen a Dockerfile before. By convention, the instructions (FROM, COPY and CMD) are uppercase and the arguments are lowercase, but that's not mandatory. Also by convention, you save the text in a file called Dockerfile, but that's not mandatory either (a file with no extension looks odd in Windows, but remember that Docker's heritage is in Linux).

Let's take a look at the instructions in that Dockerfile line by line:

- FROM microsoft/nanoserver uses the image called microsoft/nanoserver as the starting point for this image
- COPY scripts/print-env-details.ps1 c:\\print-env.ps1 copy the PowerShell script from the local computer into a specific location on the image
- CMD ["powershell.exe", "c:\\print-env.ps1"] specifies the startup command when a container runs, in this case running the PowerShell script

There are a few obvious questions here. Where does the base image come from? Built into Docker is the concept of an image registry, which is a store for container images. The default registry is a free public service called **Docker Hub**. Microsoft has made the Nano Server image available on Docker Hub, and that image is called microsoft/nanoserver. The first time you use the image, Docker will download it to your local machine and then cache it for further use.

Where does the PowerShell script get copied from? When you build an image, the directory containing the Dockerfile is used as the context for the build. When you build an image from this Dockerfile, Docker will expect to find a folder called scripts in the context directory, containing a file called print-env-details.ps1. If it doesn't find that file, the build will fail.

 Dockerfiles use the backslash as an escape character in order to continue instructions onto a new line. This clashes with Windows file paths, so you have to write c:\print.ps1 as c:\\print.ps1 or c:/print.ps1. There is a nice way to get around this, using a processor directive at the start of the Dockerfile, which I'll demonstrate later in the chapter.

How do you know PowerShell is available for use? It's part of the Nano Server base image, so you can rely on it being there. You can install any software that isn't in the base image with additional Dockerfile instructions. You can add Windows features, copy or download files into the image, extract ZIP files and do whatever else you need.

This is a very simple Dockerfile but even so, two of the instructions are optional. Only the FROM instruction is mandatory, so if you wanted to build an exact clone of Microsoft's Nano Server image, you could do that with just a FROM statement in your Dockerfile.

Building an image from a Dockerfile

Now that you have a Dockerfile, you use the docker command line to build it into an image. Like most Docker commands, the image build command is straightforward and has very few required options, preferring conventions instead. To build an image, open a command line and navigate to the directory where your Dockerfile is. Then, run docker image build and give your image a tag, which is the name that will identify the image:

```
docker image build --tag dockeronwindows/ch02-powershell-env .
```

Every image needs a tag, specified with the --tag option, which is a unique identifier for the image in your local image cache and in image registries. The tag is how you'll refer to the image when you run containers. A full tag specifies the registry to use, the repository name, which is the identifier for the application and a suffix, which is the identifier for this version of the image.

When you're building an image for yourself, you can call it anything, but the convention is to name your repository as your username for the registry, followed by the application name: {user}/{app}. You can use also the tag to identify application versions or variations, such as sixeyed/hadoop-dot-net:latest and sixeyed/hadoop-dot-net:2.7.2, which are two of my images on Docker Hub.

The period at the end of the image build command tells Docker the location of the context to use for the image, . is the current directory. Docker copies the contents of the directory tree into a temporary folder for the build, so the context needs to contain any files you reference in the Dockerfile. After copying the context, Docker starts executing the instructions in the Dockerfile.

Examining how Docker builds an image

Understanding how Docker images are constructed will help you build efficient images. The `image build` command produces a lot of output, which tells you exactly what Docker does for each step of the build. Each instruction in the Dockerfile is executed as a separate step that produces a new image layer, and the final image will be the combined stack of all the layers. This is the output from building my image:

```
> docker image build --tag dockeronwindows/ch02-powershell-env .

Sending build context to Docker daemon 3.584kB
Step 1/3 : FROM microsoft/nanoserver
 ---> d9bccb9d4cac
Step 2/3 : COPY scripts/print-env-details.ps1 c:\\print-env.ps1
 ---> a44026142eaa
Removing intermediate container 9901221bbf99
Step 3/3 : CMD powershell.exe c:\print-env.ps1
 ---> Running in 56af93a47ab1
 ---> 253feb55a9c0
Removing intermediate container 56af93a47ab1
Successfully built 253feb55a9c0
Successfully tagged dockeronwindows/ch02-powershell-env:latest
```

This is what's happening in these execution steps:

- **Step 1**: The FROM image already exists in my local cache, so Docker doesn't need to download it. The output is the ID of Microsoft's Nano Server image (starting d9b).
- **Step 2**: Docker creates a temporary, intermediate container from the base image and copies the script file from the build context into the container. Then it saves the container as a new image layer (ID a44) and removes the intermediate container (ID 990).
- **Step 3**: Docker configures the command to execute when a container is run from the image. It creates a temporary container from the *Step 2* image, configures the startup command, saves the container as a new image layer (ID 253), and deletes the intermediate container (ID 56a).

The final layer is tagged with the image name, but all the intermediate layers are also added to the local cache. The layered approach means Docker can be very efficient when it builds images and runs containers. The latest Windows Nano Server image is over 900 MB uncompressed, but when you run multiple containers based from Nano Server they will all use the same base image layers, you don't end up with multiple copies of the 900 MB image.

You'll understand more about image layers and storage later in the chapter, but first I'll look at some more complex Dockerfiles that package .NET and .NET Core applications.

Packaging your own applications

The goal of building an image is to package your application in a portable, self-contained unit. The image should be as small as possible, so it's easy to move around when you want to run the application, and it should have as few OS features as possible, so it has a fast startup time and a small attack vector.

Docker doesn't impose restrictions on the image size. Your long-term goal may be to build minimal images that run lightweight .NET Core applications on Linux or Nano Server. But you can start by packaging your existing ASP.NET apps in their entirety as Docker images to run on Windows Server Core. Docker also doesn't impose restrictions on how to package your app, so you can choose from different approaches.

Compiling the application during the build

There are two common approaches to packaging your own apps in Docker images. The first is to use a base image that contains the application platform and the build tools, so in your Dockerfile, you copy the source code into the image and compile the app as a step during the image building process.

This is a popular approach for public images because it means that anyone can build the image without having the application platform installed locally. It also means the tooling for the application is bundled with the image, so that can make it possible to debug and troubleshoot the application running in the container.

Here's an example with a simple .NET Core application. This Dockerfile is for the image `dockeronwindows/ch02-dotnet-helloworld`:

```
FROM microsoft/dotnet:1.1-sdk-nanoserver

WORKDIR /src
COPY src/ .
```

```
RUN dotnet restore; dotnet build
CMD ["dotnet", "run"]
```

The Dockerfile uses Microsoft's .NET Core image from Docker Hub as the base image. It's a specific variation of the image, one which is based on Nano Server and has the .NET Core 1.1 SDK installed. The build copies in the application source code from the context, and compiles the application as part of the container build process.

There are two new instructions in this Dockerfile which you haven't seen before:

- WORKDIR specifies the current working directory. Docker creates the directory in the intermediate container, if it doesn't already exist, and sets it to be the current directory. It remains the working directory for the subsequent instructions in the Dockerfile, and for containers when they run from the image.
- RUN executes a command inside an intermediate container and saves the state of the container after the command completes, creating a new image layer.

When I build this image, you'll see the dotnet command output, which is the application being compiled from the RUN instruction in the image build:

```
> docker image build --tag dockeronwindows/ch02-dotnet-helloworld .
Sending build context to Docker daemon 367.1kB
Step 1/5 : FROM microsoft/dotnet:1.1-sdk-nanoserver
 ---> 80950bc5c558
Step 2/5 : WORKDIR /src
 ---> 00352af1c40a
Removing intermediate container 1167582ec3ae
Step 3/5 : COPY src/ .
 ---> abd047ca95d7
Removing intermediate container 09d543e402c5
Step 4/5 : RUN dotnet restore; dotnet build
 ---> Running in 4ec42bb93ca1
 Restoring packages for C:\src\HelloWorld.NetCore.csproj...
 Generating MSBuild file
C:\src\obj\HelloWorld.NetCore.csproj.nuget.g.props.
 Writing lock file to disk. Path: C:\src\obj\project.assets.json
 Restore completed in 10.36 sec for C:\src\HelloWorld.NetCore.csproj.
 ...
```

You'll see this approach a lot on Docker Cloud for applications built with platforms like .NET Core, Go, and Node.js, where the tooling is easy to add to a base image. It means that you can set up an automated build on Docker Cloud so Docker's servers build your image from the Dockerfile when you push code changes to GitHub. The servers can do that without having .NET Core, Go, or Node.js installed because all the build dependencies are inside the base image.

This option means that the final image will be a lot bigger than it needs to be for a production application. Platform tooling will probably use more disk than the app itself, and your end result is meant to be the application - all the build tools taking up space in your image will never be used when the container runs in production. An alternative is to build the application first and then package the compiled binaries into your container image.

Compiling the application before the build

Building the application first fits in neatly with existing build pipelines. Your build servers need to have all the application platforms and build tools installed, but your finished container image only has the minimum it needs to run the app. With this approach, the Dockerfile for my .NET Core app becomes even simpler:

```
FROM microsoft/dotnet:1.1-runtime-nanoserver

WORKDIR /dotnetapp
COPY ./src/bin/Debug/netcoreapp1.1/publish .

CMD ["dotnet", "HelloWorld.NetCore.dll"]
```

This Dockerfile uses a different `FROM` image, one that contains just the .NET Core 1.1 runtime and not the tooling (so it can run a compiled application, but it can't compile one from source). You can't build this image without building the application first, so you'll need to wrap the `docker image build` command in a build script that also runs the `dotnet publish` command to compile the binaries.

A simple build script that compiles the application and builds the Docker image looks like this:

```
dotnet restore src; dotnet publish src

docker image build --file Dockerfile.slim --tag dockeronwindows/ch02-
dotnet-helloworld:slim .
```

If you put your Dockerfile instructions in a file called something other than **Dockerfile**, you can build it by specifying the filename with the `--file` option, as shown in this example: `image build --file Dockerfile.slim`.

I've moved the requirements for the platform tooling from the image to the build server, and that results in a smaller final image: 1.15 GB for this version compared to 1.68 GB for the previous one. You can see the size difference by listing images, and filtering on the image repository name:

```
> docker image ls --filter reference=dockeronwindows/ch02-dotnet-helloworld
```

REPOSITORY	TAG	IMAGE ID	CREATED SIZE
dockeronwindows/ch02-dotnet-helloworld	latest	ebdf7accda4b	6 minutes ago 1.68GB
dockeronwindows/ch02-dotnet-helloworld	slim	63aebf93b60e	13 minutes ago 1.15GB

This new version is also a more restricted image. The source code and the .NET Core SDK aren't packaged in the image, so you can't connect to a running container and inspect the application code, or make changes to the code and recompile the app.

For enterprise environments, or for commercial applications, you're likely to already have a well-equipped build server, and packaging the built app can be part of a more comprehensive workflow:

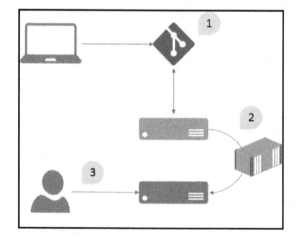

In this pipeline, the developer pushes their changes to the central source code repository (**1**). The build server compiles the application and runs unit tests - if they pass, then the container image is built and deployed in a staging environment (**2**). Integration tests and end-to-end tests are run against the staging environment, and if they pass, then your versioned container image is a good release candidate for testers to verify (**3**).

You deploy a new release by running a container from the image in production, and you know that your whole application stack is the same set of binaries which passed all the tests.

The downside with this approach is that you need to have the application SDK installed on all your build agents, and the versions of the SDK and all its dependencies need to match what the developers are using. Often in Windows projects, you find CI servers with Visual Studio installed, to ensure the server has the same tools as the developer. That makes for heavy build servers which take a lot of effort to commission and maintain.

 It also means that you can't build this Docker image yourself unless you have the .NET Core 1.1 SDK installed on your machine.

You can get the best of both options by using a *multi-stage build*, where your Dockerfile defines one step to compile your application, and another step to package it into the final image. Multi-stage Dockerfiles are portable, so anyone can build the image with no pre-requisites, but the final image only contains the minimum needed for the app.

Compiling with multi-stage builds

In a multi-stage build, you have multiple FROM instructions in your Dockerfile, where each FROM instruction starts a new stage in the build. Docker executes all the instructions when you build the image, and later stages can access the output from earlier stages, but only the final stage is used for the completed image.

I can write a multi-stage Dockerfile for the .NET Core console app by combining the previous two Dockerfiles into one:

```
# build stage
FROM microsoft/dotnet:1.1-sdk-nanoserver AS builder
WORKDIR /src
COPY src/ .
RUN dotnet restore; dotnet publish

# final image stage
```

```
FROM microsoft/dotnet:1.1-runtime-nanoserver
WORKDIR /dotnetapp
COPY --from=builder /src/bin/Debug/netcoreapp1.1/publish .
CMD ["dotnet", "HelloWorld.NetCore.dll"]
```

There are a couple of things that are new here. The first stage uses the large base image, with the .NET Core SDK installed. I've named that stage `builder`, using the `AS` option in the `FROM` instruction. The rest of that stage goes on to copy in the source code and publish the application. When the builder stage completes, the published application will be stored in an intermediate container.

The second stage uses the runtime .NET Core image, which doesn't have the SDK installed. In that stage I copy the published output from the previous stage, specifying `--from=builder` in the `COPY` instruction. Anyone can compile this application from source, without needing .NET Core installed on their machine.

Multi-stage Dockerfiles for Windows apps are completely portable. To compile the app and build the image, the only pre-requisite is to have a Windows machine with Docker installed, and a copy of the code. The builder stage contains the SDK and all the compiler tools, but the final image just has the minimum needed to run the application.

This approach isn't just for .NET Core. You can write a multi-stage Dockerfile for a .NET Framework app, where the first stage uses an image with MSBuild installed, which you use to compile your application. There are plenty of examples of that later in this book.

Whichever approach you take, there are just a few more Dockerfile instructions you need to understand in order to build more complex application images, which can integrate with other systems.

Using the main Dockerfile instructions

The Dockerfile syntax is very simple. You've already seen FROM, COPY, RUN, and CMD which are enough to package up a basic application to run as a container. For real-world images, you'll need to do more than that, and there are three more key instructions to understand.

Here's a Dockerfile for a simple static website - it uses **Internet Information Services (IIS)** and serves an HTML page in the default website, which shows some basic details:

```
# escape=`
FROM microsoft/iis
SHELL ["powershell"]

ARG ENV_NAME=DEV

EXPOSE 80

COPY template.html C:\template.html

RUN (Get-Content -Raw -Path C:\template.html) `
  -replace '{hostname}', [Environment]::MachineName `
  -replace '{environment}',
[Environment]::GetEnvironmentVariable('ENV_NAME') `
  | Set-Content -Path C:\inetpub\wwwroot\index.html
```

This Dockerfile starts differently, with the `escape` directive. That tells Docker to use the backtick ` for the escape character, to split commands over multiple lines, rather than the default backslash \. With the escape directive, I can use backslashes in file paths and backticks to split long PowerShell commands - which is more natural to Windows users.

The base image is `microsoft/iis` which is a Microsoft Windows Server Core image with IIS already set up. I copy an HTML template file from the Docker build context into the root folder. Then I run a PowerShell command to update the content of the template file and save it in the default website location for IIS.

In this Dockerfile, I use two new instructions:

- `ARG` specifies a build argument to use in the image with a default value
- `EXPOSE` will make a port available in the image, so containers from the image can have traffic sent in by the host

This static website has a single home page, which tells you the name of the server that sent the response, with the name of the environment in the page title. The HTML template file has placeholders for the host name and the environment name. The RUN command executes a PowerShell script to read the file contents, replace the placeholders with the actual host name and environment value, and then write the contents out.

Containers run in an isolated space, and the host can only send network traffic into the container if the image has explicitly made the port available for use. That's the EXPOSE instruction, which you can use to expose the ports that your application is listening on. When you run a container from this image, port 80 is available to be published so Docker can serve web traffic from the container.

I can build this image in the usual way, and make use of the ARG specified in the Dockerfile to override the default value at build-time with the --build-arg option:

```
docker image build --build-arg ENV_NAME=TEST --tag dockeronwindows/ch02-
static-website .
```

Docker processes the new instructions in the same way as those you've already seen—it creates a new, intermediate container from the previous image in the stack, executes the instruction, and extracts a new image layer from the container. After the build, I have a new image that I can run to start the static web server:

```
> docker container run --detach --publish 80 dockeronwindows/ch02-static-
website

3472a4f0efdb7f4215d49c44dcbfc81eae0426c1fc56ad75be86f63a5abf9b0e
```

This is a detached container so it runs in the background, and the --publish option makes port 80 in the container available to the host. Published ports mean traffic coming into the host can be directed into containers by Docker. But when I'm logged into the host like on my dev machine - I need to use the container's IP address to use the app. I can find the IP address with docker container inspect. The inspect command returns a lot of data, but I can pass a format string to just return the attribute I want, so this gives me the IP address of the container:

```
> docker container inspect --format '{{
.NetworkSettings.Networks.nat.IPAddress }}' 3472
172.26.204.5
```

That's a virtual IP address assigned by Docker, which I can use on the host to communicate with the container. I can browse to that IP address and see the response from IIS running inside the container, showing me the host name - which is actually a container ID, and in the title bar there is the name of the environment:

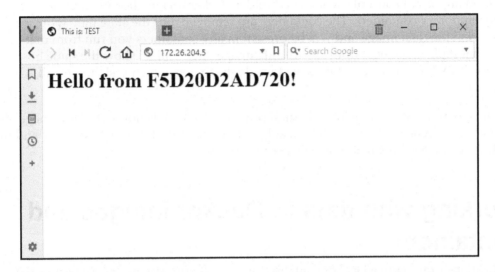

The environment name is just a text description, but the value came from the argument passed to the `docker image build` command - which overrides the default value from the `ARG` instruction in the Dockerfile. The hostname should show the container ID, but there's a problem with the current implementation.

On the web page, the hostname starts **F5D2**, but my container ID actually starts with `3472`. To understand that, I'll look again at the temporary containers used during image builds.

Understanding temporary containers and image state

My website container has an ID that starts `3472`, which is the hostname the application inside the container should see, but that's not what the website claims. So what went wrong? Remember that Docker executes every build instruction inside a temporary, intermediate container.

The RUN instruction to generate the HTML ran in a temporary container, so the PowerShell script wrote that container's ID as the hostname in the HTML file. The intermediate container gets removed by Docker, but the HTML file it created is persisted in the image.

This is an important concept - when you build a Docker image, the instructions execute inside temporary containers. The containers are removed, but the state they write is persisted in the final image and will be present in any containers you run from that image. If I run multiple containers from my website image, they will all show the same hostname from the HTML file, because that's saved inside the image, which is shared by all containers.

Of course you can store state in individual containers, which is not part of the image so it's not shared between containers. I'll look at how to work with data in Docker now and then finish the chapter with a real-world Dockerfile example.

Working with data in Docker images and containers

Applications running in a Docker container see a single filesystem that they can read from and write to in the usual way for the operating system. The container sees a single filesystem drive but it's actually a virtual filesystem, and the underlying data can be in many different physical locations.

Files that a container can access on its C drive could actually be stored in an image layer, in the container's own storage layer, or in a volume that is mapped to a location on the host. Docker merges all these locations into a single virtual filesystem.

Data in layers and the virtual C drive

The virtual filesystem is how Docker can take a set of physical image layers and treat them as one logical container image. Image layers are mounted as read-only parts of the filesystem in a container, so they can't be altered, and that's how they can be safely shared by many containers.

Each container has its own writable layer on top of all the read-only layers, so every container can modify its own data without affecting any other containers:

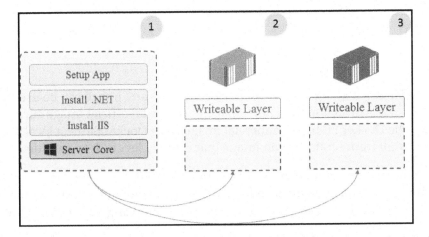

This diagram shows two containers running from the same image. The image (**1**) is physically composed of many layers - one built from each instruction in the Dockerfile. The two containers (**2 and 3**) use the same layers from the image when they run, but they each have their own isolated, writeable layers.

Docker presents a single filesystem to the container. The concept of layers and read-only base layers is hidden, and your container just reads and writes data as if it had a full native filesystem, with a single drive. If you create a file when you build a Docker image and then edit the file inside a container, Docker actually creates a copy of the changed file in the container's writable layer and hides the original read-only file. So the container has edited a copy of the file, but the original file in the image is unchanged.

You can see this by creating some simple images with data in different layers. The Dockerfile for the image `dockeronwindows/ch02-fs-1` uses Nano Server as the base image, creates a directory, and writes a file into it:

```
# escape=`
FROM microsoft/nanoserver

RUN md c:\data `
    echo 'from layer 1' > c:\data\file1.txt
```

The Dockerfile for the image `dockeronwindows/ch02-fs-2` creates an image based from that image, and adds a second file to the data directory:

```
# escape=`
FROM dockeronwindows/ch02-fs-1

RUN echo 'from image 2' > c:\data\file2.txt
```

There's nothing special about *base* images - any image can be used in the `FROM` instruction for a new image. It can be an official image curated on the Docker Hub, a commercial image from Docker Store, a local image built from scratch, or an image that is many levels deep in a hierarchy.

I'll build both images and run an interactive container from `dockeronwindows/ch02-fs-2`, so I can take a look at the files on the `C` drive. This command starts a container and gives it an explicit name, `c1`, so I can work with it without using the random container ID:

docker container run -it --name c1 dockeronwindows/ch02-fs-2 powershell

Many options in Docker commands have short and long forms. The long form starts with two dashes, like `--interactive`. The short form is a single letter and starts with a single dash, like `-i`. Short tags can be combined, so `-it` is equivalent to `-i -t`, which is equivalent to `--interactive --tty`. Run `docker --help` to navigate the commands and their options.

The `ls` command is a PowerShell alias for `Get-ChildItem`, which I can use to list the directory contents inside the container:

```
> ls C:\data

    Directory: C:\data

Mode        LastWriteTime       Length   Name
----        -------------       ------   ----
-a----      6/22/2017 7:35 AM   17       file1.txt
-a----      6/22/2017 7:35 AM   17       file2.txt
```

Both the files are there for the container to use in the `C:\data` directory - the first file is in a layer from the `ch02-fs-1` image, and the second file is in a layer from the `ch02-fs-2` image. The PowerShell executable is available from another layer in the base Nano Server image, and the container sees them all in the same way.

I'll append some more text to one of the existing files and create a new file in the `c1` container:

```
PS C:\> echo ' * ADDITIONAL * ' >> c:\data\file2.txt
PS C:\> echo 'New!' > c:\data\file3.txt
PS C:\> ls c:\data

 Directory: C:\data

Mode        LastWriteTime        Length    Name
----        -------------        ------    ----
-a----      6/22/2017 7:35 AM    17        file1.txt
-a----      6/22/2017 7:47 AM    53        file2.txt
-a----      6/22/2017 7:47 AM    14        file3.txt
```

From the file listing, you can see that `file2.txt` from the image layer has been modified and there is a new file, `file3.txt`. Now I'll exit this container and create a new one using the same image:

```
PS C:\> exit
PS> docker container run -it --name c2 dockeronwindows/ch02-fs-2 powershell
```

What are you expecting to see in the `C:\data` directory in this new container? Let's take a look:

```
> ls C:\data

Directory: C:\data

Mode        LastWriteTime        Length    Name
----        -------------        ------    ----
-a----      6/22/2017 7:35 AM    17        file1.txt
-a----      6/22/2017 7:35 AM    17        file2.txt
```

You know that image layers are read-only and every container has its own writeable layer, so the results should be clear. The new container `c2` has the original files from the image without the changes from the first container `c1` - which are stored in the writeable layer for `c1`. Each container's filesystem is isolated, so one container doesn't see any changes made by another container.

If you want to share data between containers, or between containers and the host, you can use Docker volumes.

Sharing data between containers with volumes

Volumes are defined in an image with the VOLUME instruction, specifying a directory path. When you run a container with a volume defined, the volume is mapped to a physical location on the host, which is specific to that one container. More containers running from the same image will have their volume mapped to a different host location.

In Windows, volume directories need to be empty - in your Dockerfile, you can't create files in a directory and then expose it as a volume. Volumes also need to be defined on a disk that exists in the image. In the Windows base images, there is only a C drive available, so volumes need to be created on the C drive.

The Dockerfile for dockeronwindows/ch02-volumes creates an image with two volumes:

```
# escape=`
FROM microsoft/nanoserver

VOLUME C:\app\config
VOLUME C:\app\logs

ENTRYPOINT powershell
```

When I run a container from that image, Docker creates a virtual filesystem from three sources. The image layers are read-only, the container's layer is writeable, and the volumes can be set to read-only or writeable:

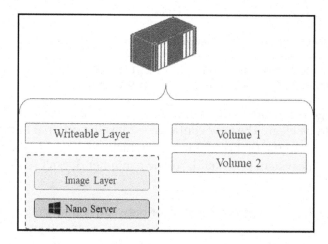

Because volumes are separate from the container, they can be shared with other containers even if the source container isn't running. I can run a task container from this image, with a command to create a new file in the volume:

```
docker container run --name source dockeronwindows/ch02-volumes "echo
'start' > c:\app\logs\log-1.txt"
```

Docker starts the container, which writes the file, and then exits. The container and its volumes haven't been deleted, so I can connect to the volumes in another container using the `--volumes-from` option and by specifying my first container's name:

```
docker container run -it --volumes-from source dockeronwindows/ch02-volumes
```

This is an interactive container, and when I list the contents of the C:\app directory, I'll see the two directories `logs` and `config`, which are volumes from the first container:

```
> ls C:\app

    Directory: C:\app

Mode        LastWriteTime       Length  Name
----        -------------       ------  ----
d----l      6/22/2017 8:11 AM           config
d----l      6/22/2017 8:11 AM           logs
```

The shared volume has read and write access, so I can see the file created in the first container and append to it:

```
PS C:\> cat C:\app\logs\log-1.txt
start

PS C:\> echo 'more' >> C:\app\logs\log-1.txt

PS C:\> cat C:\app\logs\log-1.txt
start
more
```

Sharing data between containers like this is very useful - you can run a task container that takes a backup of data or log files from a long-running background container. The default access is for volumes to be writeable, but that's something to be wary of, as you could edit data and break the application running in the source container.

Docker lets you mount volumes from another container in the read-only mode instead by adding the :ro flag to the name of the container in the --volumes-from option. This is a safer way to access data if you want to read it without making changes. I'll run a new container, sharing the same volumes from the original container in read-only mode:

```
> docker container run -it --volumes-from source:ro dockeronwindows/ch02-
volumes

PS C:\> cat C:\app\logs\log-1.txt
start
more

PS C:\> echo 'more' >> C:\app\logs\log-1.txt
out-file : Access to the path 'C:\app\logs\log-1.txt' is denied.
At line:1 char:1
+ echo 'more' >> C:\app\logs\log-1.txt
+ ~~~~~~~~~~~~~~~~~~~~~~~~~~~~~~~~~~~~~
  + CategoryInfo : OpenError: (:) [Out-File], UnauthorizedAccessException
  + FullyQualifiedErrorId :
FileOpenFailure,Microsoft.PowerShell.Commands.OutFileCommand
```

In the new container, I can't write to the log file. However I can see the content in the log file from the original container, and the line appended by the second container.

Sharing data between container and host with volumes

Container volumes are stored on the host, so you can access them directly from the machine running Docker - but they'll be in a nested directory somewhere in Docker's program data directory. The docker container inspect command tells you the physical location for a container's volumes, along with a lot more information - I've used it previously to fetch the container's IP address.

I can use explicit JSON formatting in the container inspect command, and extract just the volume information which is in the Mounts field. This command pipes the Docker output into a PowerShell cmdlet to show the JSON in a friendly format:

```
> docker container inspect --format '{{ json .Mounts }}' source |
ConvertFrom-Json

Type : volume
Name : 3514e9620e667028b7e3ca8bc42f3615ea94108e2c08875d50c102c9da7cbc06
Source : C:\ProgramData\Docker\volumes\3514e96...\_data
Destination : c:\app\config
```

```
Driver : local
RW : True

Type : volume
Name : a342dc516e19fe2b84d7514067d48c17e5324bbda5f3e97962b1ad8fa4043247
Source : C:\ProgramData\Docker\volumes\a342dc5...\_data
Destination : c:\app\logs
Driver : local
RW : True
```

I've abbreviated the output, but in the source file you can see the full path where the volume data is stored on the host. I can access the container's files directly from the host, using the source directory. When I run this command on my Windows machine, I'll see the file created inside the container volume:

```
> ls C:\ProgramData\Docker\volumes\a342dc5...\_data

Directory: C:\ProgramData\Docker\volumes\a342dc5...\_data


Mode        LastWriteTime        Length   Name
----        -------------        ------   ----
-a----      22/06/2017 08:13 28           log-1.txt
```

Accessing the files on the host is possible this way, but it's awkward to use the nested directory location with the volume ID. Instead, you can mount a volume from a specific location on the host when you create a container.

Mounting volumes from host directories

You use the `--volume` option to explicitly map a directory in a container from a known location on the host. The target location in the container can be a directory created with the `VOLUME` command, or any directory in the container's filesystem. The source is the location on the host filesystem.

I'll create a dummy configuration file for my app in a directory on the `C` drive on my Windows machine:

```
PS> mkdir C:\app-config | Out-Null
PS> echo 'VERSION=17.06' > C:\app-config\version.txt
```

Now I'll run a container which maps a volume from the host, and read the configuration file which is actually stored on the host:

```
> docker container run `
    --volume C:\app-config:C:\app\config `
    dockeronwindows/ch02-volumes `
    cat C:\app\config\version.txt
VERSION=17.06
```

The --volume option specifies the mount in the format {source}:{target}. The source is the host location, which needs to exist. The target is the container location, which does not need to exist - but needs to be empty if it does exist.

 Volume mounts are different in Windows and Linux containers. In Linux the target folder does not need to be empty, and Docker will merge the contents from the source into the target. Docker on Linux also lets you mount a single file location, but on Windows you can only mount whole directories.

Volume mounts are useful for running stateful applications in containers, like databases. You can run SQL Server in a container, and have the database files stored in a location on the host - which could be a RAID array on the server. When you have schema updates, you remove the old container and start a new container from the updated Docker image. You use the same volume mount for the new container, so the data is preserved from the old container.

Using volumes for configuration and state

Application state is an important consideration when you're running applications in containers. Containers can be long-running, but they are not intended to be permanent. One of the biggest advantages with containers over traditional compute models is that you can easily replace them, and the replacement starts in seconds. When you have a new feature to deploy, or a security vulnerability to patch, you just build an upgraded image, stop the old container, and start a replacement from the new image.

Volumes let you manage that upgrade process by keeping your data separate from your application container. I'll demonstrate this with a simple web application that stores the hit count for a page in a text file - each time you browse to the page, the site increments the count.

The Dockerfile for the image `dockeronwindows/ch02-hitcount-website` uses multi-stage builds, compiling the application using the `microsoft/dotnet` image and packaging the final app using `microsoft/aspnetcore` as the base:

```
# escape=`
FROM microsoft/dotnet:1.1.2-sdk-nanoserver AS builder
WORKDIR C:\src
COPY src .
RUN dotnet restore; dotnet publish

# app image
FROM microsoft/aspnetcore:1.1.2-nanoserver
WORKDIR C:\dotnetapp
RUN New-Item -Type Directory -Path .\app-state

CMD ["dotnet", "HitCountWebApp.dll"]
COPY --from=builder C:\src\bin\Debug\netcoreapp1.1\publish .
```

In the Dockerfile I create an empty directory at `C:\dotnetapp\app-state` which is where the application will store the hit count in a text file. I've built the first version of the app into an image with the `v1` tag:

```
docker image build --tag dockeronwindows/ch02-hitcount-website:v1 .
```

I'll create a directory on the host to use for the container's state, and run a container that mounts the application state directory from a directory on the host:

```
mkdir C:\app-state

docker container run -d -P `
 -v C:\app-state:C:\dotnetapp\app-state `
 --name appv1
 dockeronwindows/ch02-hitcount-website:v1
```

I can get the IP address of the container from `docker container inspect`, and then browse to the site. When I refresh the page a few times I'll see the hit count increasing:

Now when I have an upgraded version of the app to deploy, I can package it into a new image tagged with v2. When the image is ready, I can stop the old container and start a new one, using the same volume mapping:

```
PS> docker container stop appv1
appv1

PS> docker container run -d -P `
 -v C:\app-state:C:\dotnetapp\app-state `
 --name appv2
 dockeronwindows/ch02-hitcount-website:v2

f6433a09e9479d76db3cd0bc76f9f817acfc6c52375c5e33dbc1d4c9780feb6d
```

The volume containing the application state is being reused, so the new version will continue using the saved state from the old version. I have a new container with a new IP address. When I browse to it for the first time, I see the updated UI with an attractive icon, but the hit count is carried forward from version 1:

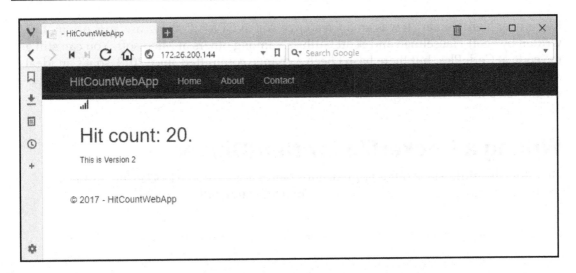

Application state can have structural changes between versions, which is something you will need to manage yourself. The Docker image for the open source Git server, GitLab, is a good example of this - the state is stored in a database on a volume, and when you upgrade to a new version, the app checks the database and runs upgrade scripts, if needed.

Application configuration is another place to make use of volumes. You can ship your application with a default configuration set built into the image but with a volume created for users to override the base configuration with their own values.

You'll see these techniques put to good use in the next chapter.

Packaging a traditional ASP.NET web app as a Docker image

Microsoft has made the Windows Server Core base image available on Docker Hub, and that's a version of Windows Server 2016 which has much of the functionality of the full server edition but without the UI. As base images go, it's very large - 5 GB compressed on Docker Hub, compared to 380 MB for Nano Server, and 2 MB for the tiny Alpine Linux image. But it means you can Dockerize pretty much any existing Windows app, and that's a great way to start migrating your systems to Docker.

Remember NerdDinner? It was an open source ASP.NET MVC showcase app, originally written by Scott Hanselman and Scott Guthrie - among others at Microsoft. You can still get the code at CodePlex, but there hasn't been a change committed since 2013, so it's an ideal candidate for proving that old ASP.NET apps can be migrated to Docker, and that can be the first step in modernizing them.

Writing a Dockerfile for NerdDinner

I'll follow the multi-stage build approach for NerdDinner, so the Dockerfile for the `dockeronwindows/ch-02-nerd-dinner` images starts with a builder stage:

```
# escape=`
FROM sixeyed/msbuild:netfx-4.5.2-webdeploy-10.0.14393.1198 AS builder

WORKDIR C:\src\NerdDinner
COPY src\NerdDinner\packages.config .
RUN nuget restore packages.config –PackagesDirectory ..\packages

COPY src C:\src
RUN msbuild .\NerdDinner\NerdDinner.csproj /p:OutputPath=c:\out\NerdDinner
`
            /p:DeployOnBuild=true `
/p:VSToolsPath=C:\MSBuild.Microsoft.VisualStudio.Web.targets.14.0.0.3\tools
\VSToolsPath
```

The stage uses `sixeyed/msbuild` as the base image for compiling the application, which is an image I maintain on Docker Cloud. That image installs MSBuild, NuGet and the other dependencies you need for packaging a Visual Studio Web project, without using Visual Studio. The build stage happens in two parts:

- First, copy the NuGet `packages.config` file into the image, and then run `nuget restore`
- Next, copy the rest of the source tree and run `msbuild`

Separating those parts means Docker will use multiple image layers, the first layer will contain all the restored NuGet packages and the second layer will contain the compiled web app. This means I can take advantage of Docker's layer caching. Unless I change my NuGet references, the packages will be loaded from the cached layer and Docker won't run the restore part, which is an expensive operation. The MSBuild step will run every time any source files change.

If I had a deployment guide for NerdDinner, before the move to Docker, it would look something like this:

- Install Windows on a clean server
- Run all Windows Updates
- Install IIS
- Install .NET
- Set up ASP.NET
- Copy the web app into the C drive
- Create an application pool in IIS
- Create the website in IIS using the application pool
- Delete the default website

This will be the basis for the second stage of the Dockerfile, but I will be able to simplify all the steps. I can use `microsoft/aspnet` as the `FROM` image, which gives me a clean install of Windows with IIS and ASP.NET installed. That takes care of the first five steps in one instruction. This is the remainder of the Dockerfile for `dockeronwindows/ch-02-nerd-dinner`:

```
FROM microsoft/aspnet:windowsservercore-10.0.14393.1198
SHELL ["powershell", "-Command", "$ErrorActionPreference = 'Stop';"]

WORKDIR C:\nerd-dinner

RUN Remove-Website -Name 'Default Web Site'; `
    New-Website -Name 'nerd-dinner' -Port 80 -PhysicalPath 'c:\nerd-dinner'
-ApplicationPool '.NET v4.5'

RUN & c:\windows\system32\inetsrv\appcmd.exe unlock config
/section:system.webServer/handlers

COPY --from=builder C:\out\NerdDinner\_PublishedWebsites\NerdDinner
C:\nerd-dinner
```

Using the `escape` directive and `SHELL` instruction lets me use normal Windows file paths without double backslashes and PowerShell-style backticks to separate commands over many lines. Removing the default website and creating a new website in IIS is simple with PowerShell, and the Dockerfile clearly shows me the port the app is using and the path of the content.

I'm using the built-in .NET 4.5 application pool, which is a simplification from the original deployment process. In IIS on a VM, you'd normally have a dedicated application pool for each website in order to isolate processes from each other. But in the containerized app, there will be only one website running - another website would be in another container, so we already have isolation, and each container can use the default application pool without worrying about interference.

The final `COPY` instruction copies the published web application from the builder stage into the application image. It's the last line in the Dockerfile to take advantage of Docker's caching again. When I'm working on the app, the source code is the most frequent thing to change. The Dockerfile is structured so that when I change code and run `docker image build` the only instructions that run are MSBuild in the first stage and the copy in the second stage, so the build is very fast.

This could be all you need for a fully functioning Dockerized ASP.NET website, but in the case of NerdDinner, there is one more instruction, which proves that you can cope with awkward, unexpected details when you containerize your application. The NerdDinner app has some custom configuration settings in the `system.webServer` section of its `Web.config` file, and by default that section is locked by IIS. I need to unlock the section, which I do with `appcmd` in the second `RUN` instruction.

Now I can build the image and can run a legacy ASP.NET app in a Windows container:

```
docker container run -d -P dockeronwindows/ch02-nerd-dinner
```

I can get the container's IP address with `docker container inspect`, and browse to the NerdDinner homepage:

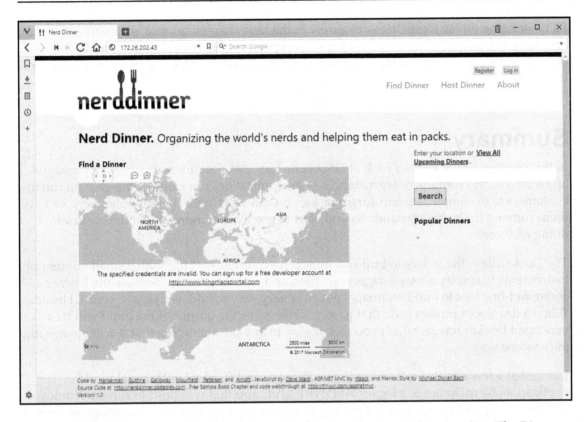

At this point, the app isn't fully functional - I just have a basic version running. The Bing Maps object doesn't show a real map because I haven't provided an API key. The API key is something that will change for every environment (each developer, the test environments, and production will have different keys). In Docker you manage environment configuration with environment variables, which I will use for the next iteration of the Dockerfile in Chapter 3, *Developing Dockerized .NET and .NET Core Applications*.

If you navigate around this version of NerdDinner and try to register a new user or search for a dinner, you'll see a yellow screen crash page telling you the database isn't available. In its original form, NerdDinner uses SQL Server LocalDB as a lightweight database and stores the database file in the app directory. I could install the LocalDB runtime into the container image, but that doesn't fit with the Docker philosophy of having one function per container. Instead, I'll build a separate image for the database so I can run it in its own container.

I'll be iterating on the NerdDinner example in the next chapter, adding environment variables, running SQL Server as a separate component in its own container, and demonstrating how you can start modernizing traditional ASP.NET apps by making use of the Docker platform.

Summary

In this chapter, I took a closer look at Docker images and containers. Images are packaged applications, and containers are instances of an application, run from an image. You can use containers to do simple fire-and-forget tasks, you can work with them interactively, or have them running in the background. As you start to use Docker more, you'll find yourself doing all three.

The Dockerfile is the source to build an image. It's a simple text file with a small number of instructions to specify a base image, copy files, and run commands. You use the Docker command-line tool to build an image, which is very easy to add as a step to your CI build. When a developer pushes code that passes all the tests, the output of the build will be a versioned Docker image, which you can deploy to any host knowing that it will always run in the same way.

I looked at a few simple Dockerfiles in this chapter, and finished with a real-world application. NerdDinner is a legacy ASP.NET MVC app that was built to run on Windows and IIS. Using multi-stage builds I packaged that legacy app into a Docker image and ran it in a container. This shows that the new model of compute that Docker offers isn't just for greenfield projects using .NET Core and Nano Server - you can migrate existing apps to Docker and put yourself in a good place to start modernizing them.

In the next chapter, I'll use Docker to modernize the architecture of NerdDinner, breaking features out into separate components and using Docker to plug them all together.

3

Developing Dockerized .NET and .NET Core Applications

Docker is a platform for packaging, distributing, and running applications. When you package your applications as Docker images, they all have the same shape—you can deploy, manage, secure, and upgrade them all in the same way. All Dockerized applications have the same requirements to run them: the Docker Engine running on a compatible operating system. Applications run in isolated environments, so you can host different application platforms and different platform versions on the same machine with no interference.

In the .NET world, this means you can run multiple workloads on a single Windows machine—they could be ASP.NET websites or **Windows Communication Foundation (WCF)** apps on .NET console applications or .NET Windows Services. You saw in the previous chapter that you can Dockerize legacy .NET applications without any code change, but Docker has some simple expectations about how applications running inside containers should behave, so they can get the full benefit of the platform.

In this chapter, you'll look at how to build applications so they can take complete advantage of the Docker platform, including the following:

- The integration points between Docker and your application
- Configuring your application with environment variables
- Monitoring applications with health checks
- Running distributed solutions with components in different containers

This will help you develop .NET and .NET Core applications that behave in the way Docker expects, so you can manage them fully with Docker.

Building good citizens for Docker

The Docker platform makes very few demands on applications that want to use it. You're not restricted to certain languages or frameworks, and you don't need to use special libraries to communicate from the app to the container and you don't need to structure your application in a certain way.

To support the widest possible range of applications, Docker uses the console to communicate between the application and the container runtime. Application logs and error messages are expected on the console output and error streams. Storage managed by Docker is presented as a normal disk to the operating system, and Docker's networking stack is transparent. The application appears to be running on its own machine, connected to other machines by a normal TCP/IP network.

A good citizen for Docker is an app that makes very few assumptions about the system it's running on and uses basic mechanisms that all operating systems support: the filesystem, environment variables, networking, and the console. Most importantly, the application should only do one thing. As you've seen, when Docker runs a container, it starts the process specified in the Dockerfile or the command line, and it watches that process. When the process ends, the container exits, so ideally, you should build your app to have a single process, which ensures Docker is watching the process that matters.

These are recommendations, though, not requirements. You can start multiple processes in a bootstrap script when a container runs and Docker will run it happily—but it will only monitor the last process that started. Your apps can write log entries to local files instead of the console and Docker will still run them, but you won't see any output if you use Docker to check the container logs.

In .NET, you can easily meet the recommendations by running a console application, which provides a simplified integration between the application and the host, and it's one reason why all .NET Core apps - including websites and web APIs—run as console applications. For legacy .NET apps, you won't be able to make them into perfect citizens, but you can extend them to make good use of the Docker platform.

Hosting Internet Information Services (IIS) applications in Docker

Complete .NET Framework apps can be easily packaged into Docker images, but there are some limitations you need to be aware of. Microsoft provides Nano Server and Windows Server Core base images on Docker Hub. The complete .NET Framework doesn't run on Nano Server, so to host your existing .NET apps in Docker, you need to use the Windows Server Core base image.

Running from Windows Server Core means your application images will be around 10 GB in size, the bulk of which is in the base image. You have a complete Windows Server operating system, with all the packages available to enable Windows Server features, such as DNS and DHCP—even though you only want to use it for a single application role. It's perfectly reasonable to run containers from Windows Server Core, but you need to be aware of the implications:

- The base image has a large surface area with a lot of software installed, which means it's likely to have more frequent security and functional patches
- The OS runs a lot of its own processes in addition to your application process, as several core parts of Windows run as background Windows services
- Windows has its own application platforms, with high-value feature sets for hosting and management, which do not natively integrate with the Docker approach

You can take an ASP.NET web application and dockerize it in a few hours. It will build into a large Docker image that takes longer to distribute and start up than an application built on a lightweight, modern application stack. But you still have a single package with your whole application deployed, configured, and ready to run. This is a big step in improving quality and reducing deployment time, and it can be the first part of a program to modernize a legacy application.

To integrate an ASP.NET app more closely with Docker, you can modify how IIS logs are written and specify how Docker checks whether the container is healthy—without any changes to the application code. If changing code is part of your modernization program, then with minimal changes, you can use the container's environment variables for application configuration.

Configuring IIS for Docker-friendly logging

IIS writes log entries to text files, recording HTTP requests and responses. You can configure exactly what fields are written, but the default installation records useful things, such as the route of the HTTP request, the response status code, and the time taken for IIS to respond. It would be good to surface these logs entries to Docker, but IIS manages its own log files, buffering entries before writing them to the disk and rotating log files to manage the disk space.

Log management is a fundamental part of application platforms, which is why IIS takes care of it for web apps, but Docker has its own logging system. Docker logging is far more powerful and pluggable than the text filesystem that IIS uses, but it only reads log entries from the container's console output stream. You can't have IIS writing logs to the console because it runs in a background Windows Service with no console attached, so you need a different approach.

There are two options for this. The first is to build an HTTP module that plugs into the IIS platform with an event handler that receives logs from IIS. This handler can publish all messages to a queue or a Windows pipe, so you don't change how IIS logs; you just add another log sink. Then, you'd package your web application together with a console app that listened for published log entries and relayed them on the console. The console app would be the entry point when a container starts, so every IIS log entry would get routed to the console for Docker to read.

The HTTP module approach is robust and scalable, but it adds more complexity than we need when we're getting started. A simpler option is to configure IIS to write all log entries to a single text file and in the startup command for the container run a PowerShell script to watch that file and echo new log entries to the console. When the container is running, all the IIS log entries get echoed to the console, which surfaces them to Docker.

To set this up in the Docker image, you first need to configure IIS so it writes all log entries from any site to a single file, and it lets the file grow without rotating it. You can do this with PowerShell, using the `Set-WebConfigurationProperty` cmdlet in the Dockerfile, modifying the central logging properties at the application host level. I use this cmdlet in the Dockerfile for the `dockeronwindows/ch03-iis-log-watcher` image:

```
RUN Set-WebConfigurationProperty -p 'MACHINE/WEBROOT/APPHOST' -fi
'system.applicationHost/log' -n 'centralLogFileMode' -v 'CentralW3C'; `
    Set-WebConfigurationProperty -p 'MACHINE/WEBROOT/APPHOST' -fi
'system.applicationHost/log/centralW3CLogFile' -n 'truncateSize' -v
4294967295; `
    Set-WebConfigurationProperty -p 'MACHINE/WEBROOT/APPHOST' -fi
'system.applicationHost/log/centralW3CLogFile' -n 'period' -v 'MaxSize'; `
    Set-WebConfigurationProperty -p 'MACHINE/WEBROOT/APPHOST' -fi
```

```
'system.applicationHost/log/centralW3CLogFile' -n 'directory' -v
'C:\iislog'
```

This configures IIS to log all entries to a file in C:\iislog, and to set the maximum file size for log rotation—letting the log file grow to 4 GB. That's plenty of room to play with; remember containers that are not meant to be long-lived, so we shouldn't have gigabytes of log entries in a single container. IIS still uses a subdirectory format for the log file, so the actual log file path will be C:\iislog\W3SVC\u_extend1.log. Now that I have a known log file location, I can use PowerShell to echo log entries to the console.

I do that in the CMD instruction, so the final command that Docker runs and monitors is the PowerShell cmdlet to echo log entries. When new entries are written to the console, they get picked up by Docker. PowerShell makes it easy to watch the file, but there's a complication because the file needs to exist before PowerShell can watch it. In the Dockerfile, I use multiple commands at startup:

```
CMD Start-Service W3SVC; `
    Invoke-WebRequest http://localhost -UseBasicParsing | Out-Null; `
    netsh http flush logbuffer | Out-Null; `
    Get-Content -path 'c:\iislog\W3SVC\u_extend1.log' -Tail 1 -Wait
```

There are four parts to this command:

- Start the IIS Windows service (W3SVC)
- Make an HTTP GET request to the localhost, which starts the IIS worker process and writes the first log entry
- Flush the HTTP log buffer, so the log file gets written to the disk and exists for PowerShell to watch
- Read the content of the log file in the tail mode, so any new lines written to the file get shown on the console.

I can run a container from this image in the usual way:

```
docker container run -d -P --name log-watcher dockeronwindows/ch03-iis-log-watcher
```

When I send some traffic to the site by browsing to the container's IP address (or using Invoke-WebRequest in PowerShell), I can see the IIS log entries that are relayed to Docker from the Get-Content cmdlet using docker container logs:

```
> docker container logs log-watcher
2017-06-22 10:38:54 W3SVC1 ::1 GET / - 80 - ::1
Mozilla/5.0+(Windows+NT;+Windows+NT+10.0;+en-
US)+WindowsPowerShell/5.1.14393.1066 - 200 0 0 251
2017-06-22 10:39:21 W3SVC1 172.26.207.181 GET / - 80 - 172.26.192.1
```

```
Mozilla/5.0+(Windows+NT+10.0;+WOW64)+AppleWebKit/537.36+(KHTML,+like+Gecko)
+Chrome/59.0.3071.90+Safari/537.36+Vivaldi/1.91.867.38 - 200 0 0 0
2017-06-22 10:39:21 W3SVC1 172.26.207.181 GET /iisstart.png - 80 -
172.26.192.1
Mozilla/5.0+(Windows+NT+10.0;+WOW64)+AppleWebKit/537.36+(KHTML,+like+Gecko)
+Chrome/59.0.3071.90+Safari/537.36+Vivaldi/1.91.867.38
http://172.26.207.181/ 200 0 0 119
```

 IIS always buffers log entries in the memory before writing them to the disk, so it micro-batches the writes to improve performance. The flush happens every 60 seconds or when the buffer is 64 KB in size. If you want to force the IIS log in a container to flush, use the same `netsh` command I used in the Dockerfile: `docker container exec log-watcher netsh http flush logbuffer`. You'll see an `Ok` output, and new entries will be there in `docker container logs`.

I've added configuration to IIS in the image and a new command, which means all IIS log entries get echoed to the console. This will work for any application hosted in IIS, so I can echo HTTP logs for ASP.NET applications and static websites without any changes to the apps or the site content. Console output is where Docker looks for log entries, so this simple extension integrates logging from the existing application into the new platform.

Promoting environment variables

Modern apps increasingly use environment variables for configuration settings because they're supported by practically every platform, from physical machines to serverless functions. All platforms use environment variables in the same way, as a store of key-value pairs, so using environment variables for configuration, you make your app highly portable.

ASP.NET apps already have a rich configuration framework in `Web.config`, but with some small code changes, you can take key settings and move them to environment variables. This lets you build one Docker image for your app, which you can run in different environments, setting environment variables in containers to change configuration.

Docker lets you specify environment variables in the Dockerfile and give them initial default values. The ENV instruction sets environment variables, and you can set either one variable or many variables in each ENV, this example is from the Dockerfile for `dockeronwindows/ch03-iis-environment-variables`:

```
ENV A01_KEY A01 value
ENV A02_KEY="A02 value" `
    A03_KEY="A03 value"
```

Settings added to the Dockerfile with ENV become part of the image, so every container you run from the image will have these values set. When you run a container, you can add new environment variables or replace the value of existing image variables using the --env or –e option. You can see how environment variables work with a simple Nano Server container:

```
> docker container run `
    --env ENV_01='Hello' --env ENV_02='World' `
    microsoft/nanoserver `
    powershell 'Write-Output $env:ENV_01 $env:ENV_02'
Hello
World
```

With apps hosted in IIS, there's a complication in using environment variables from Docker. When IIS starts, it reads all the environment variables from the system and caches them. When Docker runs a container with environment variables set, it writes them at the process level, but that's after IIS has cached the original values, so they don't get updated and IIS applications won't see the new value. IIS doesn't cache machine-level environment variables in the same way, though, so we can promote the values set by Docker to machine-level environment variables, and IIS apps will be able to read them.

Promoting environment variables can be done by copying them from the process level to the machine level. This PowerShell script does that by looping through all process-level variables and copying them to machine-level unless the machine-level key already exists:

```
  foreach($key in
[System.Environment]::GetEnvironmentVariables('Process').Keys) {
      if ([System.Environment]::GetEnvironmentVariable($key, 'Machine') -eq
$null) {
          $value = [System.Environment]::GetEnvironmentVariable($key,
'Process')
          [System.Environment]::SetEnvironmentVariable($key, $value,
'Machine')
      }
  }
```

I can use this script block to the CMD instruction in my Dockerfile, but if I add that to the block to echo the log, the command runs to 10 lines, and it gets difficult to manage inside the Dockerfile. Instead, I've put the environment commands and the log echo commands into one script file and used that as ENTRYPOINT:

```
COPY bootstrap.ps1 C:\
ENTRYPOINT ["powershell", "C:\bootstrap.ps1"]
```

> The ENTRYPOINT and CMD instructions both tell Docker how to run your application. You can combine them to specify a default entry point and allow users of your image to override the command when they start a container.

The application in the image is a simple ASP.NET Web Forms page that lists out environment variables. I can run this in a container in the usual way:

```
docker container run -d -P --name iis-env dockeronwindows/ch03-iis-
environment-variables
```

When the container starts, I can get the IP address and open a browser on the ASP.NET Web Forms page:

```
$ip = docker inspect --format '{{ .NetworkSettings.Networks.nat.IPAddress
}}' iis-env
start "http://$ip"
```

I see output like this, with the default environment variable values from the Docker image:

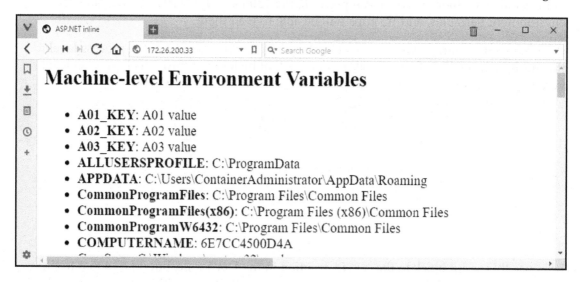

You can run the same image with different environment variables, overriding one of the image variables and adding a new variable:

```
docker run -d -P --name iis-env2 `
 -e A01_KEY='NEW VALUE!' `
 -e B01_KEY='NEW KEY!' `
 dockeronwindows/ch03-iis-environment-variables
```

Browse the container's IP address again, and you'll see the new values written out by the ASP.NET page:

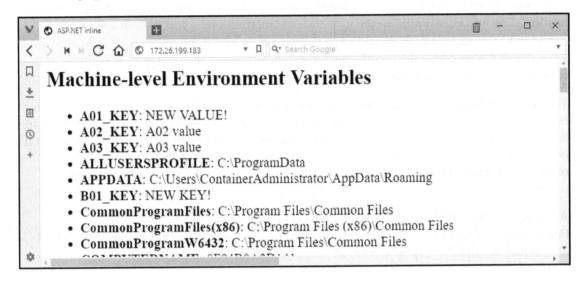

I've added support for Docker's environment variable management into an IIS image now, so ASP.NET apps can use the `System.Environment` class to read configuration settings. I've retained the IIS log echo in this new image, so this is a good Docker citizen now—you can configure the application and check the logs through Docker.

One last improvement I can make is to tell Docker how to monitor the application running inside the container, so Docker can determine whether the application is healthy and take action if it becomes unhealthy.

Building Docker images that monitor applications

When I add these new features to the NerdDinner Dockerfile and run a container from the image, I'll be able to see the web request and response logs with the `docker container logs` command, which relays all the IIS log entries captured by Docker, and I can use an environment variable to specify the database user credentials. This makes running and administering the legacy ASP.NET application consistent with how I use any other containerized application running on Docker. But I can also configure Docker to monitor the container for me, so I can manage any unexpected failures.

Docker provides the ability to monitor the application health rather than just checking whether the application process is still running, with the HEALTHCHECK instruction in the Dockerfile. With HEALTHCHECK, you tell Docker how to test whether the application is still healthy. The syntax is similar to the RUN and CMD instructions—you pass in a shell command to execute, which should have a return code of 0 if the application is healthy and 1 if it is not. Docker runs the health check periodically when the container is running and emits status events if the health of a container changes.

The simple definition of *healthy* for a web application is the ability to respond normally to HTTP requests. Which request you make depends on how thorough you want the check to be—ideally, the request should execute key parts of your application, so you're confident it is all working correctly. But equally, the request should complete quickly and have a minimal compute impact, so processing lots of health checks doesn't affect consumer requests.

A simple health check for any web application just uses the Invoke-WebRequest PowerShell cmdlet to fetch the home page and check whether the HTTP response code is 200, which means the response was successfully received:

```
try {
    $response = iwr http://localhost/ -UseBasicParsing
    if ($response.StatusCode -eq 200) {
        return 0
    } else {
        return 1
    }
}
catch { return 1 }
```

For a more complex web application, it can be useful to add a new endpoint specifically for healthchecks. You can add a diagnostic endpoint to APIs and websites that exercise some of the core logic for your app and returns a Boolean result to indicate whether the app is healthy. You can call that endpoint in the Docker health check and check the response content as well as the status code in order to give you more confidence that the app is working correctly.

The HEALTHCHECK instruction in the Dockerfile is very simple. You can configure the interval between checks and the number of checks that can fail before the container is considered unhealthy, but to use the default values, just specify the test script in HEALTHCHECK CMD . This example from the Dockerfile for the dockeronwindows/ch03-iis-healthcheck image uses PowerShell to make a GET request to the diagnostics URL and check the response status code:

```
HEALTHCHECK --interval=5s `
  CMD powershell -command `
```

```
try { `
  $response = iwr http://localhost/diagnostics –UseBasicParsing; `
  if ($response.StatusCode –eq 200) { return 0} `
  else {return 1}; `
} catch { return 1 }
```

I've specified an interval for the health check, so Docker will execute this command inside the container every five seconds (the default interval is 30 seconds if you don't specify one). The health check is very cheap to run, as it's local to the container, so you can have a short interval like this and catch any problems quickly.

The application in this Docker image is an ASP.NET Web API app, which has a diagnostics endpoint, and a controller you can use to toggle the health of the application. The Dockerfile contains a health check, and you can see how Docker uses it when we run a container from that image:

```
docker container run –d –P --name healthcheck dockeronwindows/ch03-iis-
healthcheck
```

If you run docker container ls after starting that container, you'll see a slightly different output in the status field, similar to Up 3 seconds (health: starting). Docker runs the health check every five seconds for this container, so at this point, the check hasn't been run. Wait a little longer and then the status will be something like Up 46 seconds (healthy).

This container will stay healthy until I make a call to the controller to toggle the health. I can do that with a POST request that sets the API to return HTTP status 500 for all subsequent requests:

```
$ip = docker inspect –f '{{ .NetworkSettings.Networks.nat.IPAddress }}'
healthcheck
iwr "http://$ip/toggle/unhealthy" –Method Post
```

Now the application will respond with a 500 response to all the GET requests the Docker platform makes, which will fail the health check. Docker keeps trying the health check, and if there are three failures in a row, then it considers the container to be unhealthy. At this point, the status field in the container list shows Up 3 minutes (unhealthy). Docker doesn't take automatic action on single containers that are unhealthy, so this one is left running and you can still access the API.

Health checks are important when you start running containers in a clustered Docker environment (which I cover in `Chapter 7`, *Orchestrating Distributed Solutions with Docker Swarm*), and it's a good practice to include them in all Dockerfiles. Being able to package an application that the platform can test for health is a very useful feature; this means that wherever you run the app, we can keep a check on it.

Now you have all the tools to containerize an ASP.NET application and make it a good Docker citizen, integrating with the platform so it can be monitored and administered in the same way as other containers. A full .NET Framework application running on Windows Server Core can't meet the expectation of running a single process because of the all the necessary background Windows services. But we should still build container images so they run only one logical function and separate any dependencies.

Separating dependencies

In the last chapter, I dockerized the legacy NerdDinner app and got it running but without a database. The original application expected to use SQL Server LocalDB on the same host where the app is running. LocalDB is an MSI-based installation, and I can add it to the Docker image, just by downloading the MSI and installing it with `RUN` commands in the Dockerfile. But this means that when I start a container from the image, it has two functions—hosting a web application and running a database.

Having two functions in one container is not a good idea; what would happen if you wanted to upgrade your website without changing the database? Or, what if you needed to do some maintenance on the database, which didn't impact the website? What if you need to scale out the website? By coupling the two functions together, you've added a deployment risk, test effort, and administration complexity and reduced your operational flexibility.

Instead, I'm going to package the database in a new Docker image and run it in a separate container—using Docker's network layer to access the database container from the website container. SQL Server is a licensed product, but the free variant, SQL Server Express, is available from Microsoft as an image on the Docker Hub and comes with a production license. I can use that as the base for my image, building on it to prepare a pre-configured database instance, with the schema deployed and ready to connect to the web application.

Creating Docker images for SQL Server databases

Setting up a database image is just like any other Docker image; I'll be encapsulating the setup tasks in a Dockerfile. Broadly, for a new database, the steps will be as follows:

- Install SQL Server
- Configure SQL server
- Run DDL scripts to create the database schema
- Run DML scripts to populate static data

This fits in very well with a typical build process using Visual Studio's SQL database project type and the Dacpac deployment model. The output from publishing the project is a `.dacpac` file that contains the database schema and any custom SQL scripts to run. Using the SqlPackage tool, you can deploy the Dacpac file to a SQL Server instance—and it will either create a new database if it doesn't exist, or it will upgrade an existing database so the schema matches the Dacpac.

This approach is perfect for a custom SQL Server Docker image. I can use multi-stage builds again for the Dockerfile, so you don't need Visual Studio installed to package the database from the source code. This is the first stage of the Dockerfile for the `dockeronwindows/ch03-nerd-dinner-db` image:

```
# escape=`
FROM sixeyed/msbuild:netfx-4.5.2-ssdt AS builder

WORKDIR C:\src\NerdDinner.Database
COPY src\NerdDinner.Database .

RUN msbuild NerdDinner.Database.sqlproj `
/p:SQLDBExtensionsRefPath="C:\Microsoft.Data.Tools.Msbuild.10.0.61026\lib\n
et40" `
/p:SqlServerRedistPath="C:\Microsoft.Data.Tools.Msbuild.10.0.61026\lib\net4
0"
```

The `builder` stage just copies in the SQL project source and runs MSBuild to produce the Dacpac. I'm using a variant of the public `sixeyed/msbuild` image on Docker Cloud, which includes the NuGet packages you need to compile SQL projects.

Here's the second stage of the Dockerfile, which packages the NerdDinner Dacpac to run in SQL Server Express:

```
FROM microsoft/mssql-server-windows-express

ENV ACCEPT_EULA="Y" `
    DATA_PATH="C:\data" `
    sa_password="N3rdD!Nne720^6"

VOLUME ${DATA_PATH}
WORKDIR C:\init

COPY Initialize-Database.ps1 .
CMD ./Initialize-Database.ps1 -sa_password $env:sa_password -data_path
$env:data_path -Verbose

COPY --from=builder
C:\src\NerdDinner.Database\bin\Debug\NerdDinner.Database.dacpac .
```

There are no new instructions here, beyond what you've seen so far. You'll see that there are no RUN commands, so I'm not actually setting up the database schema when I build the image; I'm just packaging the Dacpac file into the image so I have everything I need to create or upgrade the database when the container starts.

In CMD, I run a PowerShell script that sets up the database. It's usually not a good idea to hide all the startup details in a separate script because that means you can't see what's going to happen when the container runs from the Dockerfile alone. But in this case, the startup procedure has a few functions, and they would make for a huge Dockerfile if we put them all in there.

The base SQL Server Express image defines environment variables called ACCEPT_EULA, so the user can accept the license agreement and sa_password to set the administrator password. I extend this image and set default values for the variables. I'll use the variables in the same way in order to allow users to specify an administrator password when they run the container. The rest of the startup script deals with the problem of storing the database state in a Docker volume.

Managing database files for SQL Server containers

A database container is like any other Docker container, but with a focus on statefulness. You'll want to ensure your database files are stored outside of the container, so you can replace the database container without losing any data. You can easily do that with volumes, as we saw in the last chapter, but there is a catch.

If you build a custom SQL Server image with a deployed database, your database files will be inside the image in a known location. You can run a container from that image without mounting a volume and it will just work, but the data will be stored in the container's writable layer. If you replace the container, when you have a database upgrade to perform—then you'll lose all your data.

Instead, you can run the container with a volume mounted from the host, mapping the expected SQL Server data directory from a host directory so your files live outside of the container in a known location on the host. This way, you can ensure your data files are stored in a RAID array on your server. But that means you can't deploy the database in the Dockerfile because the data directory will have data files from the image and you can't mount a directory that isn't empty.

The SQL Server images from Microsoft deal with this by letting you attach database and log files when it runs, so it works on the basis that you already have your database files on the host. In this case, you can use the image directly, mount your data folder, and run a SQL Server container with arguments telling it which database(s) to attach. This is a very limited approach, though—it means you need to create the database on a different SQL Server instance first and then attach it when you run the container. This doesn't fit with an automated release process.

For my custom image, I want to do something different. The image contains the Dacpac, so it has everything it needs to deploy the database. When the container starts, I want it to check the data directory, and if it's empty, then I create a new database by deploying the Dacpac. If the database files already exist when the container starts, then attach the database files first and upgrade the database using the Dacpac.

This approach means you can use the same image to run a fresh database container for a new environment or upgrade an existing database container without losing any of its data. And this works just as well whether you mount the database directory from the host or not, so you can let the user choose how to manage the container storage, and my image supports many different scenarios.

The logic to do that is all in the `Initialize-Database.ps1` PowerShell script, which the Dockerfile sets as the entry point for containers. In the Dockerfile, I pass the data directory to the PowerShell script in the `data_path` variable, and the script checks whether the NerdDinner data (`mdf`) and log (`ldf`) files are in that directory:

```
$mdfPath = "$data_path\NerdDinner_Primary.mdf"
$ldfPath = "$data_path\NerdDinner_Primary.ldf"

# attach data files if they exist:
if ((Test-Path $mdfPath) -eq $true) {
 $sqlcmd = "IF DB_ID('NerdDinner') IS NULL BEGIN CREATE DATABASE NerdDinner
ON (FILENAME = N'$mdfPath')"
 if ((Test-Path $ldfPath) -eq $true) {
   $sqlcmd = "$sqlcmd, (FILENAME = N'$ldfPath')"
 }
 $sqlcmd = "$sqlcmd FOR ATTACH; END"
 Invoke-Sqlcmd -Query $sqlcmd -ServerInstance ".\SQLEXPRESS"
}
```

This script looks complex, but actually, it's just building a CREATE DATABASE...FOR ATTACH statement, filling in the paths of the MDF data file and LDF log file if they exist. Then, it invokes the SQL statement, which attaches the database files from the external volume as a new database in the SQL Server container.

This covers the scenario where a user runs a container with a volume mount, where the host directory has data files from a previous container. These files are attached, and the database is available in the new container. Next, the script uses the SqlPackage tool to generate a deployment script from the Dacpac. I know the SqlPackage tool exists and I know the path to it because it's built into the SQL Server Express base image:

```
$SqlPackagePath = 'C:\Program Files (x86)\Microsoft SQL
Server\130\DAC\bin\SqlPackage.exe'
& $SqlPackagePath `
 /sf:NerdDinner.Database.dacpac `
 /a:Script /op:deploy.sql /p:CommentOutSetVarDeclarations=true `
 /tsn:.\SQLEXPRESS /tdn:NerdDinner /tu:sa /tp:$sa_password
```

If the database directory was empty when the container started, there's no `NerdDinner` database on the container, and SqlPackage will generate a script with a set of `CREATE` statements to deploy the new database. If the database directory did contain files, then the existing database would have been attached. In that case, SqlPackage would generate a script with a set of `ALTER` and `CREATE` statements to bring the database in line with the Dacpac.

The `deploy.sql` script generated in this step will create the new schema or apply changes to the old schema to upgrade it. The final database schema will be the same in both cases.

Lastly, the PowerShell script executes the SQL script, passing in variables for the database name, file prefixes, and data paths:

```
$SqlCmdVars = "DatabaseName=NerdDinner", "DefaultFilePrefix=NerdDinner",
"DefaultDataPath=$data_path", "DefaultLogPath=$data_path"

Invoke-Sqlcmd -InputFile deploy.sql -Variable $SqlCmdVars -Verbose
```

After the SQL script runs, the database exists in the container with the schema modelled in the Dacpac, which was built from the SQL project in the builder stage of the Dockerfile. The database files are in the expected location with the expected names, so if this container is replaced with another one from the same image, the new container will find the existing database and attach it.

Running databases in containers

Now I have an image that can work for new deployments and upgrades. The image can be used by developers who might run it without mounting a volume while they're working on a feature, so they can start with a fresh database every time they run a container. And the same image can be used in environments where the existing database needs to be preserved by running the container with a volume that contains the database files.

This is how you run the NerdDinner database in Docker, using the default administrator password, using a host directory for the database files, and naming the container so I can access it from other containers:

```
mkdir -p C:\databases\nd

docker container run -d -p 1433:1433 `
 --name nerd-dinner-db `
 -v C:\databases\nd:C:\data `
 dockeronwindows/ch03-nerd-dinner-db
```

The first time you run that container, the Dacpac will run to create the database, saving the data and log files in the mounted directory on the host. You can check whether the files exist on your host with `ls`, and the output from `docker container logs` shows the generated SQL script running and creating resources:

```
> docker container logs nerd-dinner-db
VERBOSE: Starting SQL Server
VERBOSE: Changing SA login credentials
VERBOSE: No data files - will create new database
Generating publish script for database 'NerdDinner' on server
'.\SQLEXPRESS'.
Successfully generated script to file C:\init\deploy.sql.
VERBOSE: Changed database context to 'master'.
VERBOSE: Creating NerdDinner...
VERBOSE: Changed database context to 'NerdDinner'.
VERBOSE: Creating [dbo].[Dinners]...
...
```

The run command also publishes the standard SQL Server port `1433`, so you can connect to the database running inside the container remotely—through a .NET connection or with **SQL Server Management Studio (SSMS)**. If you already have a SQL Server instance running on your host, you can map the container's port `1433` to a different port on the host.

To connect to the SQL Server instance running in the container with SSMS, Visual Studio, or Visual Studio Code, just use the container's IP address, select SQL Server Authentication, and use the `sa` credentials:

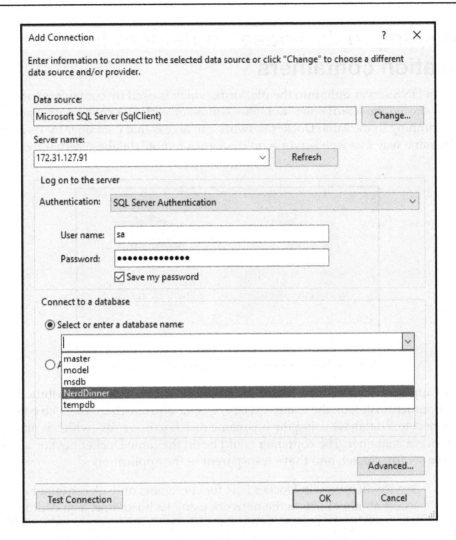

Then, you can work with the dockerized database just like any other SQL Server database, querying tables and inserting data. From the Docker host machine, you use the container's IP address as the database server name, but by publishing the port, you can access the containerized database outside of the host, using the host machine name as the server name. Docker will route any traffic on port 1433 into SQL Server running on the container.

Connecting to database containers from application containers

Docker has a DNS server built into the platform, which is used by containers for service discovery. I started the NerdDinner database container with an explicit name, and any other containers running in the same Docker network can access that container by its name—in exactly the same way as a web server would access a remote database server by its DNS hostname:

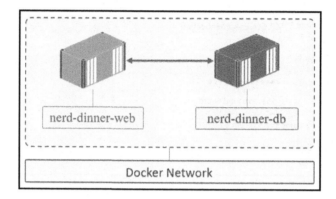

This makes application configuration much simpler than a traditional distributed solution. Every environment will look the same—in dev, QA, and production, the web container will always connect to a database using the hostname `nerd-dinner-db`, which is actually running inside a container. The container could be on the same Docker host or a separate machine in a swarm cluster, and that's transparent to the application.

Service discovery in Docker isn't for containers only. A container can access another host on the network using its hostname. You could run your web application in a container but still have it connected to SQL Server running on a physical machine rather than using a database container.

One piece of configuration could be different for each environment, and that's the SQL Server login credentials. In the NerdDinner database image, I use an environment variable with a default value to set the administrator password, and I use a similar approach in the web application container. The connection string for the database is in the `Web.config` file, with the expected hostname and user ID, but with a placeholder for the password:

```
Data Source=nerd-dinner-db,1433;Initial Catalog=NerdDinner;User
Id=sa;Password={SA_PASSWORD}
```

In the NerdDinner application image, I can add an environment variable for the password and take a similar approach to the database image—do some preprocessing in the entry point that Docker runs to start the container in order to set up the application. The Web.config file is in a known place on the image, so the startup script just needs to update the connection strings. This can be done easily with PowerShell:

```
$connectionString="Data Source=nerd-dinner-db,1433;Initial
Catalog=NerdDinner;User Id=sa;Password=$($env:sa_password)"

$file = 'C:\nerd-dinner\Web.config'
[xml]$config = Get-Content $file;
$db1Node = $config.configuration.connectionStrings.add | where {$_.name -eq
'DefaultConnection'}
$db1Node.connectionString = $connectionString
$config.Save($file)
```

 This is a simplified approach to security credentials, which I'm using to show how we can make our application more Docker-friendly without changing the code. Environment variables are not the best approach to managing secrets, though, and I'll look at this again in Chapter 9, *Understanding the Security Risks and Benefits of Docker*, when I cover security in Docker.

I've added this to a bootstrap.ps1 script file, which also has the logic from this chapter to make NerdDinner a better Docker citizen—promoting environment variables and echoing the IIS logs. I can use this script as the startup command in the Dockerfile and add a HEALTHCHECK instruction so Docker monitors the web app for me.

The Dockerfile for dockeronwindows/ch03-nerd-dinner-web has one other important instruction, which is currently needed for Windows containers to work with Docker's service discovery:

```
RUN  Set-ItemProperty -Path
'HKLM:\SYSTEM\CurrentControlSet\Services\Dnscache\Parameters' `
     -Name ServerPriorityTimeLimit -Value 0 -Type DWord
```

This command writes a registry entry that effectively turns off the Windows DNS cache. Windows caches DNS entries heavily, and this means it doesn't return to Docker frequently enough to get updated information. If a container is replaced, it will have a new IP address, and so we want containers to always use the DNS server in Docker to get the latest information and not cache any results. That's accomplished with this line.

So far in this chapter, I still haven't made any functional changes to the NerdDinner code base, only altering the database connection string in `Web.config` to use the connection details for the SQL Server database container. When I run the web application container now, it will be able to connect to the database container by name and use the SQL Server Express database running in Docker:

```
docker container run -d -P dockeronwindows/ch03-nerd-dinner-web
```

You can explicitly specify the Docker network a container should join when it's created, but on Windows, all containers default to joining the system created the `nat` network. Because of the database container and web container on the `nat` network, they can reach each other by the container name.

When the container starts up, I can now open the website using the container's IP address, click on the **Register** link, and create an account:

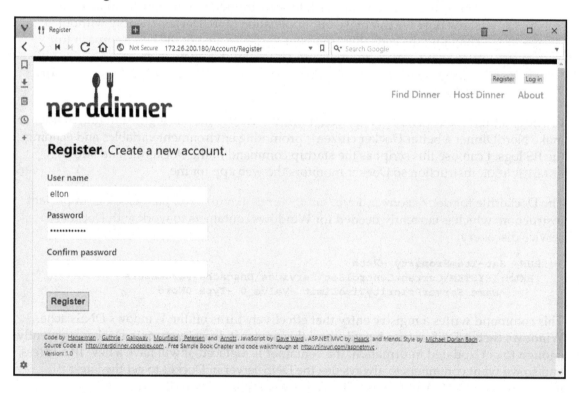

The register page queries the ASP.NET membership database, running in the SQL Server container, so if the page is functioning, then the web application has a working connection to the database. I can verify this in SSMS, querying the user table and seeing the new user row:

I've now separated the LocalDB database from the web application, and each component is running in a lightweight Docker container. On my development laptop, each container uses less than 1% of the host CPU at idle, with the database using 600 MB of memory and the web server under 300 MB. Containers are light on resources so there's no penalty in splitting functional units into different containers and then you can scale, deploy, and upgrade these components individually.

Breaking up monolithic applications

Traditional .NET web applications that rely on a SQL Server database can be migrated to Docker with minimal effort and without having to rewrite any application code. At this stage in my NerdDinner migration, I have an application Docker image and a database Docker image that I can reliably and repeatably deploy and maintain. I also have some beneficial side-effects.

Encapsulating the database definition in a Visual Studio project may be a new departure, but it adds quality assurance to database scripts and brings the schema into the code base, so it can be source-controlled and managed alongside the rest of the system. Dacpacs, PowerShell scripts, and Dockerfiles provide a new common ground for different functions of IT. Development, operations, and database administration teams can work together on the same artifacts, using the same language.

Docker is an enabler for DevOps transitions, but whether or not DevOps is on your road map, Docker provides the foundations for fast, reliable releases. To take the most advantage of that, you need to look at breaking down monolithic apps into smaller pieces, so you can release high-value components frequently without having to do a regression test on the whole of a large application.

Extracting core components from an existing application lets you bring modern, lightweight technologies into your system without having to do a large, complex rewrite. This is a microservices style of architecture applied to an existing solution, where you already understand the areas that are worth extracting into their own services.

Extracting high-value components from monoliths

The Docker platform offers a huge opportunity to modernize legacy applications, allowing you to take features out of monoliths and run them in separate containers. If you can isolate the logic in a feature, that's also an opportunity migrate it to .NET Core, which lets you package it into a much smaller .NET Core image.

Microsoft's road map for .NET Core will see it adopt more and more functionality of the full .NET Framework, but porting parts of a legacy .NET application to .NET Core could still be a large undertaking. But you don't need to take that step. The value in breaking down the monolith is having features that can be developed, deployed, and maintained independently—if the components have full .NET Framework, you still get those benefits.

The advantage of a legacy app is that you understand the feature set. You can identify the high-value functionality in your system and start by extracting those features into their own components. Good candidates would be features that offer value to the business if they change frequently, so new feature requests can be rapidly built and deployed without modifying and testing the whole application.

Equally, good candidates are features that offer value to IT if they stay the same—complex components with a lot of dependencies that the business doesn't change often. Extracting such a feature into a separate component means you can deploy upgrades to the main application without having to test the complex component because it remains unchanged. Breaking up a monolith like this gives you a set of components that each have their own delivery cadence.

In NerdDinner, there are some good candidates to break out into their own services. In the rest of this chapter, I'll focus on one of them, the home page. The home page is the feature that renders the HTML for the first page of the application. A process to deploy changes to the home page quickly and safely in production will let the business experiment with a new look and feel, evaluate the impact of the new version, and decide whether to continue with it.

The current application is distributed among two containers. For the part of this chapter, I'll break the home page out into its own component, so it will run in three containers:

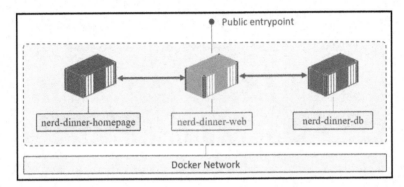

I won't change the routing for the application; users will still come to the NerdDinner application first, and the application container will call the home page service container to get the content to show. This way, I don't need to expose the new container publicly. There is only one technical requirement for the change—the main application needs to be able to communicate with the new service component.

You're free to choose how the applications in containers communicate—Docker networking gives you full protocol support for TCP/IP and UDP. You could make the whole process asynchronous, running a message queue in another container, with message handlers listening in other containers—but I'll start with something simpler in this chapter.

Hosting a UI component in an ASP.NET Core application

ASP.NET Core is a modern application stack that delivers the best of ASP.NET MVC and web API in a slim and performant runtime. ASP.NET Core websites run as console applications, they write logs to the console output stream, and they can use environment variables for configuration. The architecture makes them good Docker citizens out of the box.

The easiest way to extract the NerdDinner home page into a new service is to write it as an ASP.NET Core website with a single page and relay the new application's output from the existing application. Here's my stylish, modern redesign of the home page running in ASP.NET Core on a local machine:

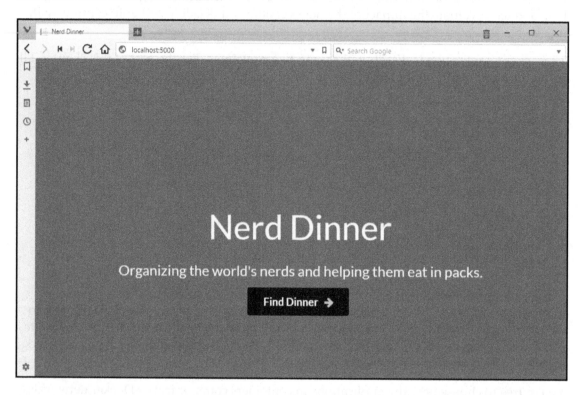

To package the home page application as a Docker image, I'm using the same multi-stage build approach I've used for the main application and the database images. In Chapter 10, *Powering a Continuous Deployment Pipeline with Docker*, you'll see how to use Docker to power a CI/CD build pipeline and tie the whole automated deployment process together.

The Dockerfile for the `dockeronwindows/ch03-nerd-dinner-homepage` image uses the same pattern I have for the full ASP.NET application, separating the package restore and the compilation steps:

```
# escape=`
FROM microsoft/dotnet:1.1.2-sdk-nanoserver AS builder

WORKDIR C:\src\NerdDinnerHomepage
COPY src\NerdDinnerHomepage\NerdDinnerHomepage.csproj .
RUN dotnet restore
```

```
COPY src\NerdDinnerHomepage .
RUN dotnet publish
```

The final stage of the Dockerfile provides a default value for the NERD_DINNER_URL environment variable. The application uses it as the target for the link on the home page. The rest of the Dockerfile instructions just copy in the published application and set up the entry point:

```
FROM microsoft/aspnetcore:1.1.2-nanoserver

ENV NERD_DINNER_URL="/home/find"
CMD ["dotnet", "NerdDinnerHomepage.dll"]

WORKDIR C:\dotnetapp
COPY --from=builder
C:\src\NerdDinnerHomepage\bin\Debug\netcoreapp1.1\publish .
```

I can run the home page component in a separate container, but it's not connected to the main NerdDinner app yet. I need to make a code change to the original app in order to integrate the new home page service.

Connecting to application containers from other application containers

Calling the new home page service from the main application container is fundamentally the same as connecting to the database—I will run the home page container with a known name, and I can access the service in other containers using its name and Docker's built-in service discovery.

A simple change to the HomeController class in the main NerdDinner application will relay the response from the new home page service instead of rendering the page from the main application:

```
static HomeController()
{
    var homepageUrl = Environment.GetEnvironmentVariable("HOMEPAGE_URL",
EnvironmentVariableTarget.Machine);
    var request = WebRequest.Create(homepageUrl);
    using (var response = request.GetResponse())
    using (var responseStream = new
StreamReader(response.GetResponseStream()))
    {
        _NewHomePageHtml = responseStream.ReadToEnd();
    }
```

```
}

public string Index()
{
    return _NewHomePageHtml;
}
```

In the new code, I get the URL for the home page service from an environment variable. Just as with the database connection, I can set a default value for that in the Dockerfile. This would be a bad practice in a distributed application where we can't guarantee where the components are running—but in a dockerized application, I can do it safely because I will control the names of the containers, so I can be sure the service names are correct when I deploy them.

I've tagged this updated image as `dockeronwindows/ch03-nerd-dinner-web:v2`. To start the whole solution now, I need to run three containers:

```
docker container run -d -p 1433:1433 --name nerd-dinner-db `
 -v C:\databases\nd:C:\data dockeronwindows/ch03-nerd-dinner-db

docker container run -d -P  --name nerd-dinner-homepage
dockeronwindows/ch03-nerd-dinner-homepage

docker container run -d -P dockeronwindows/ch03-nerd-dinner-web:v2
```

When the containers are running, I go to the NerdDinner container, and I see the home page from the new component:

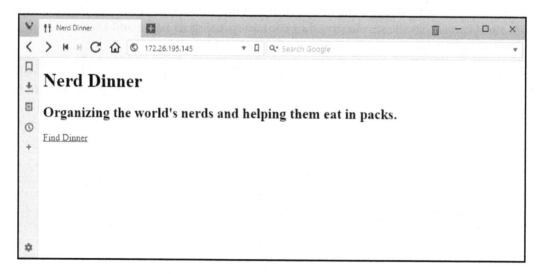

The **Find Dinner** link takes me back to the original web app, and now I can iterate over the home page and release a new UI just by replacing that container—without releasing or testing the rest of the app.

 What happened to the new UI? In this simple example, the integrated home page doesn't have the styling of the new ASP.NET Core version because the main application only reads the HTML for the page, not the CSS files or other assets. A better approach would be to run a proxy in a container and use that as the entry point to other containers, so each container serves all its assets.

Now that I have my solution split across three containers, I've dramatically improved flexibility. During build time, I can focus on features that give the highest value without spending effort to test components that haven't changed. At deployment time, I can release quickly and confidently, knowing that the new image we push to production will be exactly what was tested. And at runtime, I can scale components independently according to their requirements.

I do have a new nonfunctional requirement—which is to ensure that all the containers have the expected names, are started in the correct order, and are in the same Docker network, so the solution as a whole works correctly. Docker has support for this, which I'll show you in Chapter 6, *Organizing Distributed Solutions with Docker Compose*, which is focused on organizing distributed systems with Docker Compose.

Summary

In this chapter, we covered three main topics:

- Containerizing legacy .NET Framework applications so they are good Docker citizens and integrate with the platform for configuration, logging, and monitoring
- Containerizing database workloads with SQL Server Express and the Dacpac deployment model, building a versioned Docker image that can run as a new database or upgrade an existing database
- Extracting functionality from monolithic apps into separate containers, using ASP.NET Core and Windows Nano Server to package a fast, lightweight service that the main application consumes

You've learned how to use more images from Microsoft on Docker Hub and how to use Windows Server Core for full .NET applications, SQL Server Express for databases, and the Nano Server flavors of the .NET Core image.

In later chapters, I'll return to NerdDinner and continue to modernize it by extracting features into dedicated services. Before that, in the next chapter, I'll look more closely at Docker Hub and other registries to store images.

4

Pushing and Pulling Images from Docker Registries

Shipping applications is an integral part of the Docker platform. The Docker service can download images from a central location to run containers from them, and also upload images that were built locally to a central location. These shared image stores are called **registries**, and in this chapter I'll look more closely at how image registries work and the type of registries that are available to you.

The primary image registry is Docker Hub, which is a free online service and is the default location for the Docker service to work with images. Docker Hub is a great place for the community to share images built to package open source software that is free to redistribute. Docker Hub has been hugely successful. At the time of writing this book, there are over 600,000 images available on the Hub, with over 12 billion downloads between them.

A public registry may not be suitable for your own applications. Docker Cloud is an alternative which offers a commercial plan to host private images (in a similar way that GitHub lets you host public and private source code repositories), and there are other commercial registries. You can also run your own registry server in your environment, using an open-source registry implementation which is freely available.

In this chapter, I'll show you how to use those registries, and I'll cover the finer details of tagging images - which is how you can version your Docker images, and work with images from different registries.

Understanding registries and repositories

You download an image from a registry using the `docker image pull` command. When you run the command, the Docker service connects to the registry, authenticates - if it needs to - and pulls the image down. The pull process downloads all the image layers and stores them in the local image cache on the machine. Containers can only be run from images that are available in the local image cache, so unless they're built locally, they need to be pulled first.

One of the earliest commands you run when you get started with Docker on Windows is something simple, like this example from Chapter 2, *Packaging and Running Applications as Docker Containers_SSR*:

```
> docker container run dockeronwindows/ch02-powershell-env

Name                Value
----                -----
ALLUSERSPROFILE     C:\ProgramData
APPDATA             C:\Users\ContainerAdministrator\AppData\Roaming
...
```

This will work even if you don't have the image in your local cache because Docker can pull it from the default registry - Docker Cloud, in this case. If you try to run a container from an image that you don't have stored locally, Docker will automatically pull it before creating the container.

In this example, I haven't given Docker much information to go on - just the image name `dockeronwindows/ch02-powershell-env`. That detail is enough for Docker to find the right image in the registry, because Docker fills in some of the missing details with default values. The name of the repository is `dockeronwindows/ch02-powershell-env`; a repository is a storage unit that can contains many versions of a Docker image.

Examining image repository names

Repositories have a fixed naming scheme: `{registry-domain}/{account-id}/{repository-name}:{tag}`. All parts are required, but Docker assumes defaults for some values. So, `dockeronwindows/ch02-powershell-env` is actually a short form of the full repository name `docker.io/dockeronwindows/ch02-powershell-env:latest`.

- `registry-domain` is the domain name or IP address of the registry that stores the image. Docker Hub, Docker Cloud and Docker Store are default registries, so you can omit the registry domain when you're using those images. Docker will use `docker.io` as the registry if you don't specify one.
- `account-id` is the name of the account or organization that owns the image on the registry. On Docker Hub the account name is mandatory—my own account ID is `sixeyed`, and the organization account ID for the images that accompany this book is called `dockeronwindows`. On other registries the account ID may not be needed.
- `repository-name`: It is the name you want to give your image to uniquely identify the application, within all the repositories for your account on the registry.
- `tag`: is how you distinguish between different image variations in the repository.

You use the tag for versioning your applications or to identify variants. If you don't specify a tag when you build or pull images, Docker assumes the default tag `latest`. When you start with Docker, you will use Docker Hub and the `latest` tag, which are the defaults Docker provides to hide some of the complexity until you're ready to dig deeper. As you continue with Docker, you'll use tags to make clear distinctions between different versions of your application package.

A good example is Microsoft's .NET Core base image, which is on Docker Hub in the `microsoft/dotnet` repository. .NET Core is a cross-platform application stack that runs on Linux and Windows. You can run only Linux containers on Linux-based Docker hosts, and you can run only Windows containers on Windows-based Docker hosts, so Microsoft includes the operating system in the tag name.

At the time of writing, Microsoft has dozens of versions of the .NET Core image available for use in the `microsoft/dotnet` repository, identified with different tags. These are just some of the tags:

- `1.1.2-runtime-jessie` a Linux image based on Debian that has the .NET Core 1.1 runtime installed
- `1.1.2-runtime-nanoserver` a Nano Server image that has the .NET Core 1.1 runtime installed

- `1.1.2-sdk-jessie` a Linux image based on Debian that has the .NET Core 1.1 runtime and SDK installed
- `1.1.2-sdk-nanoserver` a Nano Server image that has the .NET Core 1.1 runtime and SDK installed

The tags make it clear what each image contains, but they are all fundamentally similar - they are all variations of `microsoft/dotnet`.

 Docker also supports multi-arch images, where a single repository name is used as an umbrella for many variations. There could be image variations based on Linux and Windows, Intel and **Advanced RISC Machines (ARM)** processors. They all use the same umbrella repository name, and when you run `docker image pull`, Docker pulls the matching image for your host's operating system and CPU architecture.

Building, tagging, and versioning images

You tag images when you first build them, but you can also explicitly add tags to an image with the `docker image tag` command. This is very useful in versioning mature applications, so users can choose which versioning level they want to work with. If you run these commands, you would build an image with five tags, with ascending levels of precision for the application version:

```
docker image build -t myapp .
docker image tag myapp:latest myapp:5
docker image tag myapp:latest myapp:5.1
docker image tag myapp:latest myapp:5.1.6
docker image tag myapp:latest myapp:bc90e9
```

The initial `docker image build` command doesn't specify a tag, so the new image will default to `myapp:latest`. Each subsequent `docker image tag` command adds a new tag to the same image. Tagging doesn't copy the image, so there's no data duplication, you just have one image which can be referred to with several tags. By adding all these tags, you give consumers the choice of image to use, or to base their own image on.

This example application uses semantic versioning. The final tag could be the ID of the source code commit that triggered the build; this might be used internally but not made public. `5.1.6` is the patch version, `5.1` is the minor version number, and `5` is the major version number.

Users can explicitly use `myapp:5.1.6`, which is the most specific version number, knowing that the tag won't change at that level and the image will always be the same. The next release will have the tag `5.1.7`, but that will be a different image with a different application version.

`myapp:5.1` will change with each patch release - with the next build, `5.1` will be a tagged alias of `5.1.7` - but users can be confident there won't be any breaking changes. `myapp:5` will change with each minor release - next month it could be an alias of myapp:5.2. Users can choose the major version if they always want the latest release for version 5, or they could use latest if they always want the latest version, and can accept the possibility of breaking changes.

As the producer of images, you can decide how to support versioning in your image tags. As the consumer, you should favor being more specific - especially with images you use as the `FROM` image for your own builds. If you're packaging a .NET Core application, you will have problems if you start your Dockerfile like this:

```
FROM microsoft/dotnet:runtime-nanoserver
```

At the time of writing, this image has version 1.1 of the .NET Core runtime installed. If your application targets version 1.1 then that's fine, the image will build and your application will run correctly in a container. But when .NET Core 1.2 or 2.0 is released, the generic `runtime-nanoserver` tag will be applied to the new image, which may not support the 1.1 target. When you use the exact same Dockerfile after that release, it will use a new base image - your image will build but the application may fail if the base image no longer supports your application.

Instead, you should use consider using a tag for the minor version of the application framework you're using:

```
FROM microsoft/dotnet:1.1-runtime-nanoserver
```

This way, you'll benefit from any patch releases to the image, but you'll always be using the 1.1 release of .NET Core, so your application will always have a matching host platform in the base image.

You can tag any image you have in your local cache, not just images you build yourself. This is useful if you want to re-tag a public image and add it to an approved set of base images in your local, private registry.

Pushing images to a registry

Building and tagging images are local operations. The end result of `docker image build` and `docker image tag` is a change to the image cache on the Docker host where you run the commands. Images need to be explicitly shared to a registry with the `docker image push` command.

Docker Hub is available for use without authenticating to pull public images, but to upload images (or pull private images), you need to register for an account. Registration is free at `https://cloud.docker.com/` - where you can create a Docker ID that you can use on Docker Hub, Docker Cloud, and other Docker services. Your Docker ID is how you authenticate with the Docker service to access Docker Hub, with the `docker login` command:

```
> docker login

Login with your Docker ID to push and pull images from Docker Hub. If you
don't have a Docker ID, head over to https://hub.docker.com to create one.
Username: dockeronwindows
Password:
Login Succeeded
```

To push images to Docker Hub, the repository name must contain your Docker ID as the account ID. You can tag an image using account account ID - like `microsoft/my-app` - but you can't push it to Microsoft's organization on the registry. The Docker ID you are logged in with needs to have permission to push to the account on the registry.

When I publish images to go along with this book, I build them with `dockeronwindows` as the account name in the repository, log in with that account, and push:

```
docker image build -t dockeronwindows/ch03-iis-healthcheck .
docker image push dockeronwindows/ch03-iis-healthcheck
```

The output from the Docker CLI shows how the image is split into layers, and it tells you the upload status for each layer:

```
The push refers to a repository [docker.io/dockeronwindows/ch03-iis-
healthcheck]
177624560099: Pushed
badbec9dc449: Pushed
f87d75e4972b: Pushing [================================>                  ]
7.925 MB/12.66 MB
0c3e4b980d94: Pushed
19150debad5f: Pushed
1225b6de9f9d: Pushed
64e9e8b7f7a8: Pushing [=================>                                 ]
22.14 MB/62.19 MB
```

```
48c58914e7a1: Pushing [===============>                          ]
20.45 MB/66.33 MB
ef215b8a1176: Pushing [==>                                       ]
14.07 MB/280.3 MB
72ee693ca2b2: Pushed
de57d9086f9a: Skipped foreign layer
f358be10862c: Skipped foreign layer
```

This image uses Windows Server Core as the base image. The base image is not publicly redistributable - it's publicly available on Docker Hub, but Microsoft have not licensed the image to be stored on other public image registries. That's why we see the lines stating *Skipped foreign layer* - Docker will not push those layers.

You can't publish to another user's account, but you can tag another user's images with your own account name. This is a perfectly valid set of commands, which I could run if I wanted to download a specific version of the Windows Server Core image, give it a friendlier name, and make it available on the Hub under that new name in my account:

```
docker image pull microsoft/windowsservercore:10.0.14393.1358
docker image tag microsoft/windowsservercore:10.0.14393.1358
sixeyed/windowsservercore:2017-07
docker image push sixeyed/windowsservercore:2017-07
```

Pushing images to a registry doesn't get any more complex than that, for the user - although under the hood Docker runs some smart logic. Image layering applies to registries as well as to the local image cache on the Docker host. When you push an image based on Windows Server Core to the Hub, Docker doesn't upload the 10 GB base image - it knows that base layer already exists on the Hub, and it will only upload the layers which are missing on the target registry.

The last example of tagging a public image and pushing it to the public Hub is valid but unlikely - you're much more likely to tag and push images to your own local, private registry.

Running a local image registry

The Docker platform is portable because it's written in Go, which is a cross-platform language. Go applications can be compiled to native binaries, so Docker can run on Linux or Windows without users having to install Go. On the Docker Hub the registry image contains a registry server written in Go, so you can host your own image registry by running a Docker container from that image.

registry is an official repository, but at the time of writing, it only has images available for Linux. It's likely that a Windows version of the registry will be published soon, but in this chapter I will walk you through building your own registry image, as it demonstrates some common Docker usage patterns.

 Official repositories are available on Docker Hub like other public images, but they have been curated by Docker, Inc, and are maintained either by Docker themselves or by the application owners. You can rely on them containing correctly packaged and up-to-date software. The majority of official images only have Linux variants, but the number of Windows-based official images is growing.

Building the registry image

Docker's registry server is an open source application. It's hosted on GitHub in the docker/distribution repository. To build the application, you need to install the Go SDK first. If you did that, you can run a simple command to compile the application:

```
go get github.com/docker/distribution/cmd/registry
```

But if you're not a regular Go developer, you don't want the overhead of installing and maintaining the Go tools on your local machine, just so you can build the registry server when you want to update it. It would be better to package the Go tools into a Docker image and set up the image so that when you run a container, it builds the registry server for you. You can do this with the same multi-stage build approach I demonstrated in Chapter 3, *Developing Dockerized .NET and .NET Core Applications*.

The multi-stage pattern has a lot of advantages. Firstly, it means that your application image can be kept as lightweight as possible - you don't need to package the build tools along with the runtime. Secondly, it means that your build agent is encapsulated in a Docker image so you don't need to install those tools on your build server. Thirdly, it means that developers can use exactly the same build process that the build server uses, so you avoid a situation where developer machines and the build server have different tool sets installed, with the risk of them drifting and causing build issues.

The Dockerfile for `dockeronwindows/ch04-registry` uses the official Go image, which has a Windows Server Core variant on Docker Hub. The builder stage uses that image to compile the registry application:

```
# escape=`
FROM golang:1.8-windowsservercore AS builder
SHELL ["powershell", "-Command", "$ErrorActionPreference = 'Stop';"]

ARG REGISTRY_VERSION=v2.6.1

WORKDIR C:\gopath\src\github.com\docker
RUN git clone https://github.com/docker/distribution.git; `
    cd distribution; `
    git checkout $env:REGISTRY_VERSION; `
    go build -o C:\out\registry.exe .\cmd\registry
```

I'm using an `ARG` instruction to specify the version of the source code to build - the GitHub repository has labels for each released version, and I'm defaulting to version 2.6.1. Then I use `git` to clone the source code and switch to the labelled version of the code, and `go build` to compile the application. The output will be `registry.exe`, a native Windows executable which doesn't need Go installed to run.

The final stage of the Dockerfile uses Nano Server as the base, which can run the Go application just fine. I'll look at this stage in detail, because the setup addresses a problem with storage in Windows containers which impacts Go and other languages. The start of the stage just specifies the version of Nano Server to use as the base, and switches to PowerShell:

```
FROM microsoft/nanoserver:10.0.14393.1358
SHELL ["powershell", "-Command", "$ErrorActionPreference = 'Stop';"]
```

Next there are instructions to configure storage for the registry server. I use environment variables to specify the paths, create a volume, and then set a Windows registry flag to create a drive mapping for the volume path:

```
ENV DATA_PATH="C:\data" `
    REGISTRY_STORAGE_FILESYSTEM_ROOTDIRECTORY="G:\\"

VOLUME ${DATA_PATH}

RUN Set-ItemProperty -Path 'HKLM:\SYSTEM\CurrentControlSet\Control\Session
Manager\DOS Devices' `
                    -Name 'G:' -Value "\??\$($env:DATA_PATH)" -Type String
```

This is a pattern you may have to use with Java, Node, PHP and even in .NET applications in Windows containers. It's necessary because of the way Windows implements volumes. My volume creates the directory path `C:\data` inside the container, but that's actually a **symbolic link (symlink)** to another directory location.

Symlinks are very common in Linux. Windows has supported them for a long time, but they're far less common. Some language rutimes see a directory is a symlink, and try to resolve the underlying path. In a container, the path will be something like `\\?\\ContainerMappedDirectories\{GUID}`. Making sense of that path can cause the app to fail.

So this setup creates a drive alias for the directory - inside the container, the `G:` drive actually maps to `C:\data`. When applications see `G:\` they don't see it as a symlink, so they don't try to resolve the path. They write directly to the `G:` drive, and Windows redirects it to `C:\data`, which is actually a volume hosted outside of the container.

 If you're interested in the mechanics of this fix, the details are in a GitHub issue: `https://github.com/moby/moby/issues/27537`.

The registry server uses the `REGISTRY_STORAGE_FILESYSTEM_ROOTDIRECTORY` environment variable to configure the storage location. That's set to `G:` so the Go runtime can work without hitting the symlink issue. The rest of the Dockerfile sets up the image to allow traffic on port `5000`, the conventional registry port, and copies in the output from the builder stage:

```
EXPOSE 5000

WORKDIR C:\registry

CMD ["registry", "serve", "config.yml"]
COPY --from=builder C:\out\registry.exe .
COPY --from=builder
C:\gopath\src\github.com\docker\distribution\...\config-example.yml
.\config.yml
```

Building the registry image is the same as any other image, but when you use it to run your own registry, there are some important factors to consider.

Running a registry container

Running your own registry lets you share images between team members and store the output of all your application builds using the fast local network instead of an internet connection. You would typically run the registry container on a server that can be widely accessed, in a configuration like this:

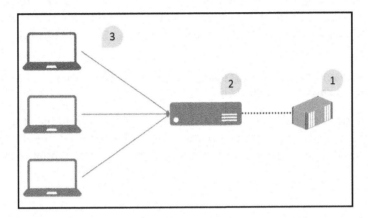

The registry is running in a container (**1**) on a server (**2**). The client machines (**3**) connected to the server to use the local registry to push and pull private images.

To make the registry container accessible, you need to publish port 5000 from the container to port 5000 on the host. Registry users can access the container using the host server's IP address or hostname, and that will be the registry domain you use in repository names. You'll also want to mount a volume from the host to store the image data in a known location. When you replace the container for a new version, it will still be available using the host's domain name, and it will still have all the image layers stored by the previous container.

On my host server I have a RAID array configured as disk E:, which I'll use for my registry data, so I can run my registry container mapping that volume:

```
mkdir E:\registry-data
docker container run -d -p 5000:5000 -v E:\registry-data:C:\data
dockeronwindows/ch04-registry
```

The volume is mapped to C:\data - the G: drive alias only exists inside the container.

In my network, I'll be running the container on a physical machine with the IP address 192.168.2.146. I could use 192.168.2.146:5000 as the registry domain to tag images, but that isn't very flexible. It's better to use the domain name of the host, so I could point that to a different physical server if I needed to, without having to re-tag all my images.

For the hostname you can use your network's **Domain Name System (DNS)** service, or a **Canonical Name (CNAME)** if you're running a public server, or you could add an entry to the hosts file on the client machines and use a custom domain name. This is the PowerShell command I use to add the host name entry for registry.local pointing to my Docker server:

```
Add-Content -Path 'C:\Windows\System32\drivers\etc\hosts' -Value
'192.168.2.146 registry.local'
```

Now my server is running a registry server in a container with reliable storage, and my client is set up to access the registry host using a friendly domain name. I can start pushing and pulling private images from my own registry, which is only available to users on my network.

Pushing and pulling images with a local registry

You can only push images to a registry if the image tag matches the registry domain. The process for tagging and pushing is the same as with Docker Hub, but you need to explicitly include the local registry domain in the new tag. These commands pull the registry server image from Docker Hub and add a new tag, making it suitable to be pushed to the local registry:

```
docker image pull dockeronwindows/ch04-registry

docker image tag dockeronwindows/ch04-registry
registry.local:5000/infrastructure/registry:v2.6.1
```

In the docker image tag command, you can change every part of the image name for the new tag. I've used the following:

- registry.local:5000 the registry domain. The original image name had an implied domain of docker.io.
- infrastructure the account name. The original account name was dockeronwindows.

- `registry` the repository name. The original was `ch04-registry`.
- `v2.6.1` the image tag. The original implied tag was `latest`.

I can try to push the new tagged image to the local registry, but Docker won't let me use the registry yet:

```
> docker push registry.local:5000/infrastructure/registry:v2.6.1

The push refers to a repository
[registry.local:5000/infrastructure/registry]
Get https://registry.local:5000/v2/: http: server gave HTTP response to
HTTPS client
```

The Docker platform is secure by default, and the same principle extends to image registries. The Docker service expects to use SSL to communicate with registries, so the traffic is encrypted. My simple registry installation uses plaintext HTTP, so I get an error saying Docker tried to use an encrypted transport for the registry but only an unencrypted transport was available.

There are two options to set up Docker to use the local registry. The first is to extend the registry server to secure the communication - the registry server image can run over HTTPS if you supply it with an SSL certificate. That's what I would do in a production environment, but to start out I can use the other option and make an exception in the Docker configuration. The Docker service will allow an HTTP registry to be used if it's explicitly named in an allowed list of insecure registries.

You can run the registry image with HTTPS using your company's SSL certificate or a self-signed certificate, which means that you don't need to configure the Docker Engine to allow insecure registries. There is a Windows registry walkthrough in Docker's lab repository on GitHub `docker/labs` which explains how to do that.

Configuring Docker to allow insecure registries

The Docker service can use a JSON configuration file to change settings, including the list of insecure registries the engine will allow. Any registry domains in that list can use HTTP rather than HTTPS, so this is not something you should do for a registry hosted on a public network.

Docker's configuration file is located at
`%programdata%\docker\config\daemon.json` (**daemon** is Linux terminology for a
background service, so this is the name of the Docker service configuration file). You can
manually edit it to add the local registry as a secure option and then restart the Docker
Windows service. This configuration allows Docker to use the local registry with HTTP:

```
{
    "insecure-registries": [
        "registry.local:5000"
    ]
}
```

If you're using Docker for Windows, the UI has a nice configuration window that takes care
of this for you. Instead of editing the file manually, just right-click on the Docker logo in the
status bar, select **Settings**, navigate to the **Daemon** page, and add an entry to the Insecure
registries list:

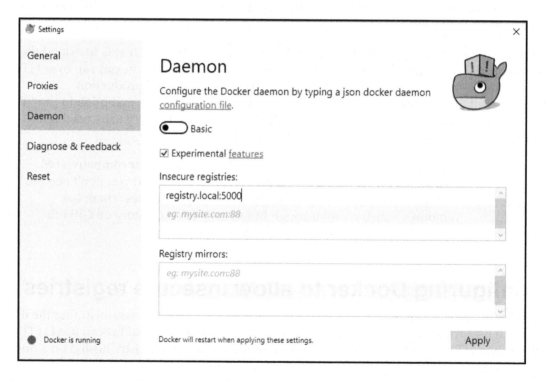

With the local registry domain added to my insecure list, I can use it to push and pull images:

```
> docker push registry.local:5000/infrastructure/registry:v2.6.1

The push refers to a repository
[registry.local:5000/infrastructure/registry]
8aef1b3b4856: Pushed
cacb6be9e720: Pushed
415729850f90: Pushed
ff6770fbf55c: Pushed
9acef5971c00: Pushed
45049fa42adf: Pushed
3c7d57559064: Pushed
f6f3d7c5a77c: Pushed
c5dc94330b3f: Pushed
e6537bd7a896: Skipped foreign layer
6c357baed9f5: Skipped foreign layer
v2.6.1: digest:
sha256:970ea320b67116cea565f5af24ed99dea65b6e3d8ae1dbb285acfb2673d4307b
size: 2615
```

Any users with network access to my Docker server can use images stored in the local registry with the `docker image pull` or `docker image run` commands. You can also use local images as the base image in other Dockerfiles, specifying the name with the registry domain, the repository name, and the tag in the FROM instruction:

```
FROM registry.local:5000/infrastructure/registry:v2.6.1
CMD ["powershell", "Write-Output", "Hello from Chapter 4."]
```

 There is no way to override the default registry, so you can't set your local registry to be the default when a domain isn't specified - the default is always Docker Hub. If you want to use a different registry for images, the registry domain always has to be specified in the image name. Any image names you use without a registry address will be assumed to refer to images from `docker.io`.

Storing Windows image layers in a local registry

You are not allowed to publicly redistribute the base layers for the Microsoft images, but you are allowed to store them in a private registry. This is particularly useful for the Windows Server Core image. The compressed size of that image is 5 GB, and Microsoft release a new version of the image every month on Docker Hub with the latest security patches.

The updates usually only add one new layer to the image, but that layer could be a 1 GB download. If you have many users working with Windows images, they will all need to download those layers and that's a lot of bandwidth and a lot of time. If you run a local registry server, you can pull those layers once from Docker Hub, and push them to your local registry. Every other user then pulls from the local registry, downloading from the fast local network rather than the internet.

You need to enable this feature for specific registries in the Docker configuration file, using the `allow-nondistributable-artifacts` field:

```
{
  "insecure-registries": [
    "registry.local:5000"
  ],
  "allow-nondistributable-artifacts": [
    "registry.local:5000"
  ]
}
```

This setting isn't exposed directly in the Docker for Windows UI, but you can set it in the **Advanced** mode of the settings screen:

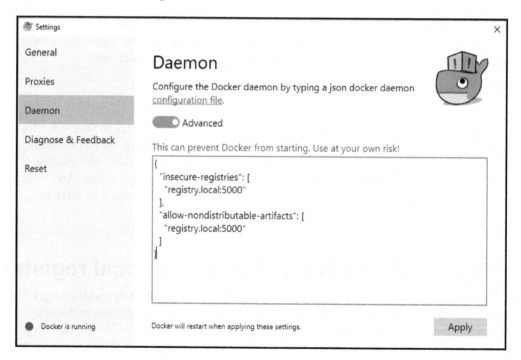

Now I can push the Windows *foreign layers* to my local registry. I can tag the latest Nano Server image with my own registry domain and push the image there:

```
PS> docker image tag microsoft/nanoserver:10.0.14393.1358
registry.sixeyed:5000/microsoft/nanoserver:10.0.14393.1358

PS> docker image push
registry.sixeyed:5000/microsoft/nanoserver:10.0.14393.1358
The push refers to a repository
[registry.sixeyed:5000/microsoft/nanoserver]
e6537bd7a896: Pushing [=====================> ] 146.1MB/344.1MB
6c357baed9f5: Pushing [===========> ] 160.3MB/700.8MB
```

On another Docker host, I can pull my local Nano Server image. But I don't need to use the custom image name `registry.sixeyed:5000/microsoft/nanoserver:10.0.14393.1358` when I want to use Nano Server - I can use the standard `microsoft/nanoserver:10.0.14393.1358` name. Docker will see that image doesn't exist and start to pull it from Docker Hub - but it will find the layers already available on the host's image cache, from the local registry, and it will use them instead of downloading from Docker Hub.

Using a commercial registry

Running your own registry is not the only way to have a secure, private store for image repositories, there are several third-party offerings you can use. In practice they all work in the same way - you need to tag your images with the registry domain and authenticate with the registry server. There are several options available, and the most comprehensive ones come from Docker, Inc, which has different products available for different levels of service.

Docker Hub

Docker Hub is the most widely used public container registry, averaging one billion image pulls per month at the time of writing. You can host unlimited public repositories on the Hub and pay a subscription to host multiple private repositories.

Docker Hub has an automated build system, so you can link image repositories to source code repositories in GitHub or BitBucket, and Docker's servers will build an image from the Dockerfile in the repository whenever you push changes - it's a simple and effective hosted **Continuous Integration (CI)** solution, especially if you are using portable multi-stage Dockerfiles.

A Hub subscription is suitable for smaller projects or teams with multiple users working on the same applications. It has an authorization framework where users can create an organization - which becomes the account name in the repository rather than an individual user's account name. Many users can be given access to the organization repositories, which allows multiple users to push images to the repository, something you can't do with individual user repositories.

Docker Cloud

Docker Cloud is a hosted platform which provides a registry and a platform for managing Docker swarms running in the cloud. You can create Docker swarms on virtual machines in AWS, Azure, DigitalOcean or other cloud providers and use Docker Cloud to deploy Docker on the VMs, and Docker for Windows to manage the remote Docker nodes.

In addition to the CI builds of Docker Hub, with Cloud you can configure automated application testing. You define tests in your source code repository, and when you push changes Docker Cloud will build the image, run a container, and execute the test suite. This means that you can use Docker Cloud for a full CI/CD pipeline, where new changes are automatically deployed to the cloud servers managed by Docker Cloud.

The registry in Docker Cloud also provides security scanning, a feature where Docker examines the contents of images, looking at the software installed and comparing it with industry-standard databases of known vulnerabilities. Docker can flag security issues with the operating system used in the base image or with software dependencies installed on top of the base image. Security scanning and organization-level authorization make Docker Cloud ideal for smaller teams and projects.

Docker Cloud is a good option to manage containerized workloads in the cloud. Docker images are portable by definition, so you can limit your cloud requirements to basic **Infrastructure as a Service (IaaS)** offerings - you just need VMs, storage, and virtual networking to support Docker workloads. You can run multi-cloud applications or move between providers easily using the consistent administration platform in Docker Cloud. I will cover Docker swarm in Chapter 7, *Orchestrating Distributed Solutions with Docker Swarm*.

Docker Store

Docker Store is a registry for commercial software distribution. It's like an app store for server-side applications. If your company produces commercial software, Docker Store could be a good choice for distributing it. You build and push images in exactly the same way, but your source can be kept private - only the packaged application is publicly available.

There is also a certification process you can go through, for images being hosted on Docker Store. Docker certification applies across software images and hardware stacks. If your image is certified, it's guaranteed to work on **Docker Enterprise Edition (Docker EE)** on any certified hardware. Docker tests all the combinations in the certification process, and that end-to-end guarantee is very attractive to large enterprises.

Docker Trusted Registry

Docker Trusted Registry (DTR) is part of the Docker EE Advanced suite, the enterprise-grade **Containers-as-a-Service (CaaS)** platform from Docker, Inc. It's aimed at enterprises running a cluster of Docker hosts in their own data centers or in a virtual private cloud. Docker EE Advanced comes with a comprehensive management suite called **Universal Control Plane (UCP)**, which provides an interface to administer all the resources in your Docker cluster - the host servers, images, containers, networks, volumes, and everything else. Docker EE Advanced also provides DTR, which is a secure, scalable registry.

DTR runs over HTTPS and is a clustered service, so you can deploy multiple registry servers across your cluster for scalability and failover. You can use local storage or cloud storage for DTR, so images can be persisted on an Azure backend with practically unlimited capacity. Like Docker Cloud, you can create organizations for shared repositories, but with DTR you manage authentication by creating your own user accounts or plugging into an **Lightweight Directory Access Protocol (LDAP)** service (such as Active Directory). Then you can configure role-based access control for fine-grained permissions.

Security scanning is also available in DTR, so you can have the service running in your own environment. You can configure scans to run whenever an image is pushed, or on a schedule. Scheduled scans can alert you when a new vulnerability is found in one of the dependencies for an old image. The DTR UI lets you drill down into the details of the vulnerability and see the exact file and the exact exploit.

There is one other major security feature that is only available in Docker EE Advanced, and that is **content trust**. Docker content trust lets users digitally sign images to capture an approval workflow - so QA and security teams may run an image version through their test suites and sign it to confirm that they approve a release candidate for production. Those signatures are stored in DTR. UCP can be configured to only run images that have been signed by certain teams, so you get close control over what software your cluster will run, together with an audit trail proving who built and approved the software.

Docker EE Advanced has a rich suite of features that can be accessed through friendly web UIs as well as through the standard Docker command line. Security, reliability, and scalability are major factors in the feature set, which makes it a good choice for enterprise users looking for a standard way to manage images, containers, and Docker hosts. I will cover UCP in Chapter 8, *Administering and Monitoring Dockerized Solutions* and DTR in Chapter 9, *Understanding the Security Risks and Benefits of Docker*.

Other registries

Many third-party services have added an image registry to their existing offerings. On the cloud, you have the **EC2 Container Registry (ECR)** from **Amazon Web Services (AWS)**, Azure Container Registry from Microsoft, and Container Registry on Google Cloud Platform. All these offerings integrate with the standard Docker command line and with the other products in each respective platform, so they can be good options if you are heavily invested in one cloud service provider.

There are also standalone registry offerings, including Artifactory from JFrog, and Quay.io - which are hosted services. Having a hosted registry
removes the management overhead of running your own registry server, and if you are already using a platform that provides a registry, it makes sense to evaluate that option.

All the registry providers have different feature sets and service levels - you should compare the offerings and most importantly, check the level of Windows support. Most of the existing platforms were originally built to support Linux images and Linux clients, and there may not be feature parity for Windows.

Summary

In this chapter, you learned what an image registry does and how you work with it using Docker. I covered repository names and image tagging to identify application versions or platform variations, and how to run and use a local registry server - running in a container.

Using a private registry is something you're likely to do quite early in your Docker journey. As you start to Dockerize existing applications and experiment with new software stacks, it may be useful to push and pull images across the fast local network - or use Docker Cloud if local storage space is an issue. As you use Docker more and progress to production implementation, you may have a roadmap to upgrade to DTR for a supported registry with rich security features.

Now that you have a good understanding on how to share images and use images shared by other people, you can look at bringing tried and trusted software components into our own applications with a container-first solution design.

5
Adopting Container-First Solution Design

Adopting Docker as your application platform brings clear operational benefits. Containers are a much lighter unit of compute than virtual machines, but they still provide isolation, so you can run more workloads on less hardware. All these workloads have the same shape in Docker, so operations teams can manage .NET, Java, Go, and Node.js applications in the same way. The Docker platform also has benefits in application architecture. In this chapter, I'll look at how container-first solution design helps you add features to your application with high quality and low risk.

I'll be returning to NerdDinner in this chapter, picking up from where I left off in Chapter 3, *Developing Dockerized .NET and .NET Core Applications*. NerdDinner is a traditional .NET application, a monolithic design with tight coupling between components, where all communication is synchronous. There is no unit testing, integration testing, or end-to-end testing. NerdDinner is like millions of other .NET apps - it may have the features the users need, but it's difficult and dangerous to modify. Moving apps like this to Docker lets you take a different approach to modifying or adding features.

Two aspects of the Docker platform change the way you think about solution design. First, networking and service discovery means you can distribute applications across multiple components, each running in containers that can be moved, scaled, and upgraded independently. Second, the expanding range of production-grade software available on Docker Hub and Docker Store means you can use off-the-shelf software for many generic services and manage them in the same way as your own components. This gives you the freedom to design better solutions without infrastructure or technology restrictions.

In this chapter I'll show you how to modernize a traditional .NET application, by adopting container-first design:

- Splitting functionality into separate containers, to address performance issues and add features
- Adding enterprise-grade software to your solution by running containers from official images
- Building hybrid .NET Framework and .NET Core solutions in Docker
- Moving from monoliths to distributed solutions

Design goals for NerdDinner

In Chapter 3, *Developing Dockerized .NET and .NET Core Applications*, I extracted the NerdDinner home page into a separate component, which enabled rapid delivery of UI changes. Now I'm going to make some more fundamental changes. The data layer in NerdDinner uses **Entity Framework (EF)**, and all database access is synchronous. A lot of traffic to the site will create a lot of open connections to SQL Server and run a lot of queries. Performance will deteriorate as load increases, to the point where queries time out or the connection pool is starved, and the site will show errors to the users.

One way to improve this would be to make all the data access methods async, but that's an invasive change - all the controller actions would need to be made async too, and there is no automated test suite to verify such a wholesale set of changes. Alternatively, I could add a cache for data retrieval so GET requests would hit the cache and not the database. That's also a complex change, and I would need to cache data for long enough to make a cache hit likely while keeping the cache in sync when data changes. Again, the lack of tests means complex changes like this are hard to verify, so this is also a risky approach.

It would be hard to estimate the benefit if I did implement these complex changes. If all the data access moves to asynchronous methods, will that make the website run faster and able to handle more traffic? If I can integrate a cache that is efficient enough to take reads away from the database, will that improve the overall performance? These benefits are difficult to quantify until you've actually made the change, when you might find that the improvement doesn't justify the investment.

With a container-first approach, you can look at the design differently. If you identify one feature that makes expensive database calls but doesn't need to run synchronously, you can move the database code to a separate component. Then you use asynchronous messaging between the components, publishing an event from the main web app onto a message queue and acting on the event message in the new component. With Docker, each of these components will run in one or more containers:

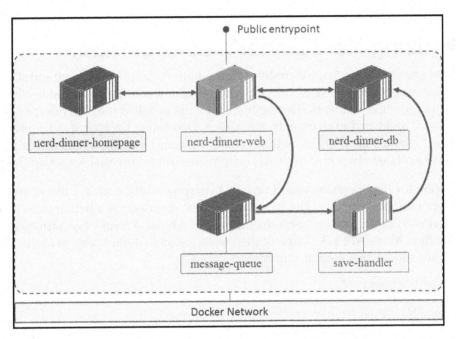

If I focus on just one feature then I can implement the change quickly. This design has none of the drawbacks of the other approaches:

- It's a targeted change and only one controller action changes in the main application
- The new message handler component is small and highly cohesive, so it will be easy to test
- The web layer and the data layer are being decoupled, so they can be scaled independently
- I'm moving work away from the web application, so we can be sure of a performance improvement.

There are other advantages too. The new component is completely independent of the original application, it just needs to listen for an event message and act on it. You can use .NET, .NET Core or any other technology stack for the message handler; you don't need to be constrained to a single stack. And you also have events being published from the app, so you have the option to add other features later by adding new handlers listening for these events.

Dockerizing NerdDinner's configuration

NerdDinner uses `Web.config` for configuration - both for application configuration values that are constant between releases, and for environmental configuration values that change between different environments. The configuration file is baked into the release package, which makes it awkward to change. In `Chapter 3`, *Developing Dockerized .NET and .NET Core Applications*, I worked around this without changing code by using a start up script in the Dockerfile to update values in `Web.config` from environment variables set by Docker.

In preparation for the bigger changes to come, I've updated the code for this chapter to use environment variables directly. The `Env` class in the web project is a helper class that fetches values for known configuration items, including the database connection strings and secrets such as the Bing Maps API key. Some of these settings have default values in the Dockerfile, but others need to be provided at runtime:

```
ENV BING_MAPS_KEY="" `
    IP_INFO_DB_KEY="" `
    HOMEPAGE_URL="http://nerd-dinner-homepage" `
    MESSAGE_QUEUE_URL="nats://message-queue:4222" `
    AUTH_DB_CONNECTION_STRING="Data Source=nerd-dinner-db..." `
    APP_DB_CONNECTION_STRING="Data Source=nerd-dinner-db..."
```

Using default values for the database connection strings means that the app is usable when you start the database and web containers without having to specify any environment variables. The app isn't 100% functional, though, because the API keys are needed for Bing Maps and the IP geolocation services. These are rate-limited services, so you are likely to have different keys for each developer and each environment.

To keep environment values safe, Docker lets you load them from a file rather than specifying them in plaintext in the `docker container run` command. Isolating values in a file means that the file itself can be secured, so only administrators and the Docker service account can access it. The environment file is a simple text format, with one line for each environment variable, written as a key-value pair. For the web container, my environment file contains the secret API keys:

```
BING_MAPS_KEY=*my key*
IP_INFO_DB_KEY=*my key*
```

To run the container and load the file contents as environment variables, you can use the `--env-file` option.

I've packaged those changes in a new version of the NerdDinner Docker image, `dockeronwindows/ch05-nerd-dinner-web`. Like other examples from Chapter 3, *Developing Dockerized .NET and .NET Core Applications*, the Dockerfile uses a bootstrap script as the entry point, which promotes environment variables to the machine level so the ASP.NET application can read them.

The new version of the NerdDinner website runs in Docker with this command:

```
docker container run -d -P `
  --name nerd-dinner-web `
  --env-file api-keys.env `
  dockeronwindows/ch05-nerd-dinner-web
```

The application needs these API keys set in the environment variables to run properly, but that's a runtime requirement that is not clear from the Dockerfile alone. I have a PowerShell script that starts containers in the right order, with the right options, but by the end of the chapter, that script will be unwieldy. I'll address this in the next chapter when I look at composition.

Splitting out the create dinner feature

In the `DinnerController` class, the `Create` action is a relatively expensive database operation, which doesn't need to be synchronous. This feature is a good candidate for splitting into a separate component. I can publish a message from the web app instead of saving to the database while the user waits - if the site is experiencing high load, the message may wait in the queue for seconds or even minutes before being processed, but the response back to the user will be almost instant.

There are two pieces of work to split the feature into a new component. The web application needs to publish a message to a queue when a dinner is created, and a message handler needs to listen on the queue and save the dinner when it receives a message. In NerdDinner, there's a bit more work to do because the existing code base is a physical monolith as well as a logical monolith, and there's just one Visual Studio project that contains everything: all the model definitions as well as the UI code.

In this chapter's source code, I've added a new .NET assembly project called `NerdDinner.Model` to the solution and moved the EF classes to that project, so they can be shared between the web app and the message handler. The model project targets the full .NET Framework rather than .NET Core, so I can use the existing code as it is and I don't need to bring an upgrade of EF into scope for this feature change. This choice restricts the message handler to being a full .NET application too.

There's also a shared assembly project to isolate the message queue code in `NerdDinner.Messaging`. I'll be using the nats message system, which is a high-performance open source message queue. There is a nats client package on NuGet which targets .NET Standard, so it can be used in both .NET and .NET Core, and my messaging project does the same. This means that I can be flexible, so other message handlers that don't use the EF model could be written in .NET Core.

In the model project, the original definition of the `Dinner` class is polluted with a lot of EF and MVC code to capture validation and storage behavior, like this definition for the description property:

```
[Required(ErrorMessage = "Description is required")]
[StringLength(256, ErrorMessage = "Description may not be longer than 256
characters")]
[DataType(DataType.MultilineText)]
public string Description { get; set; }
```

The class should be a simple POCO definition, but these attributes mean the model definition is not portable because any consumers also need to reference EF and MVC. To avoid that in the messaging project, I have a simple `Dinner` entity defined without any of these attributes, and that class is the one I use to send dinner information in messages. I can use the `AutoMapper` NuGet package to convert between dinner class definitions, as the properties are fundamentally the same.

 This is the sort of challenge you will find in lots of older projects - there's no clear separation of concerns, so breaking out features is not straightforward. You can take this approach and restructure the code base without fundamentally changing logic, which will help in modernizing the app.

The main code in the `Create` method of the `DinnersController` class now maps the dinner model to the clean dinner entity and publishes an event instead of writing to the database:

```
if (ModelState.IsValid)
{
  dinner.HostedBy = User.Identity.Name;
  var eventMessage = new DinnerCreatedEvent
  {
    Dinner = Mapper.Map<entities.Dinner>(dinner),
    CreatedAt = DateTime.UtcNow
  };
  MessageQueue.Publish(eventMessage);
  return RedirectToAction("Index");
}
```

This is the fire-and-forget messaging pattern. The web application is the producer, publishing an event message. The producer doesn't wait for a response and doesn't know which components—if any, will consume the message and act on it. It's loosely coupled and fast, and it puts the responsibility to deliver the message onto the message queue, which is where it should be.

Listening for this event message is a new .NET console project in `NerdDinner.MessageHandlers.CreateDinner`. The `Main` method of the console app uses the shared messaging project to open a connection to the message queue and subscribe to these dinner-created event messages. When a message is received, the handler maps the dinner entity in the message back to a dinner model and saves the model to the database using code taken from the original implementation in the `DinnersController` class (and tidied up a little):

```
var dinner = Mapper.Map<models.Dinner>(eventMessage.Dinner);
using (var db = new NerdDinnerContext())
{
  dinner.RSVPs = new List<RSVP>
  {
    new RSVP
    {
      AttendeeName = dinner.HostedBy
    }
  };
  db.Dinners.Add(dinner);
  db.SaveChanges();
}
```

Now the message handler can be packaged into its own Docker image and run in a container alongside the website container.

Packaging .NET console apps in Docker

Console apps are easy to build as good citizens for Docker. The compiled executable for the app will be the main process Docker starts and monitors, so you just need to make use of the console for logging, and environment variables for configuration.

For my message handler I'm using a multi-stage build with a slightly different pattern. I have a separate image for the builder stage, which I use to compile the whole solution - the web project and the new projects I've added. I'll walk through the builder image later in the chapter, when you've seen all the new components.

The builder compiles the solution, and the Dockerfile for the console application references the `dockeronwindows/ch05-nerd-dinner-builder` image in a stage called **builder**. The final stage packages the compiled executable from the builder stage and sets up default configuration values:

```
# escape=`
FROM dockeronwindows/ch05-nerd-dinner-builder AS builder

# app image
FROM microsoft/windowsservercore:10.0.14393.1198
SHELL ["powershell", "-Command", "$ErrorActionPreference = 'Stop';"]

CMD ["NerdDinner.MessageHandlers.SaveDinner.exe"]

ENV APP_DB_CONNECTION_STRING="Data Source=nerd-dinner-db..." `
    MESSAGE_QUEUE_URL="nats://message-queue:4222"

WORKDIR C:\save-handler
COPY --from=builder C:\src\NerdDinner.MessageHandlers.SaveDinner\bin\Debug\
    .
```

The new message handler needs to access the message queue and the database, and the connection strings for each are captured as environment variables. In the code for the project, there is an `Env` class to read these values from environment variables.

In the Dockerfile, the entry point in the `CMD` instruction is the console executable, so the container will keep running as long as the console app is running. The listener for the message queue runs asynchronously on a separate thread. The handler code will fire when a message is received, so there's no polling of the queue and the app runs very efficiently.

Keeping the console app running indefinitely is straightforward, using a
`ManualResetEvent` object. In the `Main` method, I wait for a reset event that never happens,
so the program keeps running:

```
class Program
{
  private static ManualResetEvent _ResetEvent = new
ManualResetEvent(false);

  static void Main(string[] args)
  {
    // set up message listener
    _ResetEvent.WaitOne();
  }
}
```

This is a simple and efficient way of keeping a .NET (or .NET Core) console app alive.
When I start a message handler container, it will keep running in the background and listen
for messages until the container is stopped.

Running a message queue in Docker

The web application now publishes messages, and a handler listens for them, so the final
component I need is a message queue to connect the two. Queues need the same level of
availability as the rest of the solution, so they're good candidates for running in Docker
containers. In a distributed solution deployed on many servers, the queue can be clustered
across multiple containers for performance and redundancy.

Your choice of messaging technology depends on the features you need, but there are
plenty of options with .NET client libraries—**Microsoft Message Queue** (**MSMQ**) is the
native Windows queue, RabbitMQ is a popular open source queue that supports durable
messaging, and nats is an open source in-memory queue that is hugely performant.

The high throughput and low latency of nats messaging make it a good choice to
communicate between containers, and there is an official image for nats on Docker Hub.
nats is a Go application that runs cross-platform and there are Linux, Windows Server Core,
and Nano Server variants of the Docker image.

You run the nats message queue like any other container, publishing port `4222` which is the port clients use to connect to the queue:

```
docker container run --detach `
 --publish 4222 `
 --name message-queue `
 nats:nanoserver
```

 I'm using the Nano Server version of the nats image because the lighter profile means it starts more quickly, runs more efficiently, and exposes a smaller attack surface.

The nats server application logs messages to the console, so the log entries are collected by Docker. When the container is running, you can verify that the queue is listening using `docker container logs`:

```
> docker container logs message-queue
[1416] 2017/06/23 09:20:41.329327 [INF] Starting nats-server version 0.9.6
[1416] 2017/06/23 09:20:41.329327 [INF] Starting http monitor on
0.0.0.0:8222
[1416] 2017/06/23 09:20:41.331269 [INF] Listening for client connections on
0.0.0.0:4222
[1416] 2017/06/23 09:20:41.331269 [INF] Server is ready
[1416] 2017/06/23 09:20:41.334275 [INF] Listening for route connections on
0.0.0.0:6222
```

The message queue is an infrastructure-level component with no dependencies on other components. It can be started before other containers and left running when application containers are stopped or upgraded.

Starting a multi-container solution

As you make more use of Docker, your solution will become distributed across more containers - either running custom code that you split out from a monolith, or tried and trusted third-party software from Docker Hub or Docker Store.

NerdDinner now runs across four containers - SQL Server, the web app, the nats message queue, and the message handler. There are dependencies between the containers, and they need to be started in the correct order and created with the correct names so that components can be found using Docker's service discovery.

In the next chapter, I'll use Docker Compose to declaratively map out these dependencies. For now, I have a PowerShell script `ch05-run-nerd-dinner_part-1.ps1` which explicitly starts the containers with the correct configuration:

```
docker container run -d -p 4222 `
  --name message-queue `
  nats:nanoserver;

docker container run -d -p 1433 `
  --name nerd-dinner-db `
  -v C:\databases\nd:C:\data `
  dockeronwindows/ch03-nerd-dinner-db;

docker container run -d -p 80 `
  --name nerd-dinner-homepage `
  dockeronwindows/ch03-nerd-dinner-homepage;

docker container run -d `
  --name nerd-dinner-save-handler `
  dockeronwindows/ch05-nerd-dinner-save-handler;

docker container run -d -p 80 `
  --name nerd-dinner-web `
  --env-file api-keys.env `
  dockeronwindows/ch05-nerd-dinner-web;
```

In this script I'm using the SQL database and home page images from `Chapter 3`, *Developing Dockerized .NET and .NET Core Applications* - these components haven't changed, so they can be run alongside the new components.

If you want to run this yourself with full functionality, you will need to populate your own API keys in the file `api-keys.env`. You'll need to sign up to the Bing Maps API and the IP information database. You can run the app without those keys, but not all features will work correctly.

When I run the script with my own API keys set and inspect the web container to get the IP address, I can browse to the application. It's a fully featured version of NerdDinner now. I can log in and complete the create dinner form, complete with map integration:

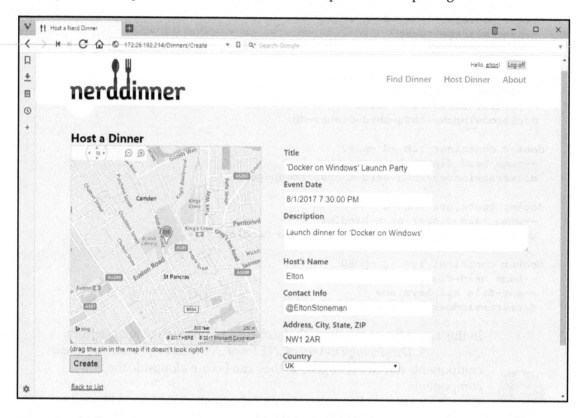

When I submit the form, the web app publishes an event message to the queue. That is a very cheap operation, so the web app returns to the user almost immediately. Listening for messages is the console application, running in a different container - potentially on a different host. It picks up the message and processes it. The handler logs the activity to the console, so admin users can monitor it using `docker container logs`:

```
> docker container logs nerd-dinner-save-handler

Connecting to message queue url: nats://message-queue:4222
Listening on subject: events.dinner.created, queue: save-dinner-handler
Received message, subject: events.dinner.created
Saving new dinner, created at: 6/24/2017 8:44:21 PM; event ID: b7ecb300-
af6f-4f2e-ab18-19bea90d4684
Dinner saved. Dinner ID: 1; event ID: b7ecb300-af6f-4f2e-ab18-19bea90d4684
```

The functionality of the create dinner feature is the same - data entered by the user is saved to SQL Server, and the user experience is the same, but the scalability of this feature is massively improved. Designing for containers lets me extract the persistence code into a new component, knowing the component can be deployed on the same infrastructure as the existing solution and that it will inherit the existing levels of scalability and failover, if the application is deployed on a cluster.

I can rely on the Docker platform and take a dependency on a new core component, the message queue. The queue technology itself is enterprise-grade software, capable of processing hundreds of thousands of messages per second. nats is free open source software that is available on Docker Hub to drop straight into your solution, running as a container and connected to other containers in the Docker network.

So far, I've used the container-first design and the power of Docker to modernize one part of NerdDinner. Targeting a single feature means I can release this new version confidently, after testing only the feature that's changed. If I wanted to add auditing to the create dinner feature, I would just make an update to the message handler and I wouldn't need to do a full regression test of the web application, because that component is not going to be updated.

Designing with containers in mind also gives me a foundation to add more features.

Adding new features in containers

Decoupling components from a monolith has a beneficial side effect. The approach I've taken has introduced a style of event-driven architecture for one feature. I can build on that to add new features, again taking a container-first approach.

In NerdDinner there is a single data store, a transactional database stored in SQL Server. That's fine to service the website, but it's limited when it comes to user-facing features, such as reporting. There's no user-friendly way to search the data, build dashboards, or enable self-service reporting.

An ideal solution for this would be to add a secondary data store, a reporting database, using a technology which does provide self-service analytics. Without Docker that would be a major project, needing a redesign or additional infrastructure or both. With Docker, I can leave the existing application alone and add new features running in containers on the existing servers.

Elasticsearch is another enterprise-grade open source project which is available as a Windows image on Docker Hub. Elasticsearch is a full search document data store which works well as a reporting database, along with the companion product Kibana which provides a user friendly web front end.

I can add self-service analytics for the dinners created in NerdDinner by running Elasticsearch and Kibana in containers in the same network as the other containers. The current solution already publishes events with dinner details, so to add dinners to the reporting database I need to build a new message handler which subscribes to the existing events and saves the details in Elasticsearch.

When the new reporting feature is ready, it can be deployed to production without any changes to the running application. Zero-downtime deployment is another benefit of container-first design. Features are built to run in decoupled units, so individual containers can be started or upgraded without affecting other containers.

For the next feature, I'll add a new message handler which is independent of the rest of the solution. If I needed to replace the implementation of the save-dinner handler, I could also do that with zero-downtime, using the message queue to buffer events while replacing the handler.

Using Elasticsearch with Docker and .NET

Elasticsearch is such a widely useful technology that it's worth looking at in a little detail. It's a Java application, but running in Docker you can treat it as a black box and manage it in the same way as all other Docker workloads - you don't need to install Java or configure the JDK. Elasticsearch exposes a REST API for writing, reading, and searching data, and there are client wrappers for the API available in all major languages.

Data in Elasticsearch is stored as JSON documents, and every document can be fully indexed so you can search for any value in any field. It's a clustered technology that can run across many nodes for scale and resilience. In Docker, you can run each node in a separate container and distribute them across your server estate to gain scale and resilience, but add the ease of deployment and management you get with Docker.

The same storage considerations apply to Elasticsearch as with any stateful workload - in development, you can save data inside the container, so when the container is replaced, you start with a fresh database. In test environments, you can use a Docker volume mounted to a drive on the host to keep persistent storage outside of the container. In production, you can use a volume with a driver for an on-premises storage array or a cloud storage service.

There's an official Elasticsearch image on Docker Hub, but currently it only has Linux variants. I have my own image on Docker Cloud which packages Elasticsearch into a Windows Docker image. Running Elasticsearch in Docker is the same as starting any container. This command exposes port 9200, which is the default port for the REST API:

```
docker container run -d -p 9200 `
  --name elasticsearch `
  --env ES_JAVA_OPTS='-Xms512m -Xmx512m' `
sixeyed/elasticsearch:nanoserver
```

Elasticsearch is a memory-hungry application, and by default it allocates 2 GB of system memory when it starts. In a development environment I don't need that much memory for the database. I can configure that by setting the ES_JAVA_OPTS environment variable. In this command I limit Elasticsearch to 512 MB of memory.

 Elasticsearch is a cross-platform application like nats. As with nats, I'm using the Nano Server image to get the most lightweight runtime.

There is a NuGet package for Elasticsearch called **NEST**, which is an API client for reading and writing data, and is targeted for the .NET Framework and .NET Core. I use that package in a new .NET Core console project, NerdDinner.MessageHandlers.IndexDinner. The new console app listens for the create dinner event message from nats and writes the dinner details as a document in Elasticsearch.

The code to connect to the message queue and subscribe to messages is the same as the existing message handler. I have a new Dinner class, which represents the Elasticsearch document, so the message handler code maps from the dinner entity to the dinner document and saves it in Elasticsearch:

```
var eventMessage =
MessageHelper.FromData<DinnerCreatedEvent>(e.Message.Data);
var dinner = Mapper.Map<documents.Dinner>(eventMessage.Dinner);
var node = new Uri(Env.ElasticsearchUrl);
var client = new ElasticClient(node);
client.Index(dinner, idx => idx.Index("dinners"));
```

Elasticsearch and the document message handler will run in a container, all in the same Docker network as the rest of the NerdDinner solution. I can start the new containers while the existing solution is running, as there are no changes to the web application or the SQL Server message handler. Adding this new feature with Docker is a zero-downtime deployment.

The Elasticsearch message handler has no dependency on EF or any of the legacy code. I've taken advantage of that to write the app in .NET Core, which gives me the freedom to run it in a Docker container on Linux or Windows hosts. That means the Visual Studio solution has both .NET Framework and .NET Core application projects, and the apps both refer to a .NET Standard assembly project. That setup needs a slightly more complicated build agent.

Building hybrid .NET Framework and .NET Core solutions in Docker

The multi-stage builds you've seen up until now have all used my `sixeyed/msbuild` images on Docker Cloud. Those images provide MSBuild and NuGet, and any extra packages needed to build specific project types - like web projects and SQL Server projects. You can find the Dockerfiles for those images on GitHub at `sixeyed/dockerfiles-windows`, and you'll see they're all very simple.

I've been using the `sixeyed/msbuild` image as the build agent to compile individual .NET Framework projects. You can build Visual Studio solutions with the MSBuild tool, and if there are multiple .NET projects with project references, MSBuild will compile them in the correct order. If your Visual Studio solution contains both .NET and .NET Core projects, you can't build it with MSBuild alone - you need the .NET Core SDK too.

That's the case with NerdDinner in this chapter, so I have a new Docker image which packages MSBuild and the .NET Core SDK and I can use that to compile the solution. The Dockerfile for `dockeronwindows/ch05-msbuild-dotnet` is itself a multi-stage build, and the output is an image that can be used to compile a hybrid .NET Framework and .NET Core solution.

The Dockerfile starts by installing Chocolatey and then using the `choco` command to install the Visual Studio 2017 build tools and the NuGet command line. The build tools package contains the latest release of MSBuild:

```
FROM microsoft/windowsservercore:10.0.14393.1198 AS buildtools
SHELL ["powershell", "-Command", "$ErrorActionPreference = 'Stop';"]

RUN Invoke-WebRequest -UseBasicParsing https://chocolatey.org/install.ps1 |
```

```
Invoke-Expression; `
    choco install -y visualstudio2017buildtools --version
15.2.26430.20170605; `
    choco install -y nuget.commandline --version 4.1.0
```

Running this in a separate stage means I can use Chocolatey for easy package install. In the final image I'll copy the package output from this stage - but I won't copy Chocolatey itself. That makes for a smaller and cleaner image for my build agent. The next stage uses Microsoft's .NET Core image with the SDK installed. I don't add anything to this stage, I just reference the image so I can copy the SDK from it in the final image:

```
FROM microsoft/dotnet:1.1.2-sdk-nanoserver AS dotnet
```

The last stage puts together the build agent. It starts from Windows Server Core, sets file paths as environment variables and copies the .NET Core SDK, MSBuild and NuGet from the earlier stages:

```
FROM microsoft/windowsservercore:10.0.14393.1198
SHELL ["powershell", "-Command", "$ErrorActionPreference = 'Stop'"]

ENV MSBUILD_PATH="C:\Program Files (x86)\Microsoft Visual
Studio\2017\BuildTools\MSBuild\15.0\Bin" `
    NUGET_PATH="C:\ProgramData\chocolatey\lib\NuGet.CommandLine\tools" `
    DOTNET_PATH="C:\Program Files\dotnet"

COPY --from=dotnet ${DOTNET_PATH} ${DOTNET_PATH}
COPY --from=buildtools ${MSBUILD_PATH} ${MSBUILD_PATH}
COPY --from=buildtools ${NUGET_PATH} ${NUGET_PATH}
```

Next I add packages for the .NET 4.5.2 targeting pack, web deploy, and the build targets for web projects:

```
RUN Install-PackageProvider -Name chocolatey -RequiredVersion 2.8.5.130 -
Force; `
    Install-Package -Name netfx-4.5.2-devpack -RequiredVersion 4.5.5165101
-Force; `
    Install-Package -Name webdeploy -RequiredVersion 3.6.0 -Force; `
    & nuget install MSBuild.Microsoft.VisualStudio.Web.targets -Version
14.0.0.3
```

I build this Dockerfile in the usual way, and the output is an image which has the complete toolchain to compile a Hybrid .NET Framework and .NET Core solution.

Compiling the hybrid NerdDinner solution

I'm taking a different approach to building NerdDinner in this chapter, one which fits nicely with a CI process if you're mixing .NET Core and .NET Framework projects (I cover CI and CD with Docker in Chapter 10, *Powering a Continuous Deployment Pipeline with Docker*). I'll compile the whole solution in one image, and use that image as the build stage in my application Dockerfiles.

This is how the build agent and builder images are used to package the application images for this chapter:

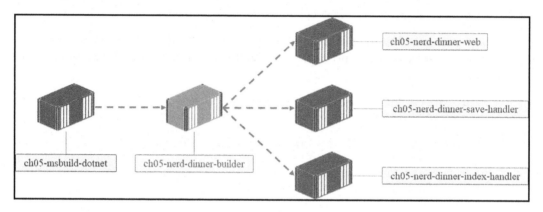

All the tools I need to build the solution are in the build agent, so the Dockerfile for `dockeronwindows/ch05-nerd-dinner-builder` is straightforward. It starts from the build agent and copies in the source tree for the solution:

```
# escape=`
FROM dockeronwindows/ch05-msbuild-dotnet

WORKDIR C:\src
COPY src .
```

Next it restores all the packages used in the projects, using `dotnet restore` for the .NET Core projects and NuGet restore for the .NET Framework projects:

```
RUN dotnet restore; `
    nuget restore -msbuildpath $env:MSBUILD_PATH
```

The two steps are necessary, because the tooling is different. Package references for .NET Core projects are listed inside the `.csproj` files, whereas for .NET Framework projects they're in `packages.config`. Both commands run from the `NerdDinner.sln` file, so I don't need to list individual projects, and as the solution grows I won't need to update the builder.

There are only two more instructions in the builder, and they compile all the projects and publish the applications:

```
RUN dotnet build .\NerdDinner.Messaging\NerdDinner.Messaging.csproj; `
    dotnet msbuild NerdDinner.sln

RUN dotnet publish .\NerdDinner.MessageHandlers.IndexDinner; `
    msbuild .\NerdDinner\NerdDinner.csproj `
        /p:DeployOnBuild=true /p:OutputPath=c:\out\NerdDinner `
/p:VSToolsPath=C:\MSBuild.Microsoft.VisualStudio.Web.targets.14.0.0.3\tools
\VSToolsPath
```

Again there are separate steps for the .NET Core and .NET Framework apps, because the tooling is not yet integrated. I expect later releases of MSBuild and .NET Core will have integrated tooling, so the complexity of managing multiple toolchains will go away. Until then, you can use Docker to isolate the complexity - building all the tools into one image, which lets you have a clean builder image with no clutter for the tooling.

The disadvantage of this approach is that there's no use of the Docker cache. The whole source tree is copied into the image as the first step. Whenever there is a code change the build will update the packages, even if the package references haven't changed. You could write this builder differently, to copy in the `.sln`, `.csproj`, and `package.config` files first for the restore phase, and then copy in the rest of the source for the build phase.

That would give you package caching and a faster build, at the cost of a more brittle Dockerfile - you'd need to edit the initial file list every time you add or remove a project.

You can choose the approach that works best with your processes. In the case of a more complex solution like this, developers may build and run the app from Visual Studio, and only build the Docker images to run tests before checking in code. In that case, the slower Docker image build is not an issue (I discuss the options for running your application in Docker while you're developing it in `Chapter 11`, *Debugging and Instrumenting Application Containers*).

One thing is different in how this image is built. The Dockerfile copies in the `src` folder, which is one level higher than the folder where the Dockerfile lives. To make sure the `src` folder is included in the Docker context, I need to run the `build image` command from the `ch05` folder, and specify the path to the Dockerfile with the `--file` option:

```
docker image build `
    --tag dockeronwindows/ch05-nerd-dinner-builder `
    --file ch05-nerd-dinner-builder\Dockerfile .
```

Building the image compiles and packages all the projects, so I can use that image as the source stage in the application Dockerfiles. I only need to build the builder once, and then I can use it to build all the other images.

Packaging .NET Core console apps in Docker

In Chapter 3, *Developing Dockerized .NET and .NET Core Applications*, I built the replacement NerdDinner home page as an ASP.NET Core web application, and in this chapter, I have the Elasticsearch message handler as a .NET Core console application. In this case the application can be packaged as a Docker image using the `microsoft/dotnet` image from Microsoft on Docker Hub.

The Dockerfile for `dockeronwindows/ch05-index-handler` uses multi-stage builds, with the builder image as the source:

```
# escape=`
FROM dockeronwindows/ch05-nerd-dinner-builder AS builder

# app image
FROM microsoft/dotnet:1.1.2-runtime-nanoserver
SHELL ["powershell", "-Command", "$ErrorActionPreference = 'Stop';"]

ENV ELASTICSEARCH_URL="http://elasticsearch:9200" `
    MESSAGE_QUEUE_URL="nats://message-queue:4222"

CMD ["dotnet", "NerdDinner.MessageHandlers.IndexDinner.dll"]

WORKDIR /index-handler
COPY --from=builder
C:\src\NerdDinner.MessageHandlers.IndexDinner\bin\Debug\netcoreapp1.1\publi
sh\ .
```

The content is very similar to the .NET Frameworks console app used for the SQL Server message handler. The differences are the FROM image—here I'm using the .NET Core runtime image, and the CMD instruction—here it's the `dotnet` command running the console application DLL. Both the message handlers use the builder image as the source for copying the compiled application, and then set up the environment variables and startup commands they need.

The index handler application uses environment variables for configuration, specifying the URLs for the message queue and the Elasticsearch API. These values have defaults set in the Dockerfile in the same way as the other NerdDinner components, because I'll control the deployment stack and can safely rely on these values. The start up command runs the .NET Core application, which writes log entries to the console and stays alive with a `ManualResetEvent` object, so it integrates well with Docker.

When the application runs, it will listen for messages from nats, with the create dinner message subject. When events are published from the web application, nats will send copies to every subscriber, so the SQL Server save handler and the Elasticsearch index handler will both get copies of the event. The event message contains enough detail for both handlers to operate. If a future feature requires more detail, then the web app can publish a new version of the event with additional information, but the existing message handlers would not need to change.

Running another container with Kibana will complete this feature and add self-service analytics to NerdDinner.

Providing analytics with Kibana

Kibana is an open source web frontend for Elasticsearch, which gives you visualizations for analytics and the ability to search for specific data. It's produced by the company behind Elasticsearch and is very widely used because it provides a user friendly way to navigate around huge quantities of data. You can explore the data interactively, and power users can build comprehensive dashboards to share with others.

The latest version of Kibana is a Node.js application, so like Elasticsearch and nats, it's a cross-platform application, which you can find packaged on Docker Hub with Linux and Windows variants. The Kibana image is built using the same convention-based approach that I've used in the message handlers—it expects to connect to a container called `elasticsearch` on the default API port 9200.

In the source code directory for this chapter, there is a second PowerShell script which deploys the containers for this feature. `ch05-run-nerd-dinner_part-2.ps1` starts the additional Elasticsearch, Kibana, and index handler containers—it assumes the other components are already running from the part-1 script:

```
docker container run -d -p 9200 `
--name elasticsearch `
sixeyed/elasticsearch:nanoserver

docker container run -d -p 5601 `
--name kibana `
sixeyed/kibana:nanoserver;

docker container run -d `
 --name nerd-dinner-index-handler `
dockeronwindows/ch05-nerd-dinner-index-handler;
```

The full stack is running now. When I add a new dinner, I will see the logs from the message handler containers showing the data is now being saved to Elasticsearch as well as to SQL Server:

```
> docker container logs nerd-dinner-save-handler
Connecting to message queue url: nats://message-queue:4222
Listening on subject: events.dinner.created, queue: save-dinner-handler
Received message, subject: events.dinner.created
Saving new dinner, created at: 6/24/2017 10:58:31 PM; event ID: a7530414-
d2ad-407a-9b03-ade7a22f1f7e
Dinner saved. Dinner ID: 2; event ID: a7530414-d2ad-407a-9b03-ade7a22f1f7e

> docker container logs nerd-dinner-index-handler
Connecting to message queue url: nats://message-queue:4222
Listening on subject: events.dinner.created, queue: index-dinner-handler
Received message, subject: events.dinner.created
Indexing new dinner, created at: 6/25/2017 12:13:13 AM; event ID: a7530414-
d2ad-407a-9b03-ade7a22f1f7e
```

Kibana runs on port `5601`, so I can fetch the container IP address and navigate to that port in the browser. The only configuration the launch screen needs is the name of the document collection - which Elasticsearch calls an index. In this case, the index is called **dinners.** I've already added a document Kibana, so can access the Elasticsearch metadata to determine the fields in the documents:

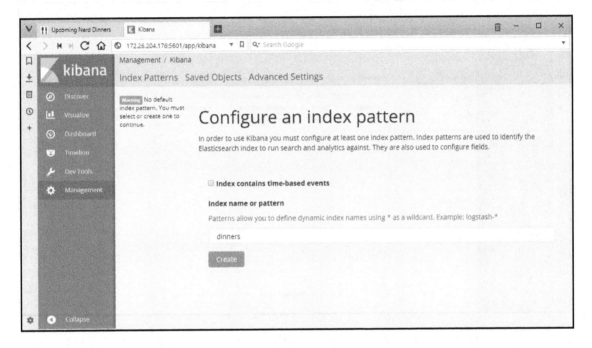

Every dinner created will now be saved in the original transactional database, SQL Server, and also in the new reporting database, Elasticsearch. Users can create visualizations over aggregated data—looking for patterns in popular times or locations, and they can search for particular dinner details and retrieve specific documents:

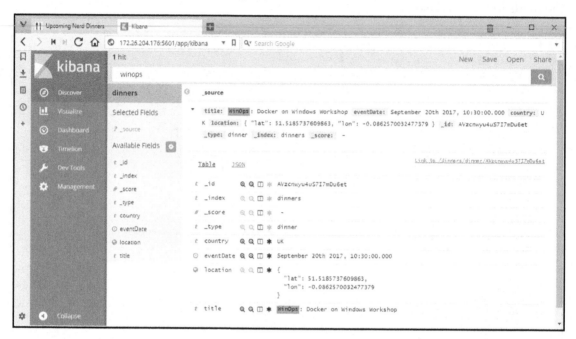

Elasticsearch and Kibana are hugely capable software systems. I won't cover them in any further detail in this book, but they are popular components with a lot of online resources if you want to learn more.

From monolith to distributed solution

NerdDinner has evolved from a legacy monolith to an easily scalable, easily extensible solution running on a modern application platform using modern design patterns. It's been a fast and low risk evolution, powered by the Docker platform and container-first design.

The project started by migrating NerdDinner to Docker as-is, running containers for the web application and the SQL Server database. Now I have eight components, each running in a lightweight Docker container and each capable of being independently deployed, so they can follow their own release cadence:

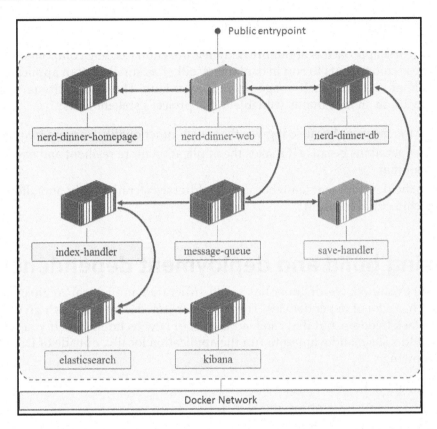

One of the great benefits of Docker is the huge library of packaged software available to add to your solution. The official images on Docker Hub are enterprise-grade open source software systems that have been tried and trusted by the community for years. Certified images on Docker Store provide commercial software which is guaranteed to work correctly on Docker EE.

More and more software packages are becoming available for Windows in easily-consumed Docker images, giving you the scope to add features to your application without significant development.

The new custom components in the NerdDinner stack are the message handlers—both simple console applications of around 100 lines of code. The save dinner handler uses the original code from the web application and uses the EF model - which I refactored into its own project to enable that reuse. The index dinner handler uses all new code written in .NET Core, which makes it efficient and portable at runtime, but at build time, all the projects are in a single Visual Studio solution.

The container-first approach is about breaking features into discrete components and designing these components to run in containers, either as small custom applications you write yourself, or as off-the-shelf images from Docker Hub. The feature-driven approach means you focus on an area that is valuable to the project's stakeholders:

- To the business because it gives them new functionality or more frequent releases
- To operations because it makes the application more resilient and easier to maintain
- To the development team because it addresses technical debt and allows greater architectural freedom

Managing build and deployment dependencies

In the current evolution, NerdDinner has a well-structured and logical architecture, but practically it has a lot of dependencies. The container-first design approach gives me technology stack freedom, but that can lead to a lot of new technologies. If you were to join the project at this stage and wanted to run the application locally, outside of Docker, you'd need the following:

- Visual Studio 2017
- .NET Core 1.1.2 runtime and SDK 1.0.4
- IIS and ASP.NET 4.5
- SQL Server
- nats, Elasticsearch, and Kibana

If you join the project and you have Docker for Windows installed, you don't need any of those dependencies. When you've cloned the source code, you can build and run the whole application stack with Docker. You can even develop and debug the solution with Docker and a lightweight editor like VS Code, removing even the dependency for Visual Studio.

This also makes continuous integration very easy - your build servers only need Docker installed to build and package the solution. You can use disposable build servers, spinning up a VM when you have builds queued and then destroying the VM when the queue is empty. You don't need complex initialization scripts for the VM, just a scripted Docker install.

There are still runtime dependencies for the solution, which I'm currently managing with a script that starts all the containers with the right options and in the right order. This is a brittle and limited approach - the script has no logic to handle any failures or to allow for a partial start where some containers are already running. I'll address this in the next chapter using Docker Compose to define and run the whole solution.

Summary

In this chapter, I looked at the container-first solution design, making use of the Docker platform at design time to easily and safely add features to your application. I covered a feature-driven approach to modernizing an existing software project, which maximizes return on investment and gives clear visibility on progress.

The container-first approach to features lets you use production-grade software from Docker Hub or Docker Store to add capabilities to your solution, with official and certified images that are high-quality curated applications. You can add these off-the-shelf components, and focus on building small custom components to complete features. Your application will evolve to be loosely coupled, so individual elements can each have the most appropriate release cycle.

The speed of development in this chapter has outpaced operations, so we currently have a well-architected solution that is fragile to deploy. In the next chapter, I'll introduce Docker Compose, which provides a clear and uniform way to describe and manage multi-container solutions.

6
Organizing Distributed Solutions with Docker Compose

Shipping software is an integral part of the Docker platform. The public registries on Docker Hub, Docker Cloud, and Docker Store make it easy to design a distributed solution using tried-and-tested components. In the previous chapter, I showed how to integrate these components into your own solution, taking a container-first design approach. The end result is a distributed solution with several moving parts. In this chapter, you'll learn how to organize all those moving parts into one unit using Docker Compose.

Docker Compose is another open source product from Docker, Inc., which extends the Docker ecosystem. The Docker **Command Line Interface** (**CLI**) and Docker API work on individual resources, such as images and containers. Docker Compose works on a higher level of services applications. An application is a single unit composed of multiple resources, which are Docker containers, networks, and volumes at runtime. You use compose to define all the resources of the application and the dependencies between them.

There are two parts to Docker Compose. The design-time element captures the application definition in a YAML file, and at runtime, Docker Compose can manage an application from the YAML file. I'll cover both these parts in this chapter, showing you how to:

- Define distributed solutions with the Docker Compose file format
- Start, stop, upgrade, and scale applications using Docker Compose
- Manage containers and images with Docker Compose
- Structure Docker Compose files to support multiple environments

Docker Compose is installed as part of Docker for Windows CE. If you install Docker using the PowerShell installer, that doesn't give you compose. You can download it from the releases on GitHub at `docker/compose`.

Defining applications with Docker Compose

The Docker Compose file format is very simple. YAML is a human-readable superset of JSON, and the Compose file specification uses descriptive attribute names. In the Compose file, you define the services, networks, and volumes that make up your application. Networks and volumes are the same concepts that you use with the Docker engine. Services are an abstraction over containers.

A container is a single instance of a component, but a service can be multiple instances of the same component running in different containers. You could have three containers in the service used for your web application and two containers in the service you use for a message handler:

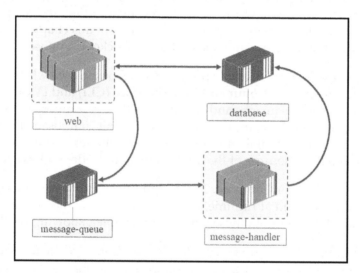

A service is like a template to run a container from an image, with a known configuration. Using services, you can scale up components of the application—running multiple containers from the same image and configuration and managing them as a single unit. Services are not used in the standalone Docker engine, but they are used in Docker Compose and also with a cluster of Docker engines running in the swarm mode (which I cover in the next chapter).

Docker provides discoverability for services in the same way that it does for containers. Consumers access the service by name, and Docker can load-balance requests across multiple containers in a service. The number of instances in the service is transparent to consumers; they always refer to the service name, and they are always directed to a single container by Docker.

In this chapter, I'll use Docker Compose to organize the distributed solution I built in the previous chapter, replacing the brittle `docker container run` PowerShell scripts with a reliable and production-ready Docker Compose file.

Capturing service definitions

Services can be defined in any order in the Compose file. To make it easier to read, I prefer to start with the simplest services, which have no dependencies—infrastructure components such as message queue and databases.

Docker Compose files are conventionally called `docker-compose.yml`, and they start with an explicit statement of the API version; the latest is version 3.3. Application resources are defined at the top level—this is a template Compose file with sections for services, networks, and volumes:

```
version: '3.3'

services:
  ...

networks:
  ...

volumes:
  ...
```

All resources need a unique name, and the name is how resources refer to other resources. Services may have a dependency on networks, volumes, and other services, which are all captured by name. The configuration for each resource is in its own section, and the attributes available are broadly the same as the respective `create` command in the Docker CLI such as `docker network create` and `docker volume create`.

In this chapter, I'll build a Compose file for the distributed NerdDinner application and show you how to use Docker Compose to manage the application. I'll start my Compose file with the common services first.

Defining infrastructure services

The simplest service I have is the message queue, nats, which has no dependencies. Each service needs a name and the image name to start containers from. Optionally, you can include start up parameters that you would use in `docker container run`. For the nats message queue, I add a network name, which means any containers created in this service will all be attached to the `nd-net` network:

```
message-queue:
  image: nats:nanoserver
  networks:
    - nd-net
```

In this service definition, I have all the parameters required to start message queue containers:

- `message-queue`: This is the name of the service; this becomes the DNS entry for other services to access nats.

- `image`: This is the full name of the image to start containers from. In this case, it's the official `nats:nanoserver` image from the public Docker Hub, but you can also use an image from a private registry by including the registry domain in the image name.

- `networks`: This is a list of the networks to connect containers to when they start. This service connects to one network named `nd-net`. This will be a Docker network used for all the services in this application. Later in the Docker Compose file, I'll explicitly capture the details of the network.

> I haven't published any ports for the nats service. The message queue is used only internally by other containers. Within a Docker network, containers can access ports on other containers without them being published to the host. This keeps the message queue secure, as it is only accessible through the Docker platform by other containers in the same network. No external server and no applications running on the server can access the message queue.

The next infrastructure service is Elasticsearch, which also has no dependencies on other services. It will be used by the message handler that also uses the nats message queue, so I will need to join all these services to the same Docker network. For Elasticsearch, I also want to limit the amount of memory it uses and use a volume for the data so it will be stored outside of the container:

```
elasticsearch:
  image: sixeyed/elasticsearch:nanoserver
  environment:
    - ES_JAVA_OPTS=-Xms512m -Xmx512m
  volumes:
    - es-data:C:\data
  networks:
   - nd-net
```

Here, `elasticsearch` is the name of the service and `sixeyed/elasticsearch` is the name of the image, which is my public image on Docker Cloud. I'm connecting the service to the same `nd-net` network, and I also mount a volume to a known location in the container. When Elasticsearch writes data to `C:\data` on the container, it will actually be stored in a volume.

Just like with networks, volumes are first-class resources in the Docker Compose file. For Elasticsearch, I'm mapping a volume called **es-data** to the data location in the container. I'll specify how the es-data volume should be created later in the Compose file.

Kibana is the first service that is available outside of the Docker network, so I need to publish ports, and it's the first that depends on another service. I can capture both these attributes in the service definition:

```
kibana:
  image: sixeyed/kibana:nanoserver
  ports:
    - "5601:5601"
  depends_on:
    - elasticsearch
  networks:
    - nd-net
```

Port publishing is the same in Docker Compose as it is when running a container. You specify which container port to publish and which host port it should publish to, so Docker routes incoming host traffic to the container. The `ports` section allows multiple mappings, and you can optionally specify TCP or UDP protocols if you have a specific requirement.

The `depends_on` attribute shows how to capture dependencies between services. In this case, as Kibana is dependent on Elasticsearch, Docker will ensure the `elasticsearch` service is up and running before starting the `kibana` service.

Containers for the Kibana service also connect to the application network. In an alternative configuration, I could have separate backend and frontend networks. All the infrastructure services would connect to the backend network, and the public-facing services would connect to the backend and frontend networks. These are both Docker networks, but separating them would give me the flexibility to configure the networks differently.

Configuring application services

The infrastructure services I've specified so far haven't needed application-level configuration. I've configured the integration points between the containers and the Docker platform with networks, volumes, and ports, but the applications use the configuration built into each Docker image.

The Kibana image connects to Elasticsearch by convention using the hostname `elasticsearch`, which is the service name I've used in the Docker Compose file to support that convention. The Docker platform will route any requests to the `elasticsearch` hostname to the service, load-balancing between containers if there are multiple containers running the service, so Kibana will be able to find Elasticsearch at the expected domain name.

My custom applications need configuration settings specified, which I can include in the Compose file using environment variables. Defining environment variables for a service in the Compose file sets these environment variables for every container running the service.

The index-dinner message handler service subscribes to the nats message queue and creates documents in Elasticsearch, so it needs to connect to the same Docker network, and it also depends on these services. I can capture these dependencies in the Compose file and specify the configuration for the application:

```
nerd-dinner-index-handler:
  image: dockeronwindows/ch05-nerd-dinner-index-handler
  depends_on:
    - elasticsearch
    - message-queue
  environment:
    - ELASTICSEARCH_URL=http://elasticsearch:9200
    - MESSAGE_QUEUE_URL=nats://message-queue:4222
  networks:
    - nd-net
```

Here, I'm using the `environment` section to specify two environment variables—each with a key-value pair—to configure the URLs for the message queue and Elasticsearch. These are actually the default values baked into the message handler image, so I don't need to include them in the Compose file, but it's useful to explicitly set them.

> You can think of the Compose file as the complete deployment guide for the distributed solution. If you explicitly specify the environment values, it makes it clear what configuration options are available.

Storing configuration variables in plain text is fine for simple application settings, but using a separate environment file is better for sensitive values, which is the approach I used in the previous chapter. This is also supported in the Compose file format. For the database service, I can use an environment file for the administrator password, specified with the `env-file` attribute:

```
nerd-dinner-db:
  image: dockeronwindows/ch03-nerd-dinner-db
  env_file:
    - db-credentials.env
  volumes:
    - db-data:C:\data
  networks:
    - nd-net
```

When the database service starts, Docker will set up the environment variables from the file called `db-credentials.env`. I've used a relative path, so that file needs to be in the same location as the Compose file. Like earlier, the contents of that file are key-value pairs, with one line per environment variable. In this file, I've included the connection strings for the application as well as the password for the database, so the credentials are all in one place:

```
sa_password=4jsZedB32!iSm__
AUTH_DB_CONNECTION_STRING=Data Source=nerd-dinner-db,1433;Initial
Catalog=NerdDinner...
APP_DB_CONNECTION_STRING=Data Source=nerd-dinner-db,1433;Initial
Catalog=NerdDinner...
```

The sensitive data is still in plain text, but by isolating it in a separate file, I can do two things. First, I can secure the file to restrict access. Second, I can take advantage of the separation of the service configuration from the application definition and use the same Docker Compose file for different environments, substituting different environment files.

Environment variables are not secure even if you secure access to the file. You can view environment variable values when you inspect a container, so anyone with access to the Docker API can read this data. For sensitive data such as passwords and API keys, you should use Docker secrets with Docker swarm, which I cover in the next chapter.

For the save-dinner message handler, I can make use of the same environment file. The handler depends on the message queue and database services, but there are no new attributes in this definition:

```
nerd-dinner-save-handler:
  image: dockeronwindows/ch05-nerd-dinner-save-handler
  depends_on:
    - nerd-dinner-db
    - message-queue
  env_file:
    - db-credentials.env
  networks:
   - nd-net
```

The last service is the website itself. Here, I will use a combination of environment variables and environment files. Variable values that are typically consistent across environments can be explicitly stated to make the configuration clear. Sensitive data can be read from separate files—in this case, containing the database credentials and the API keys:

```
nerd-dinner-web:
  image: dockeronwindows/ch05-nerd-dinner-web
  ports:
    - "80:80"
  environment:
    - HOMEPAGE_URL=http://nerd-dinner-homepage
    - MESSAGE_QUEUE_URL=nats://message-queue:4222
  env_file:
    - api-keys.env
    - db-credentials.env
  depends_on:
    - nerd-dinner-homepage
    - nerd-dinner-db
    - message-queue
  networks:
    - nd-net
```

The website containers need to be publicly available, so I publish the port exposed in the image. The application needs access to the other services, so it's connected to the same network. The home page service is also defined in the Compose file, but there is no configuration required, so that's a simple definition with just the image and network attributes.

All the services are configured now, so I just need to specify the network and volume resources to complete the Compose file.

Specifying application resources

Docker Compose separates network and volume definitions from service definitions, which allows flexibility between environments. I'll cover this flexibility later in the chapter, but to finish the NerdDinner Compose file, I'll start with the simplest approach using default values.

The services in my Compose file all use a network called `nd-net`, which needs to be specified in the Compose file. Docker networks are a good way to segregate applications. You could have several solutions that all use Elasticsearch but that have different SLAs and storage requirements. If you have a separate network for each application, you can run separate Elasticsearch services, individually configured for each application, but all named `elasticsearch`. This keeps to the expected conventions but segregates by the network so services only see the Elasticsearch instance in their own network.

Docker Compose can create networks at runtime, or you can define the resource to use an external network that already exists on the host. This specification for the NerdDinner network uses the default `nat` network that Docker creates when it is installed, so this setup will work for all standard Docker hosts:

```
networks:
  nd-net:
    external:
      name: nat
```

Volumes also need to be specified. Both of my stateful services, Elasticsearch and SQL Server—use named volumes for data storage, `es-data` and `nd-data`, respectively. Like networks, volumes can be specified as external so Docker Compose will use existing volumes. There are no default volumes, though, so if I use an external volume, I would need to create it on each host before running the application. Instead, I'll specify the volumes without any options, so Docker Compose will create them for me:

```
volumes:
  es-data:
  db-data:
```

These volumes will store the data on the host rather than in the container's writeable layer. They're not host-mounted volumes, so although the data is stored on the local disk, I'm not specifying the location. Each volume will write its data in the Docker data directory, `C:\ProgramData\Docker`. I'll look at managing these volumes later in the chapter.

My Compose file has services, networks, and volumes all specified, so it's ready to run.

Managing applications with Docker Compose

Docker Compose presents a similar interface to the Docker CLI. The `docker-compose` command uses some of the same command names and arguments for the functionality it supports—which is a subset of the functionality of the full Docker CLI. When you run commands through the compose CLI, it sends requests to the Docker engine to act on the resources in the Compose file.

Compose treats all the resources in a Compose file as a single application, and to disambiguate applications running on the same host, the runtime adds a project name to all the resources it creates for the application. When you run an application through compose and then look at the containers running on your host, you won't see a container with a name that exactly matches the service name. Compose adds the project name and an index to container names in order to support multiple containers in the service.

Running applications

I have the first Compose file for NerdDinner in the `ch06-docker-compose` directory, which also contains the environment variable files. From that directory, I can start the whole application with a single `docker-compose` command:

```
> docker-compose up -d
Creating volume "ch06dockercompose_db-data" with default driver
Creating volume "ch06dockercompose_es-data" with default driver
Creating ch06dockercompose_nerd-dinner-homepage_1 ...
Creating ch06dockercompose_elasticsearch_1 ...
Creating ch06dockercompose_nerd-dinner-db_1 ...
Creating ch06dockercompose_message-queue_1 ...
Creating ch06dockercompose_nerd-dinner-index-handler_1 ...
Creating ch06dockercompose_nerd-dinner-web_1 ...
Creating ch06dockercompose_nerd-dinner-save-handler_1 ...
```

- The `up` command is used to start the application, creating networks, and volumes and running containers
- The `-d` option runs all the containers in the background; it's the same as the `--detach` option in `docker container run`

You can see that Docker Compose creates all the services in a dependency order. Services without any dependencies are created first, and when they're running, the application services are started—the web and save-handler services are the last of all, as they have the most dependencies.

The names in the output are individual container names, with the naming format `{project}_{service}_{index}`. Each service has only one container running, which is the default, so the indexes are all 1. The project name is a sanitized version of the directory name where I ran the compose command.

When you run a `docker-compose` command and it completes, you can manage the containers with Docker Compose or with the standard Docker CLI. The containers are just normal Docker containers, with some extra metadata used by compose to manage them as a whole unit. Listing containers shows me all the service containers created by compose:

```
> docker container ls
CONTAINER ID   IMAGE                                          COMMAND
CREATED
e264defce984   dockeronwindows/ch05-nerd-dinner-save-handler
"NerdDinner.Messag..."   6 minutes ago...
d4ad2405a76b   dockeronwindows/ch05-nerd-dinner-web           "powershell
C:\\boo..."   6 minutes ago...
7a858e0d8019   sixeyed/kibana:nanoserver                      "powershell -
```

```
        Comma..."     6 minutes ago...
        2c235ad3f2ab  dockeronwindows/ch05-nerd-dinner-index-handler   "dotnet
        NerdDinner..."    6 minutes ago...
        9de3ed801ccb  sixeyed/elasticsearch:nanoserver                 "powershell -
        Comma..."     7 minutes ago...
        abb480eb4416  dockeronwindows/ch06-nerd-dinner-db              "powershell -
        Comma..."     7 minutes ago...
        a3df821d147a  nats:nanoserver                                  "gnatsd -c
        gnatsd...."    7 minutes ago...
        9e30bcae2a67  dockeronwindows/ch03-nerd-dinner-homepage        "dotnet
        NerdDinner..."    7 minutes ago...
```

The container running the website is called ch06dockercompose_nerd-dinner-web_1, and I can inspect that container to get the IP address and test the website. Both the NerdDinner site and the Kibana analytics will behave as expected because the full configuration is captured in the Compose file, and all the components are started by Docker Compose.

This is one of the most powerful features of the Compose file format. The file contains the complete specification to run your application, and anyone can use it to run your app. In this case, all the NerdDinner components are images on public registries, so anyone can start the app from this Compose file. You don't need any prerequisites other than Docker and Docker Compose to run NerdDinner, which is now a distributed application containing .NET Framework, .NET Core, Java, Go, and Node.js components.

Scaling application services

Docker Compose lets you scale services up and down easily, adding or removing containers to a running service. When a service is running with multiple containers, it's still accessible to other services in the network. Consumers use the service name for discovery and the DNS server in Docker load balances requests across all the containers in the service.

Adding more containers doesn't automatically give scale and resilience to your service, though; that depends on the application running the service. You won't get a SQL Server failover cluster just by adding another container to a SQL database service because SQL Server needs to be explicitly configured for failover. If you add another container, you'll just have two distinct database instances with separate data stores.

Web applications typically scale well if they are designed to support scale-out. Stateless applications can run in any number of containers because any container can handle any request. But if your application maintains the session state locally, requests from the same user need to be handled by the same service, which prevents you from load-balancing across many containers.

Services that publish ports to the host can't be scaled if they're running on a single Docker engine. Ports can have one only operating system process listening on them, and that's also true for Docker—you can't have the same host port mapped to multiple container ports. On a Docker swarm where you have multiple hosts, you can scale services with published ports, and Docker will run the containers on different hosts.

In NerdDinner, the message handlers are truly stateless components. They receive a message from the queue that contains all the information they need, and they process it. The nats supports grouping of subscribers on the same message queue, which means I can have several containers running the save-dinner handler, and nats will ensure only one handler gets a copy of each message, so I don't have duplicate message processing. The code in the message handlers already takes advantage of that.

Scaling up the message handler is something I can do at peak time in order to increase the throughput for message processing. I can do that with the `up` command and the `--scale` option, specifying the service name and the desired number of instances:

```
> docker-compose up -d --scale nerd-dinner-save-handler=3

ch06dockercompose_nerd-dinner-homepage_1 is up-to-date
ch06dockercompose_nerd-dinner-db_1 is up-to-date
ch06dockercompose_message-queue_1 is up-to-date
ch06dockercompose_elasticsearch_1 is up-to-date
ch06dockercompose_kibana_1 is up-to-date
ch06dockercompose_nerd-dinner-index-handler_1 is up-to-date
Starting ch06dockercompose_nerd-dinner-save-handler_1 ...
Creating ch06dockercompose_nerd-dinner-save-handler_2 ...
Creating ch06dockercompose_nerd-dinner-save-handler_3 ...
```

Docker Compose compares the state of the running application with the configuration in the Compose file and the overrides specified in the command. In this case, all the services are unchanged except for the save-dinner handler, so they are listed as up to date. The save-handler has a new service level, so Docker Compose adds two more containers.

With three instances of the save-message handler running, they share the incoming message load in a round-robin approach. That's a great way to increase the scale. The handlers concurrently process messages and write to the SQL database, which increases the throughput for saves and reduces the time taken for messages to be handled. But there is still a strict limit to the number of processes writing to SQL Server, so the database is unlikely to become a bottleneck.

I can create multiple dinners through the web application, and the message handlers will share the load when the event messages are published. I can see in the logs that different handlers process different messages, and there is no duplicate processing of events:

```
PS> docker container logs ch06dockercompose_nerd-dinner-save-handler_1
Received message, subject: events.dinner.created
Saving new dinner, created at: 6/25/2017 7:34:24 PM; event ID: 39b4c8d2-
a9ad-4bf0-9e58-f60edfc57a84
Dinner saved. Dinner ID: 1; event ID: 39b4c8d2-a9ad-4bf0-9e58-f60edfc57a84

PS> docker container logs ch06dockercompose_nerd-dinner-save-handler_2
Received message, subject: events.dinner.created
Saving new dinner, created at: 6/25/2017 7:47:37 PM; event ID:
ff636870-049b-4328-87a4-e32dfacb79db
Dinner saved. Dinner ID: 2; event ID: ff636870-049b-4328-87a4-e32dfacb79db

PS> docker container logs ch06dockercompose_nerd-dinner-save-handler_3
Received message, subject: events.dinner.created
Saving new dinner, created at: 6/25/2017 7:47:43 PM; event ID:
eedeb29d-9d4c-4411-abb5-ac65011aace6
Dinner saved. Dinner ID: 3; event ID: eedeb29d-9d4c-4411-abb5-ac65011aace6
```

Stopping and starting application services

There are several commands to manage container life cycle in Docker Compose. It's important to understand the differences between the options so you don't remove resources unexpectedly.

The up and down commands are blunt tools to start and stop the whole application. The up command creates any resources in the Compose file that don't exist, and it creates and starts containers for all the services. The down command does the reverse—it stops any running containers and removes the application resources. Containers and networks are removed if they were created by Docker Compose, but volumes are not removed—so any application data you have is retained.

The stop command just stops all the running containers without removing them or other resources. Stopping the container ends the running process with a graceful shutdown. The kill command stops all the containers by forcibly ending the running process. Stopped application containers can be started again with start, which runs the entry point program in the existing container.

Stopped containers retain all their configuration and data but don't use any compute resources. Starting and stopping containers is a very efficient way to switch context if you work on multiple projects. If I'm developing on NerdDinner when another piece of work comes in as a priority, I can stop the whole NerdDinner application to free up my development environment:

```
PS> docker-compose stop
Stopping ch06dockercompose_nerd-dinner-save-handler_3 ... done
Stopping ch06dockercompose_nerd-dinner-save-handler_2 ... done
Stopping ch06dockercompose_nerd-dinner-save-handler_1 ... done
Stopping ch06dockercompose_nerd-dinner-web_1 ... done
Stopping ch06dockercompose_kibana_1 ... done
Stopping ch06dockercompose_nerd-dinner-index-handler_1 ... done
Stopping ch06dockercompose_elasticsearch_1 ... done
Stopping ch06dockercompose_message-queue_1 ... done
Stopping ch06dockercompose_nerd-dinner-db_1 ... done
Stopping ch06dockercompose_nerd-dinner-homepage_1 ... done
```

Now I have no containers running, and I can switch to the other project. When that work is done, I can fire up NerdDinner again by running `docker-compose start`.

Stopping a container releases the IP address used by the container, and starting it again allocates a new IP address. This is transparent to other services and external consumers, but in your development environment, you will need to inspect web containers to find the new IP address to browse to.

You can also stop individual services by specifying a name, which is very useful if you want to test how your application manages failures. I can check how the index-dinner handlers behave if they can't access Elasticsearch by stopping the Elasticsearch service:

```
> docker-compose stop elasticsearch
Stopping ch06dockercompose_elasticsearch_1 ... done
```

All of these commands are processed by comparing the Compose file to the service running in Docker. You need to have access to the Docker Compose file in order to run any compose commands. This is one of the biggest drawbacks of using Docker Compose on a single host to run your applications. The alternative is to use the same Compose file but to deploy it as a stack to a Docker swarm, which I'll cover in the next chapter.

Upgrading application services

If you run `docker compose up` repeatedly from the same Compose file, no changes will be made after the first run. Docker Compose compares the configuration in the Compose file with the active containers at runtime and won't change resources unless the definition has changed. This means you can use Docker Compose to manage application upgrades.

My Compose file is currently using the database service from the image I built in Chapter 3, *Developing Dockerized .NET and .NET Core Applications*, tagged `dockeronwindows/ch03-nerd-dinner-db`. For this chapter, I've added audit fields to the tables in the database schema and built a new version of the database image, tagged `dockeronwindows/ch06-nerd-dinner-db`.

I have a second Compose file in the same `ch06-docker-compose` directory, called `docker-compose-db-upgrade.yml`. In the second file, all the service definitions are the same as the first file, except the database that uses the new image:

```
nerd-dinner-db:
  image: dockeronwindows/ch06-nerd-dinner-db
  env_file:
    - db-credentials.env
  volumes:
   - db-data:c:database
  networks:
   - nd-net
```

While the application is running, I can execute `docker compose up -d` again, specifying the new Compose filename. Docker Compose sees that the database definition has changed and recreates the service using the new database image:

```
> docker-compose -f docker-compose-db-upgrade.yml up -d

Recreating ch06dockercompose_nerd-dinner-db_1 ...
ch06dockercompose_elasticsearch_1 is up-to-date
ch06dockercompose_message-queue_1 is up-to-date
Recreating ch06dockercompose_nerd-dinner-db_1
ch06dockercompose_nerd-dinner-homepage_1 is up-to-date
ch06dockercompose_kibana_1 is up-to-date
Recreating ch06dockercompose_nerd-dinner-db_1 ... done
Recreating ch06dockercompose_nerd-dinner-web_1 ...
Recreating ch06dockercompose_nerd-dinner-web_1
Recreating ch06dockercompose_nerd-dinner-save-handler_1 ...
Recreating ch06dockercompose_nerd-dinner-save-handler_1 ... done
```

Docker Compose recreates the database service by removing the old container and starting a new one. Services that don't depend on the database are left as they are, with the log entry `up-to-date`, and any services which do depend on the database are also recreated once the new container is running.

 Compose uses the containing directory as the project name for services. You can have multiple application versions defined in different Compose files in the same directory. Docker Compose uses the same project name for them all, so you can switch between different versions by specifying the file name.

My database container uses a volume to store the data. In the Compose file, I use a default definition for the volume, so Docker Compose creates it for me. Just like the containers created by compose, volumes are a standard Docker resource and can be managed with the Docker CLI. The `docker volume ls` lists all the volumes on the host:

```
> docker volume ls

DRIVER   VOLUME NAME
local    ch06dockercompose_db-data
local    ch06dockercompose_es-data
```

I have two volumes for my NerdDinner deployment. They both use the local driver, which means the data is stored on the local disk. I can inspect the SQL Server volume to see where the data is physically stored on the host (in the `Mountpoint` attribute) and then check the contents to see the database files:

```
PS> docker volume inspect -f '{{ .Mountpoint }} 'ch06dockercompose_db-data
C:\ProgramData\Docker\volumes\ch06dockercompose_db-data\_data

PS> ls C:\ProgramData\Docker\volumes\ch06dockercompose_db-data\_data

Directory: C:\ProgramData\Docker\volumes\ch06dockercompose_db-data\_data
Mode     LastWriteTime      Length   Name
----     -------------      ------   ----
-a----  25/06/2017 21:41   8388608  NerdDinner_Primary.ldf
-a----  25/06/2017 21:41   8388608  NerdDinner_Primary.mdf
```

The volume is stored outside of the container, so when Docker Compose removes the old container database, all the data is preserved. The new database image bundles a Dacpac and is configured to do schema upgrades for the existing data file in the same way as the SQL Server database from Chapter 3, *Developing Dockerized .NET and .NET Core Applications*.

When the new container has started, I can check the logs and see that the new container attached the database files from the volume and then altered the Dinners table to add the new audit column:

```
> docker container logs ch06dockercompose_nerd-dinner-db_1

VERBOSE: Data files exist - will attach and upgrade database
Generating publish script for database 'NerdDinner' on server
'.\SQLEXPRESS'.
Successfully generated script to file C:\init\deploy.sql.
VERBOSE: Changed database context to 'NerdDinner'.
VERBOSE: Altering [dbo].[Dinners]...
VERBOSE: Update complete.
VERBOSE: Deployed NerdDinner database, data files at: C:\data
```

Docker Compose looks for any differences between resources and their definitions, not just the name of the Docker image. If you change environment variables, port mappings, volume setup, or any other configuration, compose will remove or create resources to bring the running application to the desired state.

 You need to be careful with modifying Compose files to run applications. If you remove the definition for a running service from the file, Docker Compose won't recognize that the service containers are part of the application, so they won't be included in the difference checks.

Monitoring application containers

Treating a distributed application as a single unit makes it easier to monitor and trace problems. Docker Compose provides its own `top` and `logs` commands, which operate over all the containers in the application services and display the collected results.

To check the memory and CPU usage of all the components, run `docker-compose top`:

```
> docker-compose top
ch06dockercompose_elasticsearch_1
Name          PID     CPU          Private Working Set
------------------------------------------------------
smss.exe      11620   00:00:00.031  200.7 kB
csrss.exe     6676    00:00:00.015  352.3 kB
wininit.exe   10872   00:00:00.015  606.2 kB
java.exe      1652    00:01:11.765  735.8MB
. . .
```

Containers are listed in the alphabetical order by name, and processes in each container are listed without a specific order. There's no way to change the ordering, so you can't show that the most intensive processes in the hardest working container first, but the result is in plain text, so you can manipulate it in PowerShell.

To see the log entries from all the containers, run `docker-compose logs`:

```
> docker-compose logs

nerd-dinner-save-handler_1 | Connecting to message queue url:
nats://message-queue:4222
nerd-dinner-save-handler_1 | Listening on subject: events.dinner.created,
queue: save-dinner-handler
nerd-dinner-web_1 | 2017-06-25 20:42:01 W3SVC1002144328 ::1 GET / - 80 -
::1 Mozilla/5.0+(Windows+NT;+Windows+NT+10.0;+en-
US)+WindowsPowerShell/5.1.14393.1198 - 200 0 0 13750
nerd-dinner-db_1 | VERBOSE: Starting SQL Server
nerd-dinner-db_1 | VERBOSE: Data files exist - will attach and upgrade
database
nerd-dinner-index-handler_1 | Connecting to message queue url:
nats://message-queue:4222
...
```

On screen, the container names are color-coded, so you can easily distinguish entries from different components. One advantage of reading logs through Docker Compose is that it shows output for all the containers even if the component has shown errors and the container is stopped. These error message are useful to see in context—you may see that one component throws a connection error before another component logs that it has started, which may highlight a missing dependency in the Compose file.

Docker Compose shows all the log entries for all the service containers, so the output can be extensive. You can limit this with the `--tail` option, restricting the output to a specified number of the most recent log entries for each container.

These are useful commands when you are running in development or in a low-scale project with a single server running a small number of containers. The approach doesn't work so well for large projects running on multiple containers across multiple hosts. For that, you need container-centric administration and monitoring, which I'll demonstrate in `Chapter 8`, *Administering and Monitoring Dockerized Solutions*.

Managing application images

Docker Compose can manage Docker images as well as containers. In the Compose file, you can include attributes that tell Docker Compose how to build your images. You can specify the location of the build context to send to the Docker service, which is the root folder for all your application content—and the location of the Dockerfile.

The context path is relative to the location of the Compose file, and the Dockerfile path is relative to the context. This is very useful for complex source trees such as the demo source for this book, where the context for each image is in a different folder. In the `ch06-docker-compose-build` folder, I have a Compose file with all the build attributes specified.

This is how the build details are specified for my images:

```
nerd-dinner-db:
  image: dockeronwindows/ch06-nerd-dinner-db
  build:
    context: ../ch06-nerd-dinner-db
    dockerfile: ./Dockerfile
...

nerd-dinner-save-handler:
  image: dockeronwindows/ch05-nerd-dinner-save-handler
  build:
    context: ../../ch05
    dockerfile: ./ch05-nerd-dinner-save-handler/Dockerfile
```

When you run `docker-compose build`, any services that have the `build` attribute specified will be built and tagged with the name in the `image` attribute. The build process uses the normal Docker API, so the image layer cache is still used, and only changed layers are rebuilt. Adding build details to your Compose file is a very efficient way of building all your application images, and it's also a central place to capture how the images are built.

One other useful feature of Docker Compose is the ability to manage whole groups of images. The Compose file for this chapter uses images that are all publicly available on Docker Hub, so you can run the full application with `docker-compose up`—but the first time you run it, all the images will be downloaded, which is going to take a while. You can preload images before you use them with `docker-compose pull`, which will pull all the images:

```
> docker-compose pull
Pulling message-queue (nats:nanoserver)...
nanoserver: Pulling from library/nats
Digest:
sha256:f138484bac20175e858d72297bd7770ccf854ed1ce63c7b7712ff6f850ae58d4
```

```
Status: Image is up to date for nats:nanoserver
...
```

Similarly, you can use `docker-compose push` to upload images to remote repositories. For both commands, Docker Compose uses the authenticated user from the most recent `docker login` command. If your Compose file contains images, you don't have access to push (such as the official nats image used in NerdDinner); those pushes will fail. For any repositories you are authorized to write to, whether in Docker Hub or a private registry, these images will be pushed.

Configuring application environments

When you define your full application configuration in Docker Compose, you have a single artifact that describes all the components of the application and the integration points between them. In the same way that the Dockerfile explicitly defines the steps to install and configure one piece of software, the Docker Compose file explicitly defines the steps to deploy the whole solution.

Docker Compose also lets you capture application definitions that can be deployed to different environments, so your Compose files are usable throughout the deployment pipeline. Usually, there are differences between environments, either in the infrastructure setup or the application settings. Docker Compose gives you two options to manage these environmental differences.

Infrastructure typically differs between production and non-production environments, which affects volumes and networks in Docker applications. On a development laptop, your database volume may be mapped to a known location on the local disk, which you periodically clean up. In production, you could have a volume plugin for a shared storage hardware device. Similarly, with networks, production environments may need to be explicit about subnet ranges, which are not a concern in development.

Docker Compose lets you specify resources as being external to the Compose file, so the application will use resources that already exist. These resources need to be created in advance, but that means each environment can be configured differently and still use the same Compose file.

Compose also supports an alternative approach, where you explicitly capture the configuration of your resources for each environment in different Compose files and use multiple Compose files when you run the application. I'll demonstrate both of these options. Like other design decisions, Docker doesn't impose any practices, and you can use whichever best suits your processes.

Specifying external resources

Volume and network definitions in the Compose file follow the same pattern as service definitions—each resource is named and can be configured using the same options available in the relevant `docker ... create` command. There's an extra option in Compose files to point to an existing resource.

To use existing volumes for my SQL Server and Elasticsearch data, I need to specify the `external` attribute and optionally, a name for the resource. In the `ch06-docker-compose-external` directory, my Compose file has these volume definitions:

```
volumes:
  es-data:
    external:
      name: nerd-dinner-elasticsearch-data
  db-data:
    external:
      name: nerd-dinner-database-data
```

With external resources declared, I can't just run the application using `docker-compose up`. Compose won't create volumes defined as external; they need to exist before the application starts. And these volumes are required by services, so compose won't create any containers either. Instead, you'll see an error message:

```
ERROR: Volume nerd-dinner-database-data declared as external, but could not
be found. Please create the volume manually using `docker volume create --
name=nerd-dinner-database-data` and try again.
```

The error message tells you the command you need to run in order to create the missing resource. This will create basic volumes with default configurations, and that will allow Docker Compose to start the application:

```
docker volume create --name nerd-dinner-elasticsearch-data
docker volume create --name nerd-dinner-database-data
```

 Docker lets you create volumes with different configuration options, so you can specify an explicit mount point—such as a RAID array or an NFS share. Windows doesn't support options for the local driver currently, but you can use other drivers—there are volume plug-ins to use Azure storage and enterprise storage units such as HPE 3PAR.

The same approach can be used to specify networks as external resources. In my Compose file, I initially used the default `nat` network, but in this Compose file, I specify a custom external network for the application:

```
networks:
  nd-net:
    external:
      name: nerd-dinner-network
```

Docker on Windows has several networking options. The default is network address translation, with the `nat` network, but you can also use other drivers for different network configurations. I'll create my application network with the `transparent` driver—this will give each container an IP address provided by my physical router, so containers are accessible outside of the Docker network:

```
docker network create -d transparent nerd-dinner-network --
gateway=192.168.1.1 --subnet=192.168.1.0/24
```

There's no port mapping possible with transparent networks, so I need to remove the `ports` attributes before I run `docker-compose up -d`. When the application starts, I can access the website container from an IP address in the `192.168.1.0` range, as though it were running in a server attached to my network.

Using multiple Compose files

Editing the Compose file to remove attributes means the configuration isn't portable. In this case, the behavior of the external network resource has an impact on the service specification, and that stops me from using a single Compose file for all environments. I need to have one Compose files for developers, where port publishing is specified for the `nat` network, and one for shared environments, where port publishing is removed for the transparent network.

This means two Compose files with additional overhead to keep them in sync—and more importantly, there's a risk of environments drifting if they aren't kept in sync. Using multiple Compose files addresses this and means your requirements for each environment are explicitly stated.

Docker Compose looks for files called `docker-compose.yml` and `docker-compose.override.yml` by default, and if it finds both, it will use the override file to add to or replace parts of the definitions in the main Compose file. When you run the Docker Compose CLI, you can pass additional files to be combined for the whole application specification. This lets you keep the core solution definition in one file and have explicit environment-dependent overrides in other files.

In the `ch06-docker-compose-multiple` folder, I've taken this approach. The core `docker-compose.yml` file has the service definitions that describe the structure of the solution without any environment specifics. As an example, the database service is defined with a volume and no ports published:

```
nerd-dinner-db:
  image: dockeronwindows/ch03-nerd-dinner-db
  env_file:
    - db-credentials.env
  volumes:
    - db-data:C:\data
  networks:
    - nd-net
```

Alongside the core Compose file, there is `docker-compose-local.yml`, an override file that adds environmental attributes for local development. This publishes the SQL Server port so developers can connect with SSMS and specifies the default `nat` network:

```
services:
  nerd-dinner-db:
    ports:
      - "1433"

networks:
  nd-net:
    external:
      name: nat
```

> You don't have to specify all the attributes in the override file, only the ones that change or add to the attributes in the base Compose file. The values in the override file take precedence.

I combine both files by running this:

```
docker-compose -f docker-compose.yml -f docker-compose.local.yml up -d
```

This combines the two files, which returns the application to the original development environment setup. I also have a production environment override file called `docker-compose.production.yml`, which is an override file that specifies the production attributes:

```
services:
  nerd-dinner-db:
    volumes:
      - E:\nerd-dinner-mssql:C:\data
networks:
  nd-net:
    external:
      name: nerd-dinner-network
```

There are three differences in production:

- The `ports` attribute is not specified, so there's no port publishing to the host from the container
- The `volumes` section is not specified; instead, the service volumes are explicitly mounted to a location on the host—in this case, the `E` drive, which is my RAID array
- An `external` network is used, which is a transparent network, and given containers' IP addresses from the network.

To run the application in a production configuration, I just specify the production override file:

```
docker-compose -f docker-compose.yml -f docker-compose.production.yml up -d
```

The combination of the base Compose file and the override file gives me the desired configuration, and there's no editing of files between environments. In the override file, you can add or change any attributes, including environment variables—so you could turn down the logging level in production if your app uses an environment variable to set that.

You can even combine several Compose files. If you have multiple test environments that share a lot of commonality, you can define the application setup in the base Compose file, shared test configuration in one override file, and each specific test environment in an additional override file.

As a final example, in the same folder, I have a `docker-compose.build.yml` file that isolates all the build attributes. This configuration is used only by developers and the CI process, so it doesn't need to be in the core Compose file:

```
services:
  nerd-dinner-db:
    build:
      context: ../ch06-nerd-dinner-db
      dockerfile: ./Dockerfile
```

This keeps my main Compose file clear and clean, while still allowing me to build the whole solution with a single compose command:

```
docker-compose -f docker-compose.yml -f docker-compose.local.yml -f docker-compose.build.yml build
```

Summary

In this chapter, I covered Docker Compose, the tool used to organize distributed Docker solutions. With Compose, you explicitly define all the components of your solution, the configuration of the components, and the relationship between them in a simple, clean format.

The Compose file lets you manage all the application containers as a single unit. You learned in this chapter how you can use the `docker-compose` command line to spin up and tear down the application, creating all the resources and starting or stopping containers. You also learned that you can use Docker Compose to scale components up or down and release upgrades to your solution.

Docker Compose is a powerful tool to define complex solutions. The Compose file effectively replaces lengthy deployment documents and fully describes every part of the application. With external resources and multiple Compose files, you can even capture the differences between environments and build a set of YAML files that you can use to drive your whole deployment pipeline.

The limitation of Docker Compose is that it's a client-side tool. The `docker-compose` command needs access to the Compose file to execute any commands. There is a logical grouping of resources into a single application, but that happens only in the Compose file. The Docker service sees only a set of resources, it does not recognize them as being part of the same application. Docker Compose is also limited to single-node Docker deployments.

In the next chapter, I'll move on to clustered Docker deployments, with multiple nodes running in a Docker swarm. In a production environment, this gives you high availability and scale. Docker swarm is a powerful orchestrator for container solutions, which is very easy to use. It also supports the Compose file format, so you can use your existing Compose files to deploy applications. But Docker preserves the logical architecture within the swarm, so you can manage your application without needing the Compose file.

7
Orchestrating Distributed Solutions with Docker Swarm

You can run Docker on a single PC, which is what I've done so far in this book, and it's how you would work with Docker in development and basic test environments. In more advanced test environments and in production, a single server isn't suitable. For high availability and to give you the flexibility to scale your solutions, you need multiple servers running as a single cluster. Docker has cluster support built into the platform, and you can join several Docker hosts together using the swarm mode.

All the concepts you've learned so far: images, containers, registries, networks, volumes, and services—still apply in the swarm mode. The swarm mode is an orchestration layer. It presents the same API as the standalone Docker engine, with additional functions to manage aspects of distributed computing. When you run a service in the swarm mode, Docker determines which hosts to run the containers on; it manages secure communication between containers on different hosts, and it monitors the hosts. If a server in a swarm goes down, Docker schedules the containers it was running to start on different hosts in order to maintain the service level of the application.

Swarm mode was introduced in Docker 1.12, and it provides production-grade service orchestration. All communication in a swarm is secured with TLS, so network traffic between nodes is always encrypted. You can store application secrets securely in the swarm, and Docker presents them only to those containers that need access. Swarms are scaleable, so you can easily add nodes to increase capacity or remove nodes for maintenance. Docker can also run automated rolling service updates in the swarm mode, so you can upgrade your application with zero downtime.

In this chapter, I'll set up a swarm and run NerdDinner across multiple nodes. I'll start by creating individual services and then move on to deploying the whole stack from a Compose file. You'll learn how to do the following:

- Create a swarm and join nodes
- Run, manage, scale, and update services in the swarm
- Manage sensitive data as secrets in the swarm
- Deploy a distributed application stack using a Compose file
- Isolate nodes in the swarm so you can run Windows updates

Creating a swarm and managing nodes

Docker swarm mode uses a manager-worker architecture with high availability for managers and workers. Managers are administrator-facing, and you use the active manager to manage the cluster and the resources running on the cluster. Workers are user-facing, and they run the containers for your application services.

Swarm managers can also run containers for your applications, which is unusual in manager-worker architectures. The overhead of managing a small swarm is relatively low, so if you have 10 nodes and three are managers, the managers can also run a share of the application workload.

Swarms can be practically any size. You can run a single-node swarm on your laptop to test the functionality, and you can scale up to thousands of nodes. You start by initializing the swarm with the `docker swarm init` command:

```
> docker swarm init --listen-addr 192.168.2.232 --advertise-addr
192.168.2.232
Swarm initialized: current node (60biyvlde1wche3oldbviac1v) is now a
manager.

To add a worker to this swarm, run the following command:
docker swarm join
  --token SWMTKN-1-1rmgginooh3f0t8zxhuauds7vxcqpf5g0244xtd7fnz9fn43p3-
az1n29jvzq4bdodd05zpu55vu 192.168.2.232:2377

To add a manager to this swarm, run 'docker swarm join-token manager' and
follow the instructions.
```

This creates the swarm with a single node—the Docker engine where you run the command—and that node becomes the swarm manager. My machine has multiple IP addresses, so I've specified the `listen-addr` and `advertise-addr` options that tell Docker which network interface to use for swarm communication. It's a good practice to always specify the IP address and to use static addresses for the manager nodes.

> You can keep your swarm secure using an internal private network for the swarm traffic, so that communication is not on the public network. You can even keep your managers off the public network completely. Only worker nodes with public-facing workloads need connecting to the public network in addition to the internal network.

The output from `docker swarm init` tells you how to expand the swarm by joining other nodes. Nodes can only belong to one swarm, and to join, they need to use the joining token. The token prevents rogue nodes joining your swarm if the network is compromised, so you need to treat it as a secure secret. Nodes can join as workers or managers, and there are different tokens for each. You can view and rotate the tokens with the `docker swarm join-token` command.

On a second machine running the same version of Docker, I can run the `swarm join` command to join the swarm:

```
> docker swarm join --token
SWMTKN-1-1rmgginooh3f0t8zxhuauds7vxcqpf5g0244xtd7fnz9fn43p3-
az1n29jvzq4bdodd05zpu55vu 192.168.2.232:2377
This node joined a swarm as a worker.
```

You can have a mixture of Windows and Linux nodes in the same swarm, which is a great way to manage mixed workloads. It's recommended that you have all nodes running the same version of Docker, but it can be Docker CE or EE—the swarm functionality is built into the core Docker service.

Now my Docker host is running in the swarm mode, there are more commands available to me. The `docker node` commands manage the nodes in the swarm, so I can list all the nodes in the swarm and see their current status with `docker node ls`:

```
> docker node ls
ID                            HOSTNAME          STATUS   AVAILABILITY
MANAGER STATUS
huwd8nrhikrdcbd5yficgpnry     WIN-V3VBGA0BBGR   Ready    Active
w7719btn951amwt7hcs05zn0k  *  DESKTOP-74UL7AB   Ready    Active
Leader
```

The STATUS value tells you whether the node is online in the swarm, and the AVAILABILITY value tells you whether the node is able to run containers. The MANAGER STATUS field has three options:

- Leader: The active manager controlling the swarm
- Reachable: A backup manager; it can become the leader if the current leader goes down
- No value: A worker node

Multiple managers support high availability. Docker swarm uses the Raft protocol to elect a new leader if the current leader is lost, so with an odd number of managers, three or five is common—your swarm can survive hardware failure. Worker nodes do not automatically get promoted to managers, so if all your managers are lost, then you cannot administer the swarm. In that situation, the containers on the worker nodes continue running, but there are no managers to monitor the worker nodes.

You can make worker nodes managers with docker node promote and make manager nodes workers with docker node demote—these are commands you run on a manager node. To leave a swarm, you need to run the docker swarm leave command on the node itself:

```
> docker swarm leave
Node left the swarm.
```

If you have a single-node swarm, you can exit swarm mode with the same command, but you need the --force flag.

The docker swarm and docker node commands manage the swarm. When you're running in swarm mode, you use swarm-specific commands to manage your container workload.

Creating and managing services in swarm mode

In the previous chapter, you saw how to use Docker Compose to organize a distributed solution. In a Compose file, you define the parts of your application as services using networks to connect them together. The same service concept is used in swarm mode—a service runs an application image across one or more containers called **replicas**. With the Docker command-line, you can create services on the swarm, and the swarm manager will create the replicas as containers.

I'll deploy the NerdDinner stack by creating services. All the services will run in the same Docker network, and in swarm mode, Docker has a special type of network called **overlay networking**. Overlay networks are virtual networks that span multiple physical hosts, so containers running on one swarm node can reach containers running on another node. Service discovery works in the same way; containers access each other by the service name, and Docker directs them to a container.

To create an overlay network, you need to specify the driver to be used and give the network a name. The Docker CLI returns with the ID of the new network, as it does with other resources:

```
> docker network create --driver overlay nd-swarm
j7z5fivvgpb1ou1e94oti6ra1
```

You can list the networks, and you'll see that the new network uses the overlay driver and is scoped to the swarm—which means any containers using this network can communicate with each other, whichever node they're running on:

```
> docker network ls --filter name=nd-swarm

NETWORK ID     NAME       DRIVER     SCOPE
j7z5fivvgpb1   nd-swarm   overlay    swarm
```

I'll use that network for the NerdDinner services. As with the Compose file, I'll start with the infrastructure components that have no dependencies, but now I'll use the `docker service create` command to run the services manually. I'll run a script that specifies all the services and creates them in the correct order, starting with `nats`:

```
docker service create `
  --detach=true `
  --network nd-swarm --endpoint-mode dnsrr `
  --name message-queue
  nats:nanoserver
```

There are no required options for `docker service create` other than the image name, but for a distributed application, you will want to specify the following:

- `network`: The Docker network to connect to the service containers
- `endpoint-mode`: The method of DNS name resolution that Docker uses
- `name`: The service name used as the DNS entry for other components

Docker supports two endpoint modes, vip and dnsrr. The default vip is optimized for Linux but doesn't have full support in the Windows kernel, so you need to specify dnsrr—DNS round-robin mode for Docker services on Windows.

In the source code for this chapter, the `ch07-create-services` folder has a script that starts all the services for NerdDinner in the correct order. The options for each `service create` command are the equivalent of the service definition in the Compose file for Chapter 6, *Organizing Distributed Solutions with Docker Compose*. The simplest service to create is the nats message queue, and the most complex is the NerdDinner web application:

```
docker service create `
  --network nd-swarm --endpoint-mode dnsrr `
  --env-file db-credentials.env `
  --env-file api-keys.env `
  --env HOMEPAGE_URL=http://nerd-dinner-homepage `
  --env MESSAGE_QUEUE_URL=nats://message-queue:4222 `
  --publish mode=host,target=80,published=80 `
  --name nerd-dinner-web `
  dockeronwindows/ch05-nerd-dinner-web
```

This command creates a service using the same Docker network and the same endpoint mode. The application is configured using environment variables and environment files, and port 80 is published to the host. Any traffic coming into port 80 on the host node will be directed into the container for this service.

Docker supports multiple service replicas running on a single mode but not if the ports are published using the host mode. In this case, I can run only one replica of my web application per node. The alternative is to use the ingress mode for publishing ports but that uses networking features that are not supported in Windows.

When I run the script on my swarm, I get a list of service IDs as the output:

```
> .\ch07-run-nerd-dinner.ps1
8bme2svun1222j08off2iyczo
rrgn4n3pecgf8m347vfis6mbj
lxwfb5s9erq6516whhh819588
ywrz3ecxvkiigtkpt1inid2pk
w7d7svtq2k5kp18f98wy4s1cr
ol7u97cpwdcns1abv471heh1r
deevh117z4jgaomsbrtht775b
ydzb1z1af88gvoyuyiyn9q526
```

Now I can see all the running services with `docker service ls`:

```
> docker service ls
ID              NAME                    MODE           REPLICAS IMAGE
8bme2svun122 message-queue             replicated 1/1          nats:nanoserver
deevh117z4jg nerd-dinner-homepage      replicated 1/1
dockeronwindows/ch03-nerd-dinner-homepage:latest
1xwfb5s9erq6 nerd-dinner-db            replicated 1/1
dockeronwindows/ch06-nerd-dinner-db:latest
o17u97cpwdcn nerd-dinner-index-handler replicated 1/1
dockeronwindows/ch05-nerd-dinner-index-handler:latest
rrgn4n3pecgf elasticsearch            replicated 1/1
sixeyed/elasticsearch:nanoserver
w7d7svtq2k5k nerd-dinner-save-handler  replicated 1/1
dockeronwindows/ch05-nerd-dinner-save-handler:latest
ydzb1z1af88g nerd-dinner-web           replicated 1/1
dockeronwindows/ch05-nerd-dinner-web:latest
ywrz3ecxvkii kibana                   replicated 1/1
sixeyed/kibana:nanoserver
```

Each of the services is listed as having a replica status of `1/1`, which means one replica is running out of a requested service level of one replica. Replicas are the number of containers used to run the service. Swarm mode supports two types of distributed service, and the default is to have a distributed service with a single replica, which means one container on the swarm. The service create commands in my script don't specify a replica count, so they all use the default of one.

Running services across many containers

Replicated services are how you scale in swarm mode, and you can update running services to add or remove containers. Unlike Docker Compose, you don't need a Compose file that defines the desired state of each service; that detail is already stored in the swarm from the `docker service create` command. To add more message handlers, I use `docker service scale`, passing the name of one or more services and the desired service level:

```
> docker service scale nerd-dinner-save-handler=3
nerd-dinner-save-handler scaled to 3
```

The message handler services were created with the default single replica, so this adds two more containers to share the work of the SQL Server handler service. In a multi-node swarm, the manager can schedule the containers to run on any node with a capacity. I don't need to know or care which server is actually running the containers, but I can drill down into the service list with `docker service ps` to see where the containers are running:

```
> docker service ps nerd-dinner-save-handler
ID                  NAME                              IMAGE
   NODE                  DESIRED STATE     CURRENT STATE
0m1mqtig4acm  nerd-dinner-save-handler.1  dockeronwindows/ch05-nerd-dinner-
save-handler:latest
   WIN-V3VBGA0BBGR   Running               Running 44 minutes ago
uj8lotkz28r1  nerd-dinner-save-handler.2  dockeronwindows/ch05-nerd-dinner-
save-handler:latest
   WIN-V3VBGA0BBGR   Running               Running 35 seconds ago
e3bgxfvpegy6  nerd-dinner-save-handler.3  dockeronwindows/ch05-nerd-dinner-
save-handler:latest
   WIN-V3VBGA0BBGR   Running               Running 36 seconds ago
```

In this case, I'm running a single-node swarm so all the replicas are on the same machine. Swarm mode refers to service processes as replicas, but they're actually just containers. You can log onto the nodes of the swarm and administer service containers with the same `docker ps`, `docker logs` and `docker top` commands, as usual.

Typically, you won't connect to swarm nodes directly to manage containers; you work with them as services through the manager node. Just as Docker Compose presents a consolidated view of logs for a service, you can get the same from the Docker CLI in swarm mode:

```
> docker service logs nerd-dinner-save-handler
nerd-dinner-save-handler.2.uj8lotkz28r1@WIN-V3VBGA0BBGR
   | Connecting to message queue url: nats://message-queue:4222
nerd-dinner-save-handler.3.e3bgxfvpegy6@WIN-V3VBGA0BBGR
   | Connecting to message queue url: nats://message-queue:4222
nerd-dinner-save-handler.1.0m1mqtig4acm@WIN-V3VBGA0BBGR
   | Connecting to message queue url: nats://message-queue:4222
```

Replicas are how the swarm provides fault tolerance to services. When you specify the replica level for a service with the `docker service create`, `docker service update`, or `docker service scale` command, the value is recorded in the swarm. The manager node monitors all the tasks for the service. If containers stop and the number of running services falls below the desired replica level, new tasks are scheduled to replace the stopped containers. Later in the chapter, I'll demonstrate that when I run the same solution on a multi-node swarm, then I take a node out of the swarm without any loss of service.

Global services

An alternative to replicated services is global services. In some cases, you may want the same service running on every node of the swarm as a single container on each server. To do that, you can run a service in the global mode—Docker schedules one task on each node, and any new nodes that join will also have a task scheduled.

Global services can be useful for high availability with components that are used by many services, but again, you don't get a clustered application just by running many instances of it. The nats message queue can run as a cluster across several servers, and it could be a good candidate to run as a global service. To run nats as a cluster, though, each instance needs to know the address of other instances—which doesn't work well with dynamic virtual IP addresses allocated by the Docker engine.

Instead, I can run my Elasticsearch message handler as a global service, so every node will have an instance of the message handler running. You can't change the mode of a running service, so first, I need to remove the original service:

```
> docker service rm nerd-dinner-index-handler
nerd-dinner-index-handler
```

Then, I can create a new global service:

```
docker service create `
  --mode=global `
  --detach=true `
  --network nd-swarm --endpoint-mode dnsrr `
  --env ELASTICSEARCH_URL=http://elasticsearch:9200 `
  --env MESSAGE_QUEUE_URL=nats://message-queue:4222 `
  --name nerd-dinner-index-handler `
  dockeronwindows/ch05-nerd-dinner-index-handler
```

Now I have one task running on each node in the swarm, and the total number of tasks will grow if nodes are added to the cluster or shrink if nodes are removed. This can be useful for services that you want to distribute for fault tolerance, and you want the total capacity of the service to be proportionate to the size of the cluster.

Global services are also useful in monitoring and auditing functions. If you have a centralized monitoring system such as splunk, or you're using Elasticsearch for log capture, you could run an agent on each node as a global service.

With global and replicated services, swarm mode provides the infrastructure to scale your application and maintain specified service levels. This works well for on-premises deployments if you have a fixed-size swarm but variable workloads. You can scale application components up and down to meet the demand provided they don't all require peak processing at the same time.

Deploying services manually or with scripts doesn't take full advantage of the Docker swarm. In swarm mode, you can define your application using the Docker Compose file format and deploy and manage it as a single unit called a **stack**.

Deploying stacks to Docker swarm

Stacks in Docker swarm address the limitations of using Docker Compose with a single host. You create a stack from a Compose file, and Docker stores all the metadata for the stack's services in the swarm. This means Docker is aware that the set of resources represents one application, and you can manage services from any Docker client without needing the Compose file.

You can also make use of Docker secrets to make sensitive data available to service containers instead of using environment variables.

Docker secrets

Swarm mode is inherently secure—communication between all the nodes is encrypted, and the swarm provides an encrypted data store that is distributed among the manager nodes. You can use this store for application secrets, which are a first-class resource in the Docker swarm.

Secrets are created with a name and the contents of the secret, which can be read from a file or entered into the command-line. In the ch07-docker-stack folder, I have a folder called secrets that contains all the sensitive data for the NerdDinner application. Each secret holds one piece of data, so the database connection string is in the nerd-dinner.connectionstring file:

```
Data Source=nerd-dinner-db,1433;Initial Catalog=NerdDinner;User
Id=sa;Password=N3rdD!Nne720^6; MultipleActiveResultSets=True;
```

I can create a secret named `nerd-dinner.connectionstring` and populate it with the contents of that file using `docker secret create`:

```
docker secret create nerd-dinner.connectionstring .\secrets\nerd-
dinner.connectionstring
```

Now the connection string is securely stored in the swarm. You can't view the plain text of a secret and Docker will deliver secrets only to services that explicitly request them. The secret is encrypted at rest in the managers and encrypted in transit, where it is only made available to workers who are running a replica for the service that requested the secret.

Administrators can create secrets in the swarm and make them available to the application without ever sharing the file that contained the original plain text of the secret.

The secret is decrypted only for the container, where it is presented as a text file in a known `location`. You need to change your application to read secrets from files, but that's a small change for such a big step forward in security. In the `src` folder for this chapter, I've added `Secret` classes to projects that need to read sensitive data from secrets. This example fetches the database connection string:

```
public class Secret
{
  private const string SECRET_ROOT_PATH = @"C:\ProgramData\Docker\secrets";
  public static string DbConnectionString { get { return Get("nerd-
dinner.connectionstring"); } }

  private static string Get(string name)
  {
    var path = Path.Combine(SECRET_ROOT_PATH, name);
    return File.ReadAllText(path);
  }
}
```

It's safe to hardcode the path strings, as Docker will always surface the secret file in the `C:\ProgramData\Docker\secrets` folder in the container, using the secret name as the filename.

The secret files surfaced to the container have restricted access, so only administrator accounts can read them. This is fine for the console applications that will run under the context of the container administrator, so they have access to the secret files. IIS application pools run under restricted user accounts that don't have access to read the files.

In the Dockerfile for ch07-nerd-dinner-web, I explicitly create an app pool that runs under the LocalSystem account in the container and create the NerdDinner website to use that app pool:

```
RUN Import-Module WebAdministration; `
    Remove-Website -Name 'Default Web Site'; `
    New-WebAppPool -Name 'ap-nd'; `
    Set-ItemProperty IIS:\AppPools\ap-nd -Name managedRuntimeVersion -Value
v4.0; `
    Set-ItemProperty IIS:\AppPools\ap-nd -Name processModel.identityType -
Value LocalSystem; `
    New-Website -Name 'nerd-dinner' `
     -Port 80 -PhysicalPath 'C:\nerd-dinner' -ApplicationPool 'ap-nd'
```

 Running your web application with elevated permissions is less of a concern when you run in a container, as I explain in Chapter 9, *Understanding the Security Risks and Benefits of Docker*. The Docker secrets implementation for Windows is evolving, and in a later version, you will be able to grant secret access to specific users and you won't need to run your website as LocalSystem.

You can request one or more secrets for a service in the service create and service update commands. If I wanted to run my save-dinner handler as a service, using the connection string secret, I would add the --secret option to the create command instead of using an environment file:

```
docker service create `
  --detach=true `
  --network nd-swarm --endpoint-mode dnsrr `
  --secret nerd-dinner.connectionstring `
  --name nerd-dinner-save-handler `
  dockeronwindows/ch05-nerd-dinner-save-handler
```

Instead of creating individual services, I'm going to use Compose files to define my deployment and replace environment variable files with secrets in the service definitions.

Defining a stack using Compose files

The Docker Compose file schema has evolved from supporting client-side deployments on single Docker hosts to stack deployments across Docker swarms. Different sets of attributes are relevant in different scenarios, and the tools enforce that. Docker Compose will ignore attributes that apply only to stack deployments, and Docker swarm will ignore attributes that apply only to single-node deployments.

I can make use of multiple Compose files to exploit this, defining the basic setup of my application in one file, adding local settings in one override file and swarm settings in another override file. I've done that with the Compose files in the `ch07-docker-compose` folder. The core service definitions are very simple now—they only include attributes that apply to every deployment mode, such as this example for the web service:

```
nerd-dinner-web:
  image: dockeronwindows/ch07-nerd-dinner-web
  environment:
    - HOMEPAGE_URL=http://nerd-dinner-homepage
    - MESSAGE_QUEUE_URL=nats://message-queue:4222
  networks:
    - nd-net
```

In the local override file, I add the attributes that are relevant when I'm developing the application on my laptop and deploying with Docker Compose:

```
nerd-dinner-web:
  ports:
    - "80"
  depends_on:
    - nerd-dinner-homepage
    - nerd-dinner-db
    - message-queue
  env_file:
    - api-keys.env
    - db-credentials.env
```

Swarm mode does not support the `depends_on` attribute, and when you deploy a stack, there is no guarantee which order the services will start in. If your application components are resilient and have retry logic for any dependencies, then the service startup order doesn't matter. If your components are not resilient and crash when they can't access dependencies, then Docker will restart failed containers and the application should be ready after a few retries.

Resilience is often missing from legacy applications, which assume that their dependencies are always available and respond immediately. This is not the case if you move to cloud services, and it is true of containers. Docker will keep replacing failed containers, but if you're changing code, then it's a good idea to add resilience.

My other override file specifies the attributes that are needed for the service to run in swarm mode:

```
nerd-dinner-web:
  ports:
    - mode: host
      published: 80
      target: 80
  deploy:
    endpoint_mode: dnsrr
    placement:
      constraints:
        - node.platform.os == windows
  secrets:
    - nerd-dinner.connectionstring
    - nerd-dinner-bing-maps.apikey
    - nerd-dinner-ip-info-db.apikey
```

I need to specify the ports to use host mode publishing for swarm mode, and I'm mapping port 80 in the container to port 80 on the host.

The deploy section is used only in swarm mode, and there are two extra attributes here. The first is endpoint_mode, which specifies the DNS round-robin mode needed for Windows containers. The next is constraints, which you can use to restrict the service to run only on certain nodes in the swarm. You can apply arbitrary labels to swarm nodes (which I cover in Chapter 9, *Understanding the Security Risks and Benefits of Docker*) and add constraints based on those labels. In this case, I'm using the node.platform.os label, which is a system label applied by Docker to each node.

I'll be deploying this stack to a hybrid swarm with some Windows and some Linux nodes. This constraint tells Docker to run only this service on Windows nodes, which saves time in deployment as Docker won't consider any Linux nodes as candidates to host replicas of this service. I've added these attributes to all the services in my swarm override file.

In the `secrets` section, I have named all the secrets that needs to be made available to the web service, which are the database connection string and API keys that used to be read from environment files. Secrets are top-level resources in the Compose file, so the names refer to entries later in the file, where I identify all the secrets as external resources:

```
secrets:
  nerd-dinner-bing-maps.apikey:
    external: true
  nerd-dinner-ip-info-db.apikey:
    external: true
  nerd-dinner-sa.password:
    external: true
  nerd-dinner.connectionstring:
    external: true
```

I can deploy the application with Docker Compose by specifying multiple Compose files—the core file and the local override—but the Docker command line doesn't support multiple files for stack deployment. I can still ensure the override functionality by running `docker-compose config`, which joins multiple Compose files into one output. This command generates a single Compose file called `docker-stack.yml` from the two Compose files for the stack deployment:

```
docker-compose -f docker-compose.yml -f docker-compose.swarm.yml config >
docker-stack.yml
```

Docker Compose joins the input files and checks whether the output configuration is valid. Now I can deploy my stack on the swarm, using the stack file that contains the core service descriptions plus the secrets and deployment configuration.

Deploying a stack from a Compose file

You deploy a stack from a Compose file with a single command, `docker stack deploy`. You need to pass the location of the Compose file and a name for the stack, and then Docker creates all the resources in the Compose file:

```
> docker stack deploy --compose-file docker-stack.yml nerd-dinner

Creating network nerd-dinner_nd-net
Creating service nerd-dinner_nerd-dinner-web
Creating service nerd-dinner_elasticsearch
Creating service nerd-dinner_kibana
Creating service nerd-dinner_message-queue
Creating service nerd-dinner_nerd-dinner-db
Creating service nerd-dinner_nerd-dinner-homepage
```

```
Creating service nerd-dinner_nerd-dinner-index-handler
Creating service nerd-dinner_nerd-dinner-save-handler
```

The result is a set of services that are grouped together, but unlike Docker Compose, which relies on naming conventions and labels to identify the grouping, the stack is a first-class citizen in Docker. I can list all stacks, which gives me the basic details—the stack name and the number of services in the stack:

```
> docker stack ls
NAME            SERVICES
nerd-dinner     8
```

I can also drill down into the services with docker stack services, and list the individual containers with docker stack ps:

```
> docker stack ps nerd-dinner
ID              NAME                                    IMAGE ...
d84oou5mxbr6    nerd-dinner_nerd-dinner-homepage.1
dockeronwindows/ch03-nerd-dinner-homepage:latest
unq0b6j59jcw    nerd-dinner_nerd-dinner-db.1
dockeronwindows/ch07-nerd-dinner-db:latest
n4jvdpx5hqn9    nerd-dinner_message-queue.1             nats:nanoserver
apc0djz5v37n    nerd-dinner_kibana.1
sixeyed/kibana:nanoserver
vecauuy3nhez    nerd-dinner_elasticsearch.1
sixeyed/elasticsearch:nanoserver
ixts1jeuclzi    nerd-dinner_nerd-dinner-web.1
dockeronwindows/ch07-nerd-dinner-web:latest
oalu3dpx0hsy    nerd-dinner_nerd-dinner-save-handler.1
dockeronwindows/ch07-nerd-dinner-save-handler:latest
vtans6ekbub9    nerd-dinner_nerd-dinner-index-handler.1
dockeronwindows/ch05-nerd-dinner-index-handler:latest
```

Grouping services into stacks makes it much easier to manage your application, especially when you have multiple apps running with multiple services in each. The stack is an abstraction over a set of Docker resources, but you can still manage the individual resources directly. If I run docker service rm, it will remove a service even if the service is part of a stack. When I run docker stack deploy again, Docker will see that a service is missing from the stack and will recreate it.

When it comes to updating your application with new image versions or changes to service attributes, you can modify the services directly, or you can modify the stack file and deploy it again. Docker doesn't force a process on you, but you need to be careful if you mix both approaches.

I can scale up the message handlers in my solution either by adding `replicas :2` in the deploy section of the stack file and deploying it again or by running `docker service update --replicas=2 nerd-dinner_nerd-dinner-save-handler`. If I update the service and don't change the stack file as well, the next time I deploy the stack, my handler will go down to one replica. The stack file is viewed as the desired final state, and if the current state has deviated, it will be corrected when you deploy again.

Running a single node swarm is fine for development and test environments. I can run the full NerdDinner suite as a stack, verifying that the stack file is correctly defined, and I can scale up and down to check the behavior of the app. This doesn't give me high availability because the services are all running on a single node, so if the node goes down, I will lose all my services.

You can build a swarm with greater elasticity for HA and scale by running it in the cloud. All the major cloud operators support Docker, and some provide a managed option to run a cluster of Docker nodes. The cloud container services all support the Docker image format and runtime, but some use custom orchestrators or custom deployment artifacts. Others support Docker swarm as the orchestrator, which means you can use all the same artifacts in every environment.

Running Docker swarm in the cloud

Docker has a minimal set of infrastructure requirements, so you can easily spin up a Docker host or a clustered Docker swarm in any cloud. All you need is the capacity to run Windows Server virtual machines and connect them on a network.

The cloud is a great place to run Docker, and Docker is a great way to move to the cloud. Docker gives you the power of a modern application platform without the restrictions of a **Platform as a Service (PaaS)** product. PaaS options typically have proprietary deployment systems, may need proprietary integrations in your code, and the dev experience will not use the same runtime.

Docker lets you package your applications and define your solution structure in a portable way that will run the same way on any machine and on any cloud. You can use basic **Infrastructure as a Service** (IaaS) services, which all cloud providers support, and have a consistent deployment, management, and runtime experience in every environment. The Docker Cloud editions let you choose your own cloud provider and deploy a standard Docker swarm with a production-grade configuration.

The major clouds also provide their own managed container services. If you're already using IaaS or PaaS services from Microsofr Azure, **Amazon Web Services** (**AWS**), or **Google Cloud Platform** (**GCP**), the managed option may be a good fit. If you prefer to keep your deployments portable, then the Docker Cloud editions are a better option.

Managed Docker services in the cloud

Azure, AWS, and GCP have managed container services that let you run Docker containers. AWS and GCP don't support Docker swarm mode; they use their own orchestration layers. Azure lets you choose between orchestrators, including Docker swarm, and you can add supported Windows nodes to the cluster.

These are managed services to the extent that they are simple to deploy and come with support and service-level agreements for the cloud resources that make up the service. The compute resources are all virtual machines, though, so you're billed for the VMs in your cluster, not for the containers running in the cluster.

Docker on Amazon Elastic Container Service

The **Elastic Container Service** (**ECS**) on Amazon supports Docker containers, with a custom AWS orchestration and management layer. ECS does not use swarm mode to power the cluster, so you can't use Docker secrets and you can't deploy stacks from a Compose file. The ECS command-line lets you import a Compose file, but only a subset of attributes are supported.

The ECS cluster is built from existing AWS components, using EC2 VMs for the nodes and ELB or ALB load balancers for incoming traffic. If you already have an existing investment in AWS, that may fit your current infrastructure, but you need to be aware of the disconnect between environments. If you are running Docker in a single-node swarm for development and a local multi-node swarm for testing, the production EC2 instance will need different deployment artifacts and will run on a different orchestration platform.

You can't manage the cluster remotely with the Docker CLI, so you can't use a single set of management processes for every environment. There may be technical restrictions as well. At the time of writing this, EC2 runs an older version of Docker that does not support the health check functionality. You can run Windows nodes as part of an EC2 cluster, but that's currently flagged as a beta implementation.

Docker on Google Container Platform

Google Container Platform (GKE) supports Docker containers but not the Docker swarm mode. GKE uses Kubernetes as the orchestration layer, which is an open source orchestrator originally built by Google. Kubernetes has broadly the same feature set as Docker swarm but uses its own file format to describe deployments and has its own command-line tool.

GKE deploys a Kubernetes cluster across virtual machines in the Compute Engine service. As with the other cloud options, you pay for the VMs in the cluster and not for the number of containers you're running. Setting up Kubernetes is a difficult task that GKE abstracts away, and Google adds higher-level management features, such as autoscaling for nodes (currently in beta). You can't create a GKE cluster that contains Windows nodes, so you can run only Linux workloads.

Kubernetes does have support for Windows nodes, but currently, it's in the alpha status so it's only suitable for initial testing, and you would need to deploy a custom IaaS cluster to use it in GKE. Networking in Kubernetes does not use the Docker overlay network built into Windows; it uses its own networking stack with a proxy component and a dedicated VM switch.

Docker on Azure Container Service

Microsoft has taken a different approach with the **Azure Container Service (ACS)**. Rather than building a custom management layer, they are supporting all major open source orchestrators. You can create an ACS cluster running on Apache Mesos, on Kubernetes, or using Docker swarm mode. The swarm mode option means you can use the same container runtime in Azure as you have locally and deploy to production using the same artifacts you use in dev and test.

ACS doesn't currently have an option to provision Windows nodes in the cluster. You can create a swarm using Linux nodes as managers and then create Windows VMs in the same resource group and join them to the swarm. This needs additional steps in your deployment process, but the end result is a hybrid Linux/Windows swarm, where the Windows nodes are using Docker EE in a supported configuration.

It's likely that new releases of ACS will allow you to provision Windows nodes in Docker swarm. Other orchestrators don't have the same level of Windows support—Kubernetes is in alpha, and Mesos doesn't yet have a public release for Windows.

Docker cloud editions

If you are keen on maintaining consistency between your local Docker environments and the cloud, Docker for Azure, Docker for AWS, and Docker for GCP are the best options. These are free Community Editions from Docker Store that create a Docker cluster running in swarm mode, optimized for the infrastructure on the Microsoft, Amazon, or Google clouds.

You can deploy a swarm from Docker Cloud by providing your subscription details. I've connected Docker Cloud with my Microsoft Azure subscription, so I can deploy a swarm using Docker Cloud, which will create all the resources in Azure:

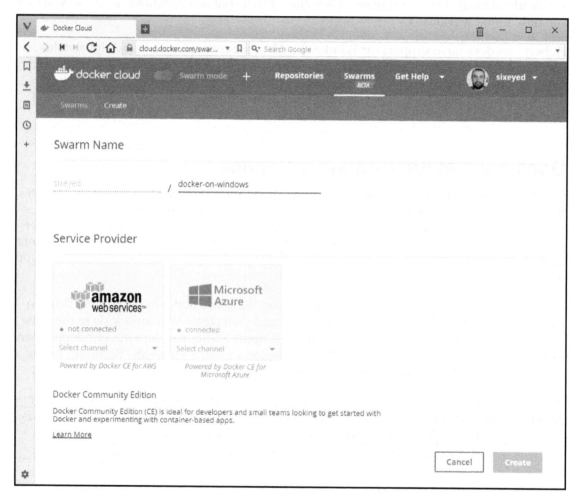

The Docker Cloud editions use a template to create IaaS components on the cloud—ARM for Azure, CloudFormation for AWS, and Deployment Manager for GCP. They give you a best-practice configuration for Docker swarm, and they're maintained by Docker, Inc. so they're kept up to date with the latest releases.

 Docker Cloud doesn't currently let you create Windows nodes in the swarm. It's worth checking whether Windows Server is an option in the latest release. If it is, this will be the easiest way to create a Windows-based Docker swarm in the cloud.

Alternatively, you can create your own template deployment, which gives you the freedom to arrange the cluster as you wish. Both AWS and Azure have VM images based on Windows Server 2016, with Docker preinstalled, which you can spin up as your swarm nodes. In Azure, you can create separate VNets and Network Security groups for managers and workers, keeping the manager nodes isolated from the Internet—a suitable approach for production clusters.

Outside of production, I use the DevTest Lab feature in Azure for my Docker swarms. The lab functionality in Azure is perfect for experimental and test environments—you can configure the whole lab to shut down and start up on daily schedules, so you only pay for compute when the swarm is in use.

I won't get into details on DevTest labs, but I can tell you that they allow you to create formulas to customize virtual machines. You can easily create a formula that uses the VM image Windows Server 2016 Datacenter—with Containers and runs a startup script to pull all the Windows images you need with PowerShell. A simple PowerShell script like this will pull the images you want:

```
$tag ='10.0.14393.1198'
docker pull "microsoft/dotnet:1.1.2-sdk-nanoserver-$tag"
docker pull "microsoft/mssql-server-windows-developer:2016-sp1-
windowsservercore-$tag"
docker pull "microsoft/aspnet:windowsservercore-$tag"
```

Running a multi-node Docker swarm in the cloud gives you a good working environment for load testing, failover testing, and to perfect deployment processes. I'll use my Azure DevTest lab to deploy NerdDinner and demonstrate zero-downtime updates, both of the application and of the Windows hosts.

Docker Cloud lets you adopt an existing swarm that you've created on a cloud provider. This associates a swarm you've created manually with your Docker ID. Docker Cloud integrates with Docker for Windows and Docker for Mac, so you can easily manage remote swarms.

I've created a custom swarm in a DevTest lab and adopted it in Docker Cloud with the name `sixeyed/docker-on-windows`. In the Docker for Windows client app, I can click on the whale icon and see a list of remote swarms that are registered with Docker Cloud:

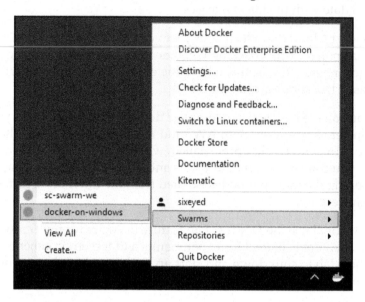

When you select a swarm, Docker opens a new command shell window, already configured to securely connect to your remote swarm. The swarm could be Windows or Linux nodes running in any cloud. In this case, I can manage the hybrid Linux/Windows swarm in my Azure DevTest lab from my Windows laptop:

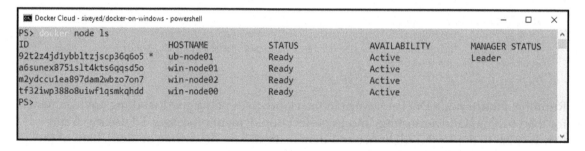

The integration between Docker Cloud and the Docker desktop editions is a very powerful feature. It's a great way to take advantage of your preferred cloud but still keep your deployment options open. From this command shell, I can run `docker stack deploy` using my local stack file. This starts the NerdDinner solution running across multiple nodes in the cloud with exactly the same deployment and management experience that I have on my laptop.

Running across multiple nodes gives me high availability so my application keeps running in case of failure, and I can take advantage of that to deploy zero-downtime updates.

Deploying updates with zero downtime

In swarm mode, Docker has two features that enable updates of the whole stack without application downtime—rolling updates and node draining. Rolling updates replace application containers with new instances from a new image—updates are staggered, so provided you have multiple replicas, there will always be tasks running to serve requests while other tasks are being upgraded.

Application updates will occur frequently, but less frequently, you will also need to update the host—either to upgrade Docker or to apply Windows patches. Docker supports draining a node, which means all the containers running on the node are stopped and no more will be scheduled. If the replica level drops for any services when the node is drained, tasks are started on other nodes. When the node is drained, you can update the host and then join it back into the swarm.

Load balancing across swarm nodes

I've connected to my Azure swarm using Docker for Windows and deployed my NerdDinner stack. The stack definition creates only one web container, so I'll scale up the web component by updating the service:

```
> docker service update --replicas=3 nerd-dinner_nerd-dinner-web
nerd-dinner_nerd-dinner-web
```

Now I have a web container running on each of my Windows worker nodes (the manager is a Linux node):

```
> docker service ps nerd-dinner_nerd-dinner-web
ID              NAME                             IMAGE
NODE ...
i83a5xzf9sai  nerd-dinner_nerd-dinner-web.1  dockeronwindows/ch07-nerd-
dinner-web:latest  win-node01
3bkm4mh26234  nerd-dinner_nerd-dinner-web.2  dockeronwindows/ch07-nerd-
dinner-web:latest  win-node00
exsb59ok6gx2  nerd-dinner_nerd-dinner-web.3  dockeronwindows/ch07-nerd-
dinner-web:latest  win-node02
```

In Azure, I've created a traffic manager profile that acts as simple load balancer across the Windows worker nodes. When I browse to `http://dow.trafficmanager.net`, Azure will direct the traffic to any one of my worker nodes, which in turn forwards the traffic to the container listening on port `80`. I see a new deployment of NerdDinner:

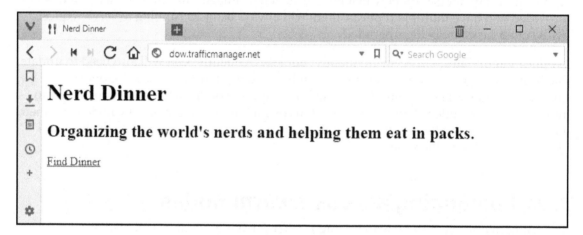

The traffic manager in Azure has its own health check, so it won't direct traffic to a node that doesn't respond on the HTTP port. This lets me perform a zero-downtime update. Docker will update one task at a time, and the Azure load balancer will direct traffic to the live tasks while the other task is being updated.

For my application update, I have an updated home page component with a restyled UI—a nice easy change to validate.

Updating application services

There are two steps to this update. First, I need to update the home page service to deploy the new UI. This is an internal component that is used only by the web application service:

```
> docker service update --image dockeronwindows/ch07-nerd-dinner-homepage
nerd-dinner_nerd-dinner-homepage
nerd-dinner_nerd-dinner-homepage
```

- `nerd-dinner-homepage` is the name of the service to update
- `--image` specifies the new image for the update

The update command doesn't have any restrictions on the image you're upgrading to. It doesn't need to be a new tag from the same repository name; it can be a completely different image. This is very flexible, but it means you need to be careful that you don't accidentally update your message handlers with a new version of the web application or vice versa.

Updating the home page component doesn't show the changed UI because the web containers cache the home page content. The web app uses a static cache, so it will not refresh the content until the app is restarted. I don't have a new image to deploy, but I can force a service update, which will restart all the containers from the current image:

```
> docker service update --force nerd-dinner_nerd-dinner-web
nerd-dinner_nerd-dinner-web
```

Docker updates one container at a time, and you can configure the delay interval between updates and the behavior to take if updates fail. While the update is in process, I can run `docker service ps` and see that the original containers are in the `Shutdown` state and the replacement containers are `Running` or `Starting`:

```
ID NAME IMAGE NODE DESIRED STATE CURRENT STATE ERROR PORTS
i83a5xzf9sai  nerd-dinner_nerd-dinner-web.1      dockeronwindows/ch07-nerd-
dinner-web:latest  win-node01
   Running    Running about an hour ago *:80->80/tcp
2d3i60h2vbvl  nerd-dinner_nerd-dinner-web.2      dockeronwindows/ch07-nerd-
dinner-web:latest  win-node00
   Running    Running about a minute ago *:80->80/tcp
3bkm4mh26234  \_ nerd-dinner_nerd-dinner-web.2  dockeronwindows/ch07-nerd-
dinner-web:latest  win-node00
   Shutdown    Shutdown 3 minutes ago
r9j83ozezdn8  nerd-dinner_nerd-dinner-web.3      dockeronwindows/ch07-nerd-
dinner-web:latest win-node02
   Running    Starting about a minute ago
exsb59ok6gx2  \_ nerd-dinner_nerd-dinner-web.3  dockeronwindows/ch07-nerd-
```

```
dinner-web:latest win-node02
  Shutdown    Shutdown about a minute ago
```

The Dockerfile for the NerdDinner web application has a health check, and Docker waits until the health check on the new container passes before it moves on to replacing the next container. During the rolling update, some users will see the old home page, and some users will see the new home page:

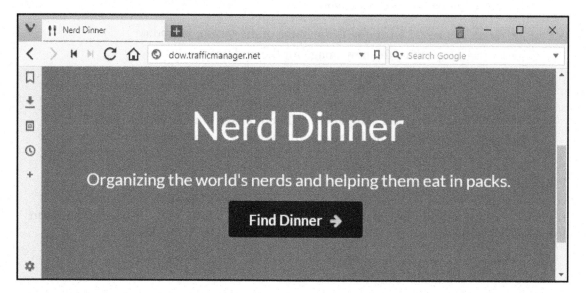

As long as the load balancer can detect status changes quickly enough, it will send traffic only to hosts that have running containers—users will get a response from a container that has been updated or one that is due to be updated. During the update, there is no container listening on port 80 on that host, so the load balancer detects that the host is unavailable and sends traffic elsewhere.

The whole update process is automated, and there will be no application downtime as tasks are updated individually and the load balancer sends traffic only to nodes that have running tasks. If it's a high-traffic application, you need to ensure there's spare capacity in your service, so when one task is being updated, the remaining tasks can handle the load.

Rolling updates give you zero downtime, but that doesn't necessarily mean your app will function correctly during the update. This process is only suitable for stateless applications—if tasks store the session state, then the user experience will be impacted. When the container holding state is replaced, the state will be lost, so if you have stateful applications, you will need to plan a more careful upgrade process.

Rolling back service updates

When you update a service in swarm mode, the swarm stores the configuration of the previous deployment. If you find a problem with the release, you can roll back to the previous state with a single command:

```
> docker service update --rollback nerd-dinner_nerd-dinner-homepage
nerd-dinner_nerd-dinner-homepage
```

The rollback is a specialized form of service update. Instead of passing an image name for tasks to update to, the `rollback` flag does a rolling update to the previous image used by the service. Again, the rollback happens one task at a time, so this is a zero-downtime process.

Service updates retain only one prior service configuration for rollbacks. If you update from version 1 to version 2 and then to version 3, the configuration of version 1 is lost. You can roll back from version 3 to version 2—but if you roll back again from version 2, it will be to the previous version, which will take you back to version 3.

Configuring update behavior

For large scale deployments, you may want to change the default update behavior, either to complete the roll out more quickly or to run a more conservative roll out strategy. The default behavior updates one task at a time, with no delay between task updates, and if a task update fails, the roll out is paused. The configuration can be overridden with three parameters:

- `update-parallelism`: The number of tasks to update concurrently
- `update-delay`: The period to wait between task updates; can be specified as hours, minutes, and seconds
- `update-failure-action`: The action to take if a task update fails; either continue or stop the roll out

You can specify the default parameters in the Dockerfile, so they're baked into the image, or the Compose file so they're set at deployment time or with the service commands. For a production deployment of NerdDinner, I might have nine instances of the SQL message handler, with `update_config` in the Compose file set to update in batches of three with a 10-second delay:

```
nerd-dinner-save-handler:
  deploy:
    endpoint_mode: dnsrr
```

```
replicas: 9
update_config:
  parallelism: 3
  delay: 10s
...
```

Update configuration for a service can also be changed with the `docker service update` command, so you can alter the update parameters and initiate a rolling upgrade with a single command.

Health checks are especially important in service updates. If a health check fails for a new task in a service update, that could mean there's a problem with the image. Completing the roll out could result in 100% unhealthy tasks and a broken application. The default update configuration prevents this, so if an updated task does not enter the running state, the roll out is paused. The update will not go ahead, but that's a better outcome than having an updated app that is broken.

Updating swarm nodes

Application updates are one part of the update routine and host updates are the other. Your Windows Docker hosts should be running a minimal operating system, preferably Windows Server 2016 Core. This version has no UI, so there's a much smaller surface area for updates, but there will still be some Windows updates that require a reboot.

Rebooting the server is an invasive process—it stops the Docker service, killing all running containers. Upgrading Docker is equally invasive for the same reason; it means a restart of the Docker service. In swarm mode, you can manage this by taking nodes of service for the update period without impacting service levels.

I'll show this with my Azure swarm. If I need to work on `win-node02`, I can gracefully reschedule the tasks it is running with `docker node update` in order to put it into drain mode:

```
> docker node update --availability drain win-node02
win-node02
```

Putting a node into drain mode means all containers are stopped, and as these are service task containers, they will be replaced with new containers on the other nodes. When the drain completes, I have no running tasks on `win-node02`: they have all been shut down. You can see that the tasks have been deliberately shut down, as Shutdown is listed as the desired state:

```
> docker node ps win-node02
ID                 NAME                                     IMAGE
NODE DESIRED STATE
rcrcwqao3c0m       nerd-dinner_message-queue.1              nats:nanoserver
    win-node02     Shutdown
zetse09726t9       nerd-dinner_kibana.1
sixeyed/kibana:nanoserver
    win-node02     Shutdown
gdg3owrdjcur       nerd-dinner_nerd-dinner-homepage.1       dockeronwindows/ch03-
nerd-dinner-homepage:latest
    win-node02     Shutdown
r9j83ozezdn8       nerd-dinner_nerd-dinner-web.3            dockeronwindows/ch07-
nerd-dinner-web:latest
    win-node02     Shutdown
exsb59ok6gx2 \_    nerd-dinner_nerd-dinner-web.3            dockeronwindows/ch07-
nerd-dinner-web:latest
    win-node02     Shutdown
```

I can check the service list and see that every service is at the required replica level except the web application service:

```
> docker service ls
ID NAME MODE REPLICAS IMAGE PORTS
4q7kmlxclwo6    nerd-dinner_elasticsearch                replicated    1/1
e2obujts50tp    nerd-dinner_message-queue                replicated    1/1
e660rl6zkk8s    nerd-dinner_nerd-dinner-db               replicated    1/1
goc2dh0rpaid    nerd-dinner_nerd-dinner-index-handler    replicated    1/1
hhfvwsuk12do    nerd-dinner_nerd-dinner-save-handler     replicated    1/1
o6mjy5jbj57x    nerd-dinner_nerd-dinner-web              replicated    2/3
qx1hhp8oo5r5    nerd-dinner_kibana                       replicated    1/1
w48ffc5ejx52    nerd-dinner_nerd-dinner-homepage         replicated    1/1
```

The swarm has created new containers to replace the replicas that were running on `win-node02`, but in the reduced swarm, there isn't any capacity to run another web container. The web application service needs to run on a Windows node and publish port 80 to the host. There are only two Windows nodes available to run containers, and both have port 80 already allocated. The web service will stay at a replica level of 2/3 until there is enough capacity in the swarm to schedule another container.

Nodes in the drain mode are considered to be not available, so if the swarm needs to schedule new tasks, none will be allocated to drained nodes. `win-node02` is effectively out of commission now, so I could log on and run a Windows update with the sconfig tool, or update the Docker service.

Updating the node may mean restarting the Docker service or rebooting the server. When that's done, I can bring the server back online in the swarm with another `docker node update` command:

```
docker node update --availability active win-node02
```

This makes the node available again. When nodes join the swarm Docker doesn't automatically rebalance the services, so the containers running on `win-node00` and `win-node01` will stay there, even though `win-node02` is available and has more capacity. The extra capacity does mean there's a Windows Server with port 80 free now, so the swarm will schedule the missing third web container onto `win-node02`:

```
> docker node ps --filter desired-state=running win-node02
ID              NAME                              IMAGE
NODE
bguu1ese91ga    nerd-dinner_nerd-dinner-web.3    dockeronwindows/ch07-nerd-
dinner-web:latest    win-node02
```

In a high-throughput environment where services are regularly started, stopped, and scaled, any nodes that join the swarm will soon be running their share of tasks. In a more static environment, you may add an extra node as a temporary increase in compute power in order to give you headroom while you update other nodes.

Swarm mode gives you the power to update any component of your application and the nodes running the swarm without any downtime. You may need to commission additional nodes in the swarm during the updates, but these can be removed afterward. You don't need any additional tooling to get rolling updates, automated rollback, and host management—it's all built into Docker.

Mixing hosts in hybrid swarms

There's one more feature of swarm mode that makes it hugely powerful. Nodes in the swarm communicate using the Docker API, and the API is cross-platform—which means you can have a single swarm running a mixture of Windows and Linux servers.

Linux isn't the focus of this book, but I will cover hybrid swarms briefly because they open up a new range of possibilities. A hybrid swarm can have Linux and Windows nodes as managers and workers. You administer the nodes and the services they're running in the same way, using the exact same Docker CLI.

One use case for hybrid swarms is to run your manager nodes on Linux to reduce licensing costs or running costs if you have your swarm in the cloud. A production swarm will need at least three manager nodes. Even if all your workloads are Windows-based, it may be more cost effective to run Linux nodes as managers and save the Windows nodes for user workloads.

The other use case is for mixed workloads. My NerdDinner solution is configured with the web service as the entry point, so HTTP requests are sent directly to the ASP.NET containers. It would be more flexible to run a reverse proxy in a container as the entry point and have requests forwarded from the proxy to the web containers.

A reverse proxy can do SSL termination, caching, load balancing, and more. You can modify HTTP headers in the proxy and disguise the fact that the actual application runs on ASP.NET. Caching is particularly important—the proxy can serve all static resources (images, style sheets, and JavaScript), reducing the number of requests to the application.

There isn't a great software reverse proxy in Windows, but in Linux, there are two—Nginx and HAProxy. Both of these are available as official images on Docker Hub, which you can drop into your solution if you have a hybrid swarm. You could have Nginx running on the Linux nodes in the swarm, forwarding traffic to the ASP.NET application on the Windows nodes.

Similarly, you could migrate any cross-platform components to run in Linux containers. That could be the .NET Core message handler from `Chapter 5`, *Adopting Container-First Solution Design*, as well as the nats message queue, Elasticsearch, Kibana, and even SQL Server. Linux images are typically much smaller and lighter than Windows images, so you should be able to run with greater density, packing more containers onto each host.

The great benefit of the hybrid swarm is that you manage all these components in the same way, from the same user interface. You can connect your local Docker CLI to the swarm manager and administer the Nginx proxy on Linux and the ASP.NET application on Windows with exactly the same commands.

Summary

This chapter was all about the Docker swarm mode, the native clustering option built right into Docker. You learned how to create a swarm and how to add and remove swarm nodes and deploy services on the swarm connected with an overlay network. I showed that you have to create services for high availability and also discussed how to use secrets to store sensitive application data securely in the swarm.

You can deploy your application as a stack on the swarm using a Compose file, which makes it very easy to group and manage your application components. I demonstrated stack deployment on a single node swarm and on a multi-node swarm running in Azure and managed with Docker Cloud.

High availability in the swarm means you can perform application updates and rollbacks without downtime. You can even take nodes out of commission when you need to update Windows or Docker and have your application still running with the same service level on the remaining nodes.

In the next chapter, I'll look more closely at the administration options for dockerized solutions. I'll start by looking at how to use your existing management tools with applications running in Docker. Then, I'll move on to managing swarms in production with Docker Enterprise Edition.

8

Administering and Monitoring Dockerized Solutions

Applications built on Docker are inherently portable, and the process of deployment is the same for every environment. As you promote your application through system tests and user tests to production, you'll use the same artifacts every time. The Docker images you use in production are the exact same versioned images that were signed off in the test environments, and any environmental differences can be captured in compose files.

In a later chapter, I'll cover how continuous deployment works with Docker, so your whole deployment process can be automated. But when you adopt Docker, you'll be moving to a new application platform, and the path to production is about more than just the deployment process. Containerized applications run in fundamentally different ways to apps deployed on VMs or bare metal servers. In this chapter, I'll look at administering and monitoring applications running in Docker.

Some of the tools you use to manage Windows applications today can still be used when the apps are moved to Docker, and I'll start by looking at some examples. But there are different management needs and opportunities for apps running in containers, and the main focus of this chapter will be management products specific to Docker.

In this chapter, I'll be using simple Dockerized applications to show how you can do the following:

- Connect **Internet Information Services (IIS)** Manager to IIS services running in containers
- Connect Server Manager to containers to see event logs and features
- Use open source projects to view and administer Docker swarms
- Use **Universal Control Plane (UCP)** with **Docker Enterprise Edition (Docker EE)**

Managing containers with Windows tools

Many of the administration tools in Windows are able to manage services running on remote machines. IIS Manager, Server Manager, and, of course, **SQL Server Management Studio (SSMS)** can all be connected to a remote server on the network for inspection and administration.

Docker containers are different from remote machines, but they can be set up to allow remote access from these tools. Typically, you need to explicitly set up access for the tool by exposing management ports, enabling Windows features, and running PowerShell cmdlets. This can all be done in the Dockerfile for your application, and I'll cover the setup steps for each of these tools.

Being able to use familiar tools can be helpful, but there are limits to what you should do with them; remember, containers are meant to be disposable. If you connect to a web application container with IIS Manager and tweak the app pool settings, that tweak will be lost when you update the app with a new container image. You can use the graphical tools to inspect a running container and diagnose problems, but you should make changes in the Dockerfile and redeploy.

IIS Manager

The IIS web management console is a perfect example. Remote access is not enabled by default in the Windows base images, but you can configure it with a simple PowerShell script. Firstly, the web management feature needs to be installed:

```
Import-Module servermanager
Add-WindowsFeature web-mgmt-service
```

Then, you need to enable remote access with a registry setting and start the web management Windows service:

```
Set-ItemProperty -Path HKLM:\SOFTWARE\Microsoft\WebManagement\Server -Name
EnableRemoteManagement -Value 1
Start-Service wmsvc
```

You also need an EXPOSE instruction in the Dockerfile to allow traffic into the management service on the expected port 8172. This will allow you to connect, but IIS management console requires user credentials for the remote machine. To support this without having to connect the container to **Active Directory (AD)**, you can create a user and password in the setup script:

```
net user iisadmin "!!Sadmin*" /add
net localgroup "Administrators" "iisadmin" /add
```

There are security issues here. You need to create an administrative account in the image, expose a port, and run an additional service - all increasing the attack surface of your application. Instead of running the setup script in the Dockerfile, it would be better to attach to a container and run the script interactively if you need remote access.

I've set up a simple web server in an image, packaged with a script to enable remote management in the Dockerfile for dockeronwindows/ch08-iis-with-management. I'll run a container from this image, publishing the HTTP and IIS management ports:

```
docker container run -d -p 80 -p 8172 --name iis dockeronwindows/ch08-iis-
with-management
```

When the container is running, I'll execute the `EnableIisRemoteManagement.ps1` script, which sets up remote access with the IIS management service:

```
docker container exec iis powershell \EnableIisRemoteManagement.ps1
```

Now I can run IIS Manager on my Windows host, choose **Start...Connect to a Server**, and enter the IP address of the container. When IIS challenges me to authenticate, I use the credentials for the `iisadmin` user I created in the setup script:

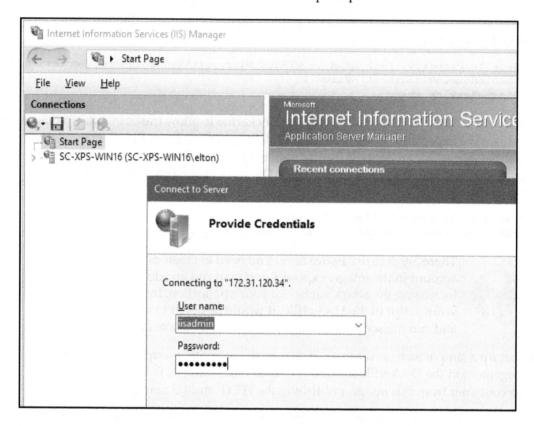

Here, I can navigate around the application pools and the website hierarchy as if I were connected to a remote server:

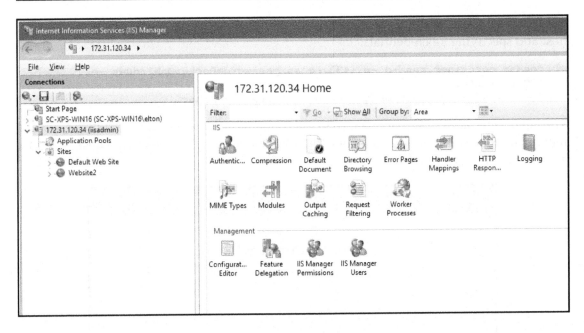

This is a good way of checking the configuration of IIS or an ASP.NET application running on IIS. You can check the virtual directory setup, application pools, and application configuration, but this should be used for investigation only.

If I find that something in the application is not configured correctly, I need to go back to the Dockerfile and fix it and not make a change to the running container. This technique can be very useful when you're migrating an existing app to Docker. If you install an MSI with the web app in the Dockerfile, you can't see what the MSI actually does - but you can connect with IIS manager and see the results.

SQL Server Management Studio

SSMS is more straightforward because it uses the standard SQL client port 1433. You don't need to expose any extra ports or start any extra services; the SQL Server images from Microsoft already have everything set up. You can connect using SQL Server authentication with the sa credentials you use when you run the container.

This command runs a SQL Server Developer Edition container, publishing port 1433 to the host and specifying sa credentials:

```
docker container run -d -p 1433 -e sa_password=DockerOnW!nd0ws -e
ACCEPT_EULA=Y `
  --name sql microsoft/mssql-server-windows-developer
```

You connect to the SQL Server instance in the container using the host's IP address from a remote machine or using the container's IP address if you're connected to the host. In SSMS, just specify the SQL credentials:

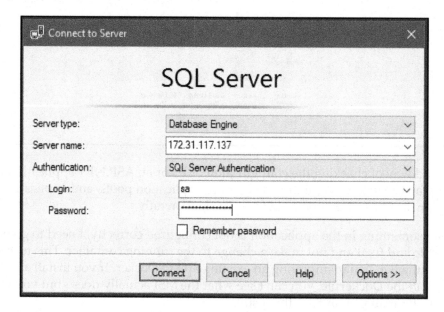

You can administer this SQL instance in the same way as any SQL Server—creating databases, assigning user permissions, restoring Dacpacs, and running SQL scripts. Remember that any changes you make won't impact the image, and you'll need to build your own image if you want the changes to be available to new containers.

This approach lets you build a database through SSMS, if that's your preference, and get it working in a container without installing and running SQL Server. You can perfect your schema, add service accounts and seed data, and then export the database as a script.

I've done this for a simple example database, exporting the schema and data to a single file called `init-db.sql`. The Dockerfile for `dockeronwindows/ch08-mssql-with-schema` takes the SQL script and packages it into a new image, with a bootstrap PowerShell script that deploys the database when you create a container:

```
# escape=`
FROM microsoft/mssql-server-windows-express
SHELL ["powershell", "-Command", "$ErrorActionPreference = 'Stop';"]

ENV sa_password DockerOnW!nd0ws
VOLUME C:\mssql

WORKDIR C:\init
COPY . .

CMD ./InitializeDatabase.ps1 -sa_password $env:sa_password -Verbose

HEALTHCHECK CMD powershell -command `
    try { `
      $result = invoke-sqlcmd -Query 'SELECT TOP 1 1 FROM Authors' -Database
DockerOnWindows; `
      if ($result[0] -eq 1) { return 0} `
      else {return 1}; `
    } catch { return 1 }
```

There's a HEALTHCHECK in the SQL Server image here, which is good practice—it lets Docker check whether the database is running correctly. In this case, the test will fail if the schema has not been created, so the container won't report as healthy until the schema deployment has completed successfully.

I can run a container from this image in the usual way:

```
docker container run -d -p 1433 --name db dockeronwindows/ch08-mssql-with-
schema
```

By publishing port `1433`, I connect to the database with SSMS and see the schema and data from the script. This represents a fresh deployment of an application database, and in this case, I've used SQL Server development edition to work out my schema but SQL Server Express for the actual database - all running in Docker with no local SQL Server instances.

If you think using SQL Server authentication is a retrograde step, you need to remember that Docker enables a different runtime model. You won't have a single SQL Server instance running multiple databases; that could all be targets if the credentials were compromised. Each SQL workload will be in a dedicated container with its own set of credentials, so you effectively have one SQL instance per database, and you could potentially have one database per service.

Security can be increased by running in Docker. Unless you need to connect to SQL Server remotely, you don't need to publish the port from the SQL container. Any applications that need database access will run as containers in the same Docker network as the SQL container and will be able to access port 1433 without publishing it to the host. This means SQL is only accessible to other containers running in the same Docker network.

 If you need to use Windows authentication with an AD account, you can still do that in Docker. Containers can be domain-joined when they start, so you can use service accounts for SQL Server instead of SQL Server authentication.

Event logs

You can connect Event Viewer on your local machine to a remote server, but currently, the remote event log services are not enabled on the Windows Server Core or Nano Server images. This means you can't connect to a container and read event log entries with the Event Viewer UI—but you can do that with the Server Manager UI, which I'll cover in the next section.

If you just want to read event logs, you can execute PowerShell cmdlets against running containers to get the log entries. This command reads the two latest event log entries for the SQL Server application from my database container:

```
> docker exec db powershell `
   "Get-EventLog -LogName Application -Source MSSQL* -Newest 2 | Format-
Table TimeWritten,Message"

TimeWritten            Message
-----------            -------
6/27/2017 5:14:49 PM Setting database option READ_WRITE to ON for database
'...
6/27/2017 5:14:49 PM Setting database option query_store to off for
database...
```

Reading event logs can be useful if you have an issue with a container that you can't diagnose any other way. But it's an approach that doesn't scale when you have dozens or hundreds of containers running. It's better to relay the event logs that are of interest to the console, so they're collected by the Docker platform and you can read them with `docker container logs`, or a management tool that can access the Docker API.

Relaying event logs is simple to do, taking a similar approach to relaying IIS logs in `Chapter` 3, *Developing Dockerized .NET and .NET Core Applications*. For any apps that write to the event log, you use a startup script as the entry point, which runs the app and then enters a read loop—getting entries from the event log and writing them out to the console.

This is a useful approach for apps that run as Windows Services, and it's an approach Microsoft has used in the SQL Server Windows images. The Dockerfile uses a PowerShell script as `CMD`, and that script ends with a loop that calls the same `Get-EventLog` cmdlet to relay logs to the console:

```
$lastCheck = (Get-Date).AddSeconds(-2)
while ($true) {
  Get-EventLog -LogName Application -Source "MSSQL*" -After $lastCheck | `
    Select-Object TimeGenerated, EntryType, Message
  $lastCheck = Get-Date
  Start-Sleep -Seconds 2
}
```

This script reads the event log every 2 seconds, gets any entries since the last read, and writes them out to the console. The script runs in the process started by Docker, so the log entries are captured and can be surfaced by the Docker API.

This is not a perfect approach - it uses a timed loop, only selects some of the data from the log, and it means storing data in both the container's event log and in Docker. It is valid if your application already writes to the event log and you want to Dockerize it without rebuilding the app. In this case, you need to be sure you have a mechanism to keep your application process running, such as a Windows Service, because Docker is monitoring only the event log loop.

Server Manager

Server Manager is a great tool to remotely administer and monitor servers, and it works well with containers based on Windows Server Core. You need to take a similar approach to the IIS management console, configuring a user in the container with administrator access and then connecting from the host.

Just like with IIS, you can add a script to the image, which enables access, so you can run it when you need it. This is safer than always enabling remote access in the image. The script just needs to add a user, configure the server to allow remote access from administrator accounts, and ensure the **Windows Remote Management (WinRM)** service is running:

```
net user serveradmin "s3rv3radmin*" /add
net localgroup "Administrators" "serveradmin" /add

New-ItemProperty -Path
HKLM:\SOFTWARE\Microsoft\Windows\CurrentVersion\Policies\System `
   -Name LocalAccountTokenFilterPolicy -Type DWord -Value 1
Start-Service winrm
```

I have a sample image, `dockeronwindows/ch08-iis-with-server-manager`, which is based on IIS and packages a script to enable remote access with Server Manager. The Dockerfile also exposes the ports used by WinRM, `5985` and `5986`. I can start a container running IIS in the background and then enable remote access:

```
> docker container run -d -P --name iis2 dockeronwindows/ch08-iis-with-
server-manager
b4d2c57d54e6c01e991dc4ed1b2a931386f9432b6f06235cc7dcac525c0bad25

> docker exec iis2 powershell .\EnableRemoteServerManagement.ps1
The command completed successfully.
```

You can connect to the container with Server Manager using the container's IP address, but the container isn't domain-joined. Server Manager will try to authenticate over a secure channel and fail, so you'll get a WinRM authentication error. To add a server that isn't domain-joined, you need to add it as a trusted host. The trusted host list needs to use the hostname of the container, not the IP address, so first, I'll get the hostname of the container:

```
> docker exec iis2 hostname
b4d2c57d54e6
```

And now, I can add the container to the trusted list. This command needs to run on the host, not in the container. You're adding the container's hostname to the local machine's list of trusted servers. I run this on my Windows Server 2016 host:

```
Set-Item wsman:\localhost\Client\TrustedHosts b4d2c57d54e6 -Concatenate -
Force
```

 I'm running Windows Server 2016, but you can use Server Manager on Windows 10 too. Install the **Remote Server Administration Tools (RSAT)** and you can use Server Manager on Windows 10 in the same way.

In Server Manager, navigate to **All Servers** | **Add Servers** and open the **DNS** tab. Here, you can enter the IP address of the container, and Server Manager will resolve the hostname:

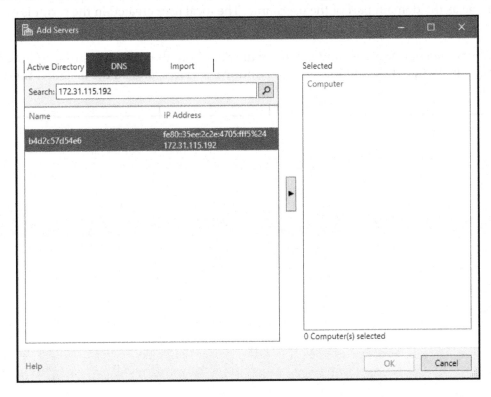

Select the server details and click on **OK**—now Server Manager will try to connect to the container. You'll see an updated status in the **All Servers** tab, which says the server is online but access is denied:

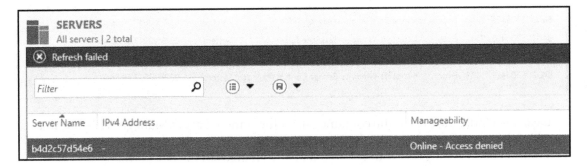

Now you can right-click on the container in the server list and click on **Manage As** to provide the credentials for the local administrator account. You need to specify the hostname as the domain part of the username. The local user created in the script is called **serveradmin**, but I need to authenticate with `b4d2c57d54e6\serveradmin`.

Now the connection succeeds and you'll see the data from the container surfaced in Server Manager, including the event log entries, Windows Services, and all the installed roles and features:

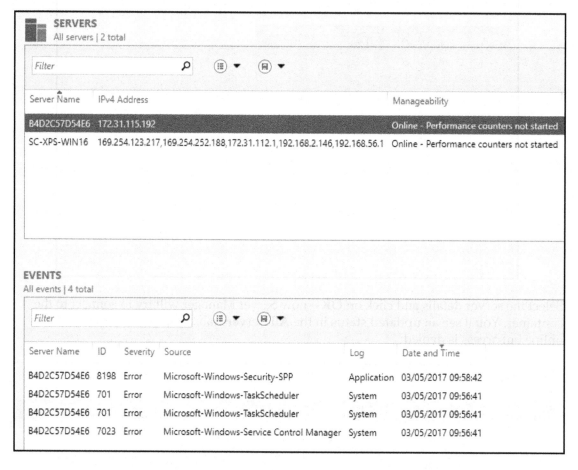

You can even add features to the container from the remote Server Manager UI—but that wouldn't be a good practice. Like the other UI management tools, it's better to use them for exploration and investigation but not to make any changes in the Dockerfile.

Managing containers with Docker tools

You've seen that you can use existing Windows tools to administer containers, but what you can do with these tools doesn't always apply in the Docker world. A container will run a single web application, so the hierarchy navigation of IIS Manager isn't really helpful. Checking event logs in Server Manager can be useful, but it is much more useful to relay entries to the console so they can be surfaced from the Docker API.

Images also need to be explicitly set up to enable access to remote management tools, exposing ports, adding users, and running additional Windows services. All this adds to the attack surface of your running container. You should look at these existing tools as useful in debugging in development and test environments, but they're not really suitable for production.

The Docker platform provides a consistent API for any type of application running in a container, and that's an opportunity for a new type of admin interface. For the rest of the chapter, I'll be looking at management tools that are Docker-aware and provide an alternative management interface to the Docker command line. I'll start with some open source tools and move on to the commercial **Containers-as-a-Service (CaaS)** platform in Docker EE.

Docker visualizer

Visualizer is a very simple web UI that shows basic information about nodes and containers in a Docker swarm. It's an open source project on GitHub in the `dockersamples/docker-swarm-visualizer` repository. It's a Node.js application, and it comes packaged in Docker images for Linux and Windows.

On my hybrid swarm in Azure, I can run the visualizer as a Linux container on the manager node. I connect to the swarm with Docker for Windows and run the following:

```
docker service create `
  --name=viz `
  --publish=8080:8080/tcp `
  --constraint=node.role==manager `
  --mount=type=bind,src=/var/run/docker.sock,dst=/var/run/docker.sock `
  dockersamples/visualizer
```

The constraint ensures the container runs only on a manager node, and as my manager runs on Linux, I can use the `mount` option to let the container talk to the Docker API. In Linux, you can treat sockets like filesystem mounts, so the container can use the API socket without having to publicly expose it over **Transmission Control Protocol (TCP)**.

> You can also run the visualizer in an all-Windows swarm. Windows doesn't currently support mounting named pipes as volumes, but there is a workaround described in the documentation for the visualizer project.

The visualizer gives you a read-only view of the containers in the swarm. The UI shows the status of hosts and containers and gives you a quick way to check the distribution of the workload on your swarm. This is how my Azure swarm looks with the NerdDinner stack deployed:

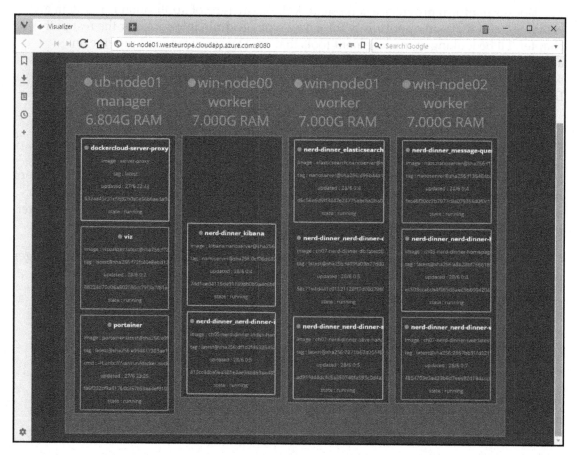

I can see at a glance that all my nodes and containers are healthy and that Docker has distributed containers across the swarm as evenly as it can. Visualizer uses the API in the Docker service, which exposes all the Docker resources with a RESTful interface.

The Docker API also provides write access, so you can create and update resources. An open source project called **Portainer** provides administration using these APIs.

Portainer

Portainer is a lightweight management UI for Docker. It runs as a container, and it can manage single Docker hosts and clusters running in swarm mode. It's an open source project hosted on GitHub in the `portainer/portainer` repository. Portainer is written in Go, so it's cross-platform and you can run it as a Linux or a Windows container.

On my hybrid swarm, I can run Portainer on the manager node:

```
docker service create `
  --name portainer `
  --publish 9000:9000 `
  --constraint 'node.role == manager' `
  --mount type=bind,src=//var/run/docker.sock,dst=/var/run/docker.sock `
  portainer/portainer -H unix:///var/run/docker.sock
```

The `portainer/portainer` image on Docker Hub is a multi-arch image, which means you can use the same image tag on Linux and Windows, and Docker will use the matching image for the host OS. You can't mount the Docker socket on Windows, but the Portainer documentation shows you how to access the Docker API on Windows.

When you first browse to Portainer, you need to specify an administrator password. Then, the service connects to the Docker API and surfaces details about all the resources. In swarm mode, I can see the nodes in the swarm, their compute capacity, Docker version, and status:

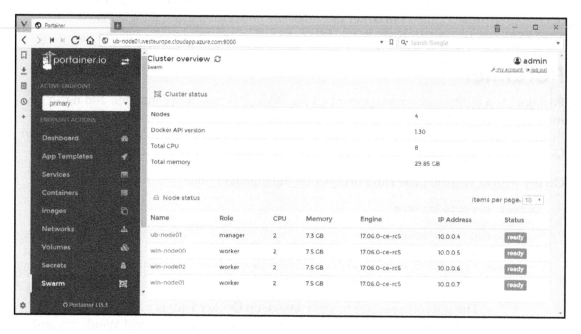

The **Services** view shows me all the running services, and from here, I can drill down into service details, and there's a quick link to update the scale of the service:

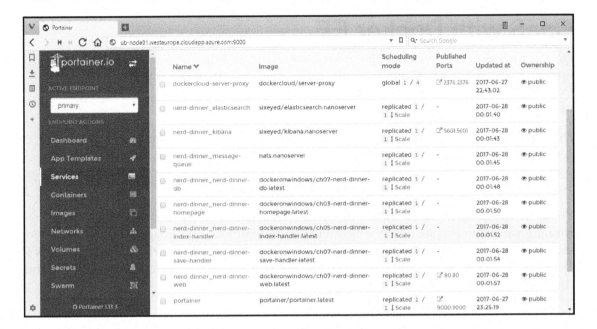

You can create containers and services from Portainer, but as of the current version (1.13), you can't deploy a stack from a compose file or manage stacks on the swarm.

Portainer is a great tool and an active open source project, but there are features where you need to understand the source of the data—some views that show the status of the node Portainer is connected to rather than the swarm as a whole. The **Services** view shows all services, but the **Volumes** and **Containers** views show only those resources on the node where Portainer is running.

You can create multiple users and teams in Portainer and apply access control to resources. You can create services that have access limited to certain teams. Authentication is managed by Portainer, so all users exist in the Portainer database and you can't connect to external identity providers.

In a production environment, you may have a requirement to run software with support. Portainer is open source, but there is a commercial support option available. For enterprise deployments or environments with strict security processes, Docker EE offers a complete feature set.

CaaS with Docker EE

Docker EE is the commercial edition from Docker, Inc. and the standard and advanced options come with the management suite called **Docker Datacenter** (**DDC**). DDC is Docker's CaaS platform and makes full use of Docker to provide a single pane of glass to manage any number of containers running on any number of hosts.

DDC is an enterprise-grade product that you run on a cluster of machines in your data center or in the cloud. The clustering functionality uses Docker swarm mode, so in production, you could have a 100-node cluster using the exact same application platform as your development laptop running as a single-node swarm.

There are two parts to DDC. There's the **Docker Trusted Registry** (**DTR**), which is like running your own private instance of Docker Hub, complete with image signing and security scanning. I'll cover DTR in Chapter 9, *Understanding the Security Risks and Benefits of Docker*, when I look at security in Docker. The administration component is called UCP, and it's a new type of management interface.

Understanding UCP

UCP is a web-based interface used to manage swarm nodes, images, services, and containers. UCP itself is a distributed application that runs in containers across connected services in the swarm. UCP gives you a single place to administer all your Docker applications in the same way. It provides role-based access control to resources so you can set fine-grained controls over who can do what.

DDC runs in swarm mode. You can deploy your application as a stack with a compose file, and UCP will create services on the cluster. UCP gives you the full range of administration features - you can create, scale and remove services, inspect, and connect to the tasks running the services and manage the nodes running the swarm. All the additional resources you need, such as Docker networks and volumes, are surfaced in UCP for management in the same way.

You can run a hybrid DDC cluster with Linux nodes for UCP and DTR and Windows nodes for your user workloads. As a subscription service from Docker, you have support from Docker's team for the setting up of your cluster and dealing with any issues, covering all the Windows and Linux nodes.

Navigating the UCP UI

You log in to UCP from the home page. You can either use the authentication built in to DDC, managing users manually from UCP, or you can connect DDC to any **Lightweight Directory Access Protocol (LDAP)** authentication store. This means you can set up DDC to use your organization's AD and log in with your Windows account.

The UCP home page is a dashboard that shows the key performance indicators of your cluster, the number of nodes, services, and containers running at that moment, together with the overall compute utilization of the cluster:

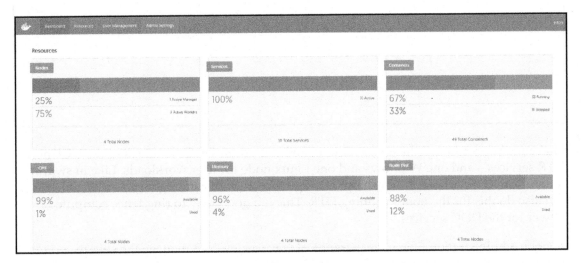

From the dashboard, you can navigate to the resource views that give you access grouped by the resource type: services, containers, images, nodes, networks, volumes, and secrets. For most of the resource types, you can list the existing resources, inspect them, delete them, and create new ones.

UCP provides **Role Based Access Control (RBAC)** for all the Docker resources. You can apply a permission label to any resource and secure access based on that label. Teams can be assigned permissions to labels—ranging from no access to full control—which secures access to team members for all the resources that have these labels.

Managing nodes

The node view shows you all the nodes in the cluster, listing the operating system and CPU architecture, the node status, and the node manager status:

I have four nodes in my cluster, two Linux nodes used for DDC workloads—the UCP and DTR services—and one Windows and one Linux node for user workloads. Like in swarm mode, I can configure DDC to exempt manager nodes from running user workloads—but I can also do this for the nodes running DTR. This is a good way to ring fence compute power for the DDC services.

In node administration, you have a graphical way to view and manage the swarm servers you have access to. You can put nodes into the drain mode, allowing you to run Windows update or upgrade Docker on the node. You can promote workers to managers, demote managers to workers, and see the tokens you need to join new nodes to the swarm.

Drilling into each node, you can see the total CPU, memory, and disk usage of the server, with a graph showing the current and recent historical usage:

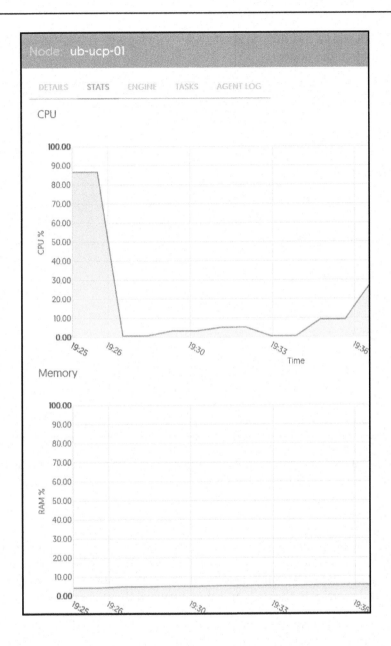

You can also list the tasks running on each node, which gives you a view of all the service containers running on the node:

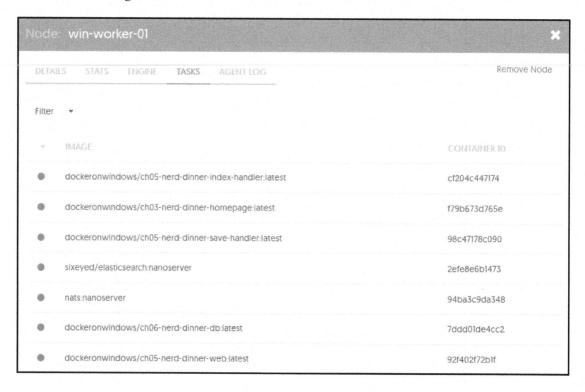

From each task, you can navigate to the container view, which I'll cover shortly.

Volumes

Volumes exist at the node level rather than the swarm level, but you can manage them in UCP across all the swarm nodes. How you manage volumes in the swarm depends on the type of volume you're using. Local volumes are fine for scenarios such as global services that write logs and metrics to the disk and then forward them centrally.

Persistent data stores running as clustered services could also use local storage. You might create a local volume on every node but add labels to servers with high-volume RAID arrays. When you create the data service, you can use a constraint to limit it to RAID nodes, so other nodes will never have a task scheduled on them, and where the tasks are running, they will write data to the volume on the RAID array.

For on-premises data centers and in the cloud, you can use shared storage with volume plugins. With shared storage, services can continue to access data even if containers move to different swarm nodes. Service tasks will read and write data to the volume that gets persisted on the shared storage device. There are many volume plugins available on Docker Store, including for cloud services such as AWS and Azure cloud, physical infrastructure from HPE and Nimble, and virtualization platforms such as vSphere.

The Docker platform is likely to add native shared storage in the future without requiring a specific provider plugin. Docker acquired a distributed storage company called **Infinit**, which built a peer-to-peer transfer mechanism. In the announcement of this acquisition, Docker shared plans to incorporate distributed storage into the Docker platform, which could allow data volumes to be accessible from any cluster node using swarm-wide storage.

Volumes have a limited number of options, so creating them is a case of specifying the driver and applying any driver options:

A permissions label can be applied to volumes, like other resources, to control availability with RBAC.

Images

UCP is not an image registry - DTR is the enterprise private registry in DDC. In the images view, UCP shows you which images have been pulled on the cluster nodes, and it also allows you to pull new images.

One drawback of swarm mode in Docker **Community Edition** (CE) is that image pulling is not done cluster-wide. On a CE swarm, you need to connect to each node and pull images if you want to preload them before starting a service. UCP doesn't have this limitation - you can use the **Pull image** function to download the image onto every node:

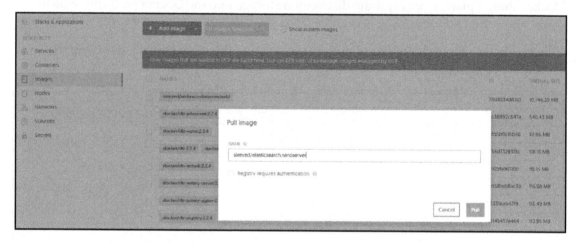

Docker images are compressed for distribution, and the Docker engine decompresses the layers when you pull an image. There are OS-specific optimizations to start containers as soon as the pull completes, which is why you can't pull Windows images on Linux hosts or vice versa. UCP will try and pull the image on every host, but if some fail because of an OS mismatch, it will continue with the remaining nodes.

In the image view, you can drill down and see the details of an image, including the history of the layers, the health check, any environment variables, and the exposed ports. The basic details also show you the OS platform of the image, the virtual size, and the date on which it was created:

Image: 7c8b98013171   ✕

DETAILS   CONFIGURATION   HISTORY   Remove Image

ID ❓   sha256:7c8b980131718da0d0ca8d47b2fecfbb6c3386dfd134d9f18d1f91338515a901

Created ❓   2017-02-13 17:12:24 +0000

Size ❓   9 GB (virtual 9 GB)

Author ❓   Unknown

Comment ❓   None

Docker Version ❓   1.13.1

Platform ❓   windows amd64

Tags ❓

  dockeronwindows/ch05-nerd-dinner-web:latest

Digests

  dockeronwindows/ch05-nerd-dinner-
  web@sha256:19615ff7ca247af15681c5475c4aa2f4aab35b826045aa9144db8cf96cf40fd8

Labels ❓

  This image does not have any labels defined

In UCP, you can also remove images from the cluster. You may have a policy of retaining just the current and previous image versions on the cluster in order to allow rollback. Other images can be safely removed from the DDC nodes, leaving all previous image versions in DTR so they can be pulled if needed.

Networks

Network management is straightforward, and UCP presents the same interface as other resource types. The network list shows you the networks in the cluster, and these can be labeled with RBAC applied, so you'll only see networks you're allowed to see.

There are several options for networks, allowing you to specify IPv6 and custom MTU packet sizes. Swarm mode supports encrypted networks, where the traffic between nodes is transparently encrypted, and it can be enabled through UCP. In a DDC cluster, you'll typically use the overlay driver to allow services to communicate in a virtual network across the cluster nodes:

Docker supports a special type of swarm network called an **ingress network**. Ingress networks have load balancing and service discovery for external requests. This makes port publishing very flexible. On a 10-node cluster, you could publish port 80 on a service with three replicas. If a node receives an incoming request on port 80 but it isn't running one of the service tasks, Docker will intelligently redirect it to a node that is running a task.

 Ingress networks are a powerful feature, but at the time of writing this, they are not supported in the Windows networking stack. Support is planned, but it will be in a future Windows update rather than a Docker release.

Networks can also be deleted through UCP but only if there are no containers attached. If you have services defined that use the network, you'll get a warning if you try to delete it.

Deploying stacks

There are two ways to deploy your applications with UCP, which are analogous to deploying individual services with `docker service create`, and deploying a full compose file with `docker stack deploy`. Stacks are the easiest to deploy and will let you use a compose file that you've verified in preproduction environments. From the stacks and applications view, click on **Deploy** and you can import a compose YML file:

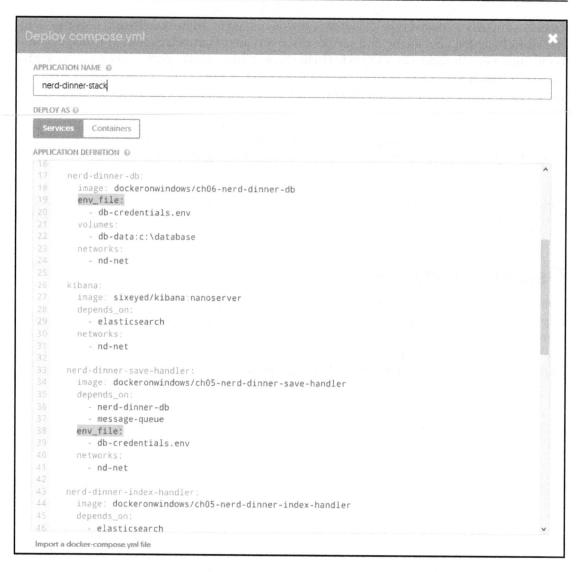

UCP validates the contents and highlights any issues - in this case, it has flagged the `env-file` option. Environment files can't be used in the same way as with the Docker Compose tool. With Docker Compose, the environment file needs to exist on the client machine where you run the `docker-compose` command. UCP deploys the compose file on the cluster without using Docker Compose, so there is no client where the environment file can be found. Similarly, options such as `build` are not supported and would show as an error.

Valid compose files are deployed as a stack, and you will see all the resources in UCP: networks, volumes, and services. Stacks are the preferred deployment model, as they continue to use the known compose file format, and they automate all the resources. But stacks are not suitable for every solution. In a stack deployment, there's no guarantee about the order in which the services will be created; the depends_on option used by Docker Compose doesn't apply. This is a deliberate design decision based on the idea that services should be resilient, but not all services are.

Modern applications should be built for failure. If a web component can't connect to the database, it should use a policy-based retry mechanism to repeatedly reconnect rather than failing to start. Traditional applications usually expect their dependencies to be available and don't have graceful retries built in. NerdDinner is like that, so if I deploy a stack from the compose file, the web app could start before the database service is created, and it will fail.

In these cases, the application will be available when all the failing tasks have been restarted and have found their dependencies available. If these restarts are likely to cause a problem with your legacy application, you may prefer to manually create services rather than deploying a stack. UCP supports this workflow too, and it lets you ensure that all the dependencies are running before you start each service.

Creating services

There are dozens of options for the docker service create command. UCP supports them all in a guided UI, which you start with **Create a Service** from the services view. First, you specify the basic details—the name of the image to use for the service, the service name (which is how other services will discover this one), the replication mode, and the number of replicas:

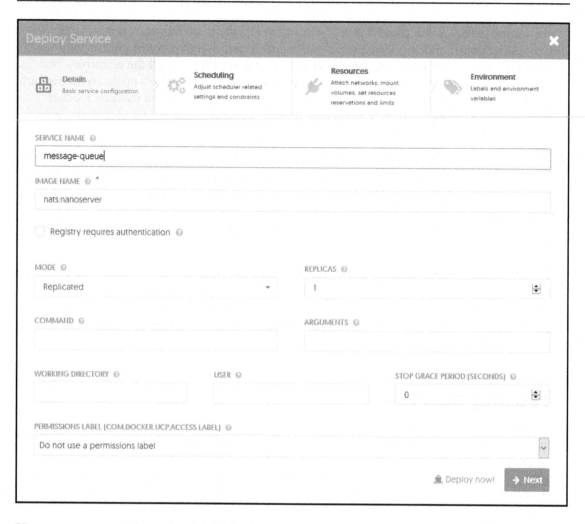

Here, you can specify credentials if the image repository is not public. You can also override the working directory, the startup command, and arguments for containers created in the service, giving you the flexibility to use the image in different ways. Next, you can configure how the service is scheduled to run on the swarm nodes:

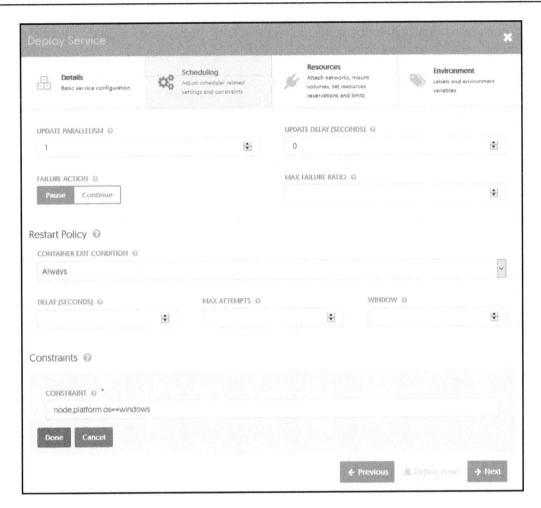

The **Restart Policy** defaults to **Always**. This works in conjunction with the replica count, so if any tasks fail or are stopped, they will be restarted to maintain the service level. You can configure the update settings for automated rollouts, and you can also add scheduling constraints. Constraints work with node labels to limit which nodes can be used to run service tasks. You can use this to restrict tasks to high-capacity nodes or to nodes that have strict access controls.

Swarm node doesn't currently evaluate the host platform when it schedules tasks, so it could try to run a Windows image on a Linux node or a Linux image on a Windows node. Adding a scheduling constraint prevents this. You can use the built-in labels that Docker applies to nodes when they join the swarm, specifying `node.platform.os==windows` to restrict to Windows nodes or `node.platform.os==linux` for Linux nodes.

Next, you can configure how the service integrates with other resources in the cluster, including networks and volumes:

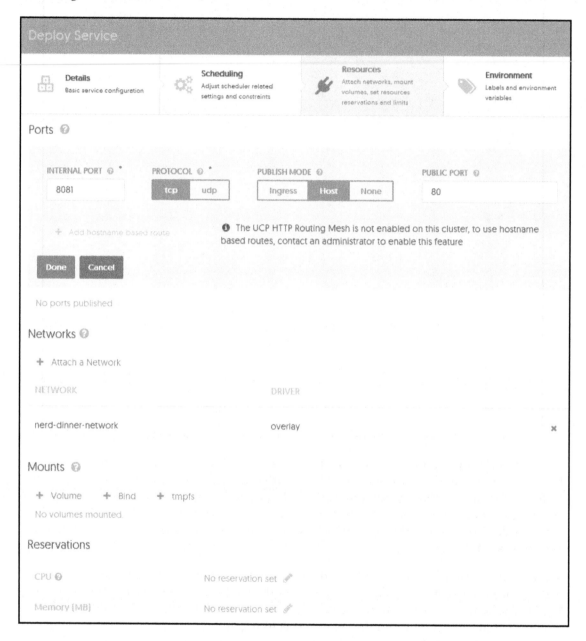

For a service that is one part of a distributed application, you would choose an existing overlay network to attach, allowing the services to communicate. Within a network, services do not need to have ports published, so the web application can reach the database without publicly exposing the ports. For external-facing services, you can publish ports and select the port mapping and publish mode. The resources section is where you can specify compute reservations and limits. You can restrict services to a share of the CPU and memory, or you can request a minimum share of CPU and memory.

The final section is to configure the service environment:

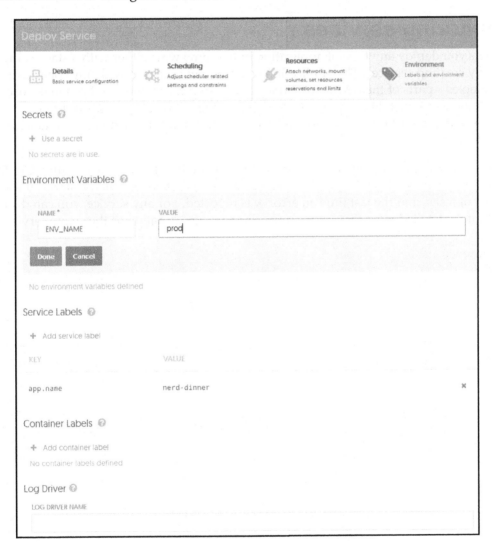

Here, you can add environment variables to be set in the service's containers and labels to apply to the service as a whole or to the containers themselves. The plug-in logging framework is exposed here, and you can specify a custom log driver. You can also select secrets to be made available to the service's containers.

When you deploy the service, UCP takes care of pulling the image onto any nodes that need it and starting the required number of containers. That would be one container per node for global services or the specified number of tasks for replicated services.

Monitoring services

UCP lets you deploy any type of application in the same way, either with a stack compose file or by creating services. The application can use many services with any combination of technologies—parts of the new NerdDinner stack can run on Linux, so I can make use of a hybrid cluster. Then, I'd be deploying Java, Go, and Node.js components as Linux containers and .NET Framework and .NET Core components as Windows containers on the same cluster.

All these different technology platforms can be managed in the same way with UCP. The service view shows all services with basic information, such as the overall status, the number of tasks, and the last time an error was reported. For any service, you can drill down into a detailed view that shows much the same information as the create service screens:

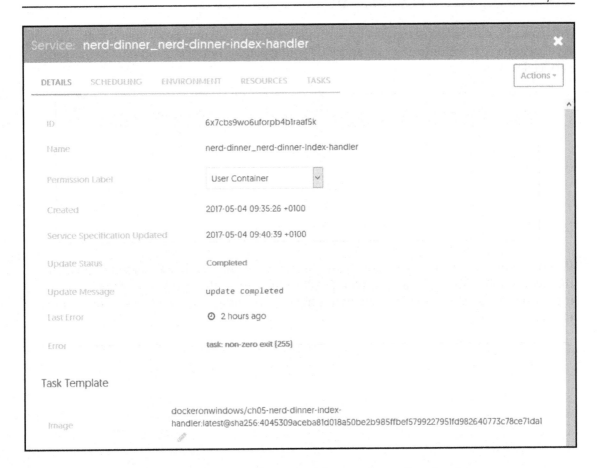

You'll use this view to check the overall status of the service and make changes—you can add environment variables, change the networks or volumes, and change the scheduling constraints. Any changes you make to the service definition will be implemented by restarting the service, so you need to understand the application impact. Stateless apps and apps that gracefully handle transient failures can be amended on the fly, but there may be application downtime—depending on your solution architecture.

You can adjust the scale of the service without restarting existing tasks. Just specify the new level of scale in the **Sheduling** tab, and UCP will create or remove containers to meet the service level:

When you increase scale, the existing containers are retained and new ones are added, so that won't affect the availability of your application (unless the app keeps the state in individual containers). However, many replicas are running, and you can see them in the task list:

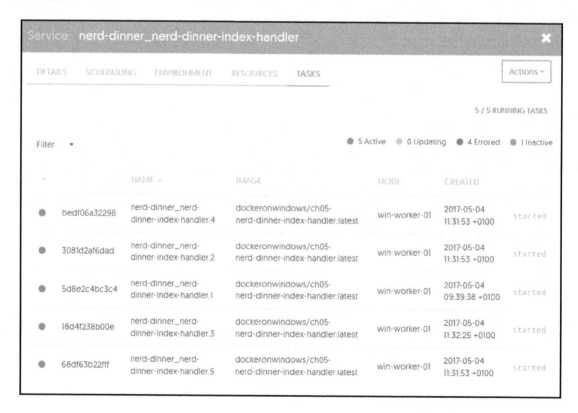

From there, you can select a task to drill down into the container view, which is where the consistent management experience makes administering Dockerized applications so straightforward. Every detail about the running container is surfaced, and you can even interact with the container. The **DETAILS** tab shows you key details, such as exposed ports, environment variables, and active processes:

Container: nerd-dinner_nerd-dinner-index-handler.1.8agaudqsriclyuhkbyaa7hmqy

| DETAILS | LOGS | STATS | CONSOLE | Container Actions |

Environment 4 variables   —

ELASTICSEARCH_URL	http://elasticsearch:9200
MESSAGE_QUEUE_URL	nats://message-queue:4222
DOTNET_VERSION	1.0.3
DOTNET_DOWNLOAD_URL	https://dotnetcli.blob.core.windows.net/dotnet/preview/Binaries/1.0.3/dotnet-win-x64.1.0.3.zip

Labels 8 labels   +

Networks nerd-dinner_nd-net   +

Ports

Processes 14 processes   —

NAME	PID	CPU	PRIVATE WORKING SET
smss.exe	11180	00:00:00.000	200.7 kB
csrss.exe	10672	00:00:00.015	340 kB

On the **LOGS** tab, you can see all the output from the container—in this case, it's the console output written by my .NET Core application, but it could by IIS logs or event logs relayed to the console:

The **STATS** tab graphically shows how much CPU and memory the container is using, and the **CONSOLE** tab lets you connect directly to a command shell running inside the container:

UCP gives you an interface that lets you drill down from the overall health of the cluster, through the status of all the running services, to the individual containers running on specific nodes. You can easily monitor the overall health of your applications, check application logs, and connect to containers for debugging—all within the same management UI. You can also download a **client bundle**, which you can use to manage the cluster from a remote Docker **Command-Line Interface (CLI)** client.

The client bundle contains a script to point your local CLI to the remote Docker API running on the cluster and also sets up client certificates for secure communication. The certificates identify a specific user in UCP, whether they have been created in UCP or whether they're an external LDAP user. So, users can log in to the UCP UI or use the `docker` commands to manage resources, and for both options, they will have the same access defined by the UCP RBAC policies.

RBAC

Authorization in UCP gives you fine-grained access control over all the Docker resources. Individual users have a default access policy, ranging from **No Access**, which means they can't view event resources in a list, to **Full Control**, which gives them read and write access to everything except the UCP admin settings. RBAC is defined at the team level—teams can have different levels of access to different permissions labels.

In my UCP instance, I have a team called **Content Management System (CMS) Admins**. Let's say the NerdDinner home page has been replaced with a CMS running in Docker and certain users need access to administer the CMS:

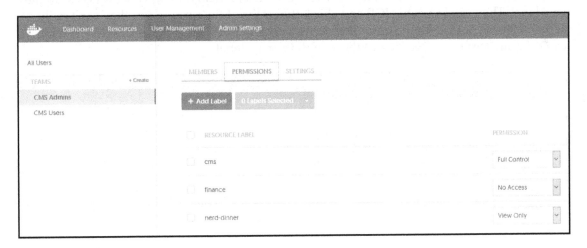

Users in this team have **Full Control** over any resources with the **cms** permission label. This means they can stop containers, scale services, and delete volumes if these resources are set up with the **cms** permissions label. This team's users also have the **View Only** permission over the **nerd-dinner** label, so they can see the NerdDinner resources and drill into the details, but they can't modify any resources. They have no access to any resources with the **finance** permission label - they won't even see these resources in the UI.

You create permissions labels by adding them here first, in the team section of **User Management**. Then, you can apply them as the permission label when you create or update a resource. Here, I've added the **cms** label to the **cms** service:

I have a second team configured to represent CMS users, who only have view access to the **cms** label. They can log in to UCP and check the status of the service, but they can't make any changes. A user with the default no-access permission who is in the CMS users team can't see any services listed except those with the **cms** label:

Also, note that the **Images** option isn't available. The images view is not available for users with a default **No Access** permission. On the service view, the user can navigate to the service and see the tasks and check the logs and resource usage, but they can't make any changes. If they try to remove the service or connect to a container, they'll see an access denied error.

Teams can have multiple permissions for different resource labels, and users can belong to multiple teams. Resource labels themselves are arbitrary strings, so the authorization system in UCP is flexible enough to suit many different security models. You could take a DevOps approach and apply labels for specific projects, with all the team members getting complete control over the project resources. Or, you could have a dedicated admin team with complete control over everything and individual developer teams, where the members have restricted control over the apps they work on.

RBAC is a major feature of UCP, and it complements the wider security story of Docker, which will be covered in `Chapter 9`, *Understanding the Security Risks and Benefits of Docker*.

Summary

This chapter focused on the operations side of running Dockerized solutions. I showed you how to use existing management tools with Docker containers and how that can be useful for investigation and debugging. The main focus was on a new way of administering and monitoring applications—using UCP to manage all kinds of workloads in the same way.

You learned how to use existing Windows management tools, such as IIS Manager and Server Manager, to administer Docker containers, and you also learned about the limitations of this approach. Sticking with the tools you know can be useful when you start with Docker, but dedicated container management tools are a better option.

I covered two open source options to manage containers: the simple visualizer and the more advanced Portainer. Both run as containers and connect to the Docker API, and they are cross-platform apps packaged in Linux and Windows Docker images.

Lastly, I walked you through the products in Docker EE used to manage production workloads. I demonstrated UCP as a single pane of glass to administer a diverse range of containerized applications and showed how RBAC lets you secure access to all of your Docker resources.

The next chapter is focused on security. Applications running in containers potentially offer a new avenue of attack. You need to be aware of the risks, but security is at the center of the Docker platform. Docker lets you easily set up an end-to-end security story, where policies are enforced by runtime—something that is very hard to do without Docker.

9
Understanding the Security Risks and Benefits of Docker

Docker is a new type of application platform, and it has been built with a strong focus on security. You can package an existing application as a Docker image, run it in a Docker container, and get significant security benefits without changing any code.

A .NET 2.0 WebForms app currently running on Windows Server 2003 will happily run under .NET 4.5 in a Windows container based on Windows Server Core 2016 with no code changes, an immediate upgrade that applies 14 years of security patches!

Security in Docker encompasses a wide range of topics, which I will cover in this chapter. I'll explain the security aspects of containers and images, the extended features in **Docker Trusted Registry (DTR)**, and the secure configuration of Docker in swarm mode.

In this chapter, I'll look at some of the internals of Docker to show how security is implemented and cover the following:

- Container processes run as an unknown user on the host, minimizing the scope for attackers
- Containers can be run with resource constraints so they can't starve the host's resources
- Images should be optimized in order to reduce the attack surface of your application
- Images can be scanned for vulnerabilities and digitally signed to record provenance
- Docker swarm encrypts communication between the nodes and encrypts stored secrets

Understanding container security

Application processes running in Windows Server containers are actually running on the host. If you run multiple ASP.NET applications in containers, you'll see multiple `w3wp.exe` processes in the task list on the host machine. Sharing the operating system kernel between containers is how Docker containers are so efficient, the container doesn't load its own kernel, so the startup and shutdown times are very fast and the overhead on runtime resources is minimal.

Software running inside a container may have security vulnerabilities, and the big question security folks ask about Docker is, how secure is the isolation between containers? If an app in a Docker container is compromised, that means a host process is compromised. Could the attacker use that process to compromise other processes, potentially hijacking the host machine or other containers running on the host.

Breaking out of a container and compromising other containers and the host could be possible if there was a vulnerability in the operating system kernel that the attacker could exploit. The Docker platform is built with the principle of security-in-depth, so even if that were possible, the platform provides multiple ways to mitigate it.

 The Docker platform has near feature parity between Linux and Windows, with the few gaps on the Windows side being actively worked on. But Docker has a longer history of production deployment on Linux and much of the guidance and tooling such as Docker Bench and the CIS Docker Benchmark is specific to Linux. It's useful to know the Linux side, but many of the practical points do not apply to Windows containers.

Container processes

All Windows processes are started and owned by a user account. The permissions of the user account determine whether the process can access files and other resources and whether they are available to modify or just to view. In the Docker base image for Windows Server Core, there is a default user account called **container administrator**. Any process you start in a container will use that user account:

```
> docker container run microsoft/windowsservercore whoami
user manager\containeradministrator
```

You can run an interactive container starting a PowerShell and find the user ID (SID) of the container administrator account:

```
> docker container run -it --rm microsoft/windowsservercore powershell

> $user = New-Object
System.Security.Principal.NTAccount("containeradministrator"); `
   $sid = $user.Translate([System.Security.Principal.SecurityIdentifier]); `
   $sid.Value
S-1-5-93-2-1
```

You'll find that the container user always has the same SID S-1-5-93-2-1, as the account is part of the Windows image so it has the same attributes in every container. The container process is really running on the host, but there is no container administrator user on the host. In fact, if you look at the container process on the host, you'll see a blank entry for the username. I'll start a long-running ping process and check the process ID (PID) inside the container:

```
> docker container run -d --name ping microsoft/windowsservercore ping -t
localhost
f8060e0f95ba0f56224f1777973e9a66fc2ccb1b1ba5073ba1918b854491ee5b

> docker container exec ping powershell Get-Process ping -IncludeUserName
Handles  WS(K)  CPU(s)  Id    UserName              ProcessName
-------  -----  ------  --    --------              -----------
  69     3828   0.00    8264  User Manager\Contai... PING
```

This is a Windows Server container running in Docker on Windows Server 2016, so the ping process is running directly on the host, and the PID inside the container will match the PID on the host. On the server, I can check the details of that same PID, 8264 in this case:

```
> Get-Process -Id 8264 -IncludeUserName
Handles  WS(K)  CPU(s)  Id    UserName  ProcessName
-------  -----  ------  --    --------  -----------
  69     3828   0.00    8264            PING
```

There is no username because the container user does not map any users on the host. Effectively, the host process is running under an anonymous user, and it has no permissions on the host, only within the sandboxed environment of one container. If a Windows Server vulnerability was found that allowed attackers to break out of a container, they would be running a host process with no access to host resources.

It's possible that a more extreme vulnerability could allow the anonymous user on the host to assume wider privileges - but that would be a major security hole in the core Windows permissions stack of the scale that typically gets a very fast response from Microsoft. The anonymous host user approach is a good mitigation to limit the impact of any unknown vulnerabilities.

Container user accounts and ACLs

In a Windows Server container, the default user account is the container administrator. This account is in the administrator group on the container, so it has complete access to the whole filesystem and all the resources on the container. The process specified in the CMD or ENTRYPOINT instruction in a Dockerfile will run under the container administrator account.

This can be problematic if there is a vulnerability in the application. The app could be compromised, and while the chances of an attacker breaking out of the container are small, the attacker could still do a lot of damage inside the application container. Administrative access means the attacker could download malicious software from the internet and run it in the container or copy state from the container to an external location.

You can mitigate this by running container processes under a nonadministrative user account. The **Internet Information Services (IIS)** and ASP.NET images from Microsoft do this. The external-facing process is the IIS Windows service, which runs under a local account in the IIS_IUSRS group. This group has read access to the IIS root path C:\inetpub\wwwroot but no write access. An attacker could compromise the web application, but they would not be able to write files, so the ability to download malicious software is gone.

In some cases, the web application needs write access to save the state, but it can be granted at a very fine level in the Dockerfile. As an example, the open source **content management system (CMS)** Umbraco can be packaged as a Docker image, but the IIS user group needs write permissions to the content folder. In the Dockerfile, you can set ACL permissions with a RUN instruction:

```
RUN $acl = Get-Acl $env:UMBRACO_ROOT; `
    $newOwner = [System.Security.Principal.NTAccount]('BUILTIN\IIS_IUSRS');

    $acl.SetOwner($newOwner); `
    Set-Acl -Path $env:UMBRACO_ROOT -AclObject $acl; `
    Get-ChildItem -Path $env:UMBRACO_ROOT -Recurse | Set-Acl -AclObject
$acl
```

I won't go into detail on Umbraco here, but you can find sample Dockerfiles in my GitHub repository at `https://github.com/sixeyed/dockerfiles-windows`.

You should use a nonadministrative user account to run processes and set ACLs as narrowly as possible. This limits the scope for any attackers who gain access to the process inside the container, but there are still attack vectors from outside the container you need to consider.

Running containers with resource constraints

You can run Docker containers with no constraints, and the container process will use as much of the host's resources as it needs. That's the default, but it could be an easy attack vector, a malicious user could generate excess load on the application in the container, which could try and grab 100% CPU and memory, starving other containers on the host. This is especially significant if you're running hundreds of containers serving multiple application workloads.

Docker has mechanisms to prevent individual containers using excessive resources. You can start containers with explicit constraints to limit the resources they can use, ensuring no single container consumes the majority of the host's compute power. You can limit a container to an explicit number of CPU cores and memory.

I have a simple .NET console app and a Dockerfile to package it in the `ch09-resource-check` folder. The app hogs compute resources, and I can run it in a container to show how Docker limits the impact of a rogue application. I can use the app to successfully allocate 600 MB of memory like this:

```
> docker container run dockeronwindows/ch09-resource-check /r Memory /p 600
I allocated 600MB of memory, and now I'm done.
```

The console application allocates 600 GB of memory in the container, which is actually 1 GB of memory from the server in a Windows Server container. I ran the container without any constraints, so the app is able to use as much memory as the server has. If I limit the container to 500 MB of memory, then the application cannot allocate 600 MB:

```
> docker container run --memory 500M dockeronwindows/ch09-resource-check /r
Memory /p 600
Unhandled Exception: OutOfMemoryException.
```

The sample application can also hog the CPU. It computes Pi to a given number of decimal places, which is a computationally expensive operation. In an unrestricted container, computing Pi to 20,000 decimal places takes just over a second on my development laptop:

```
> docker container run dockeronwindows/ch09-resource-check /r Cpu /p 20000
I calculated Pi to 20000 decimal places in 1013ms. The last digit is 8.
```

I can use a CPU restriction, and Docker will limit the compute resources available to this container, retaining more CPU for other tasks. The same computation takes twice as long:

```
> docker container run --cpus 1 dockeronwindows/ch09-resource-check /r Cpu
/p 20000
I calculated Pi to 20000 decimal places in 2043ms. The last digit is 8.
```

It can be challenging to verify that the resource constraints are in place. The underlying Windows APIs to get the CPU count and memory capacity use the OS kernel, which is the host's kernel. The kernel reports the full hardware spec, so the limits don't appear to be in place inside the container, but they are enforced. You can use WMI to check the constraints, but the output will not be as expected:

```
> docker container run --cpus 1 --memory 1G microsoft/windowsservercore
powershell `
  "Get-WmiObject Win32_ComputerSystem | select NumberOfLogicalProcessors,
TotalPhysicalMemory"

NumberOfLogicalProcessors  TotalPhysicalMemory
-------------------------  -------------------
                        8          17078218752
```

Here, the container reports eight CPUs and 16 GB of RAM even though it has been constrained to one CPU and 1 GB of RAM. The constraints are actually in place, but they operate at a level above the WMI call. If a process running inside the container tried to allocate more than 1 GB of RAM, then it would fail.

 Remember that only Windows Server containers have access to all the host's compute power, where the container process is actually running on the host. On Windows Server 10, Docker uses Hyper-V containers so each container has a lightweight VM where the process is running. That VM has its own CPU and memory restrictions, so the container can use only what's available to the VM.

Running containers with restricted capabilities

There are two useful features of the Docker platform to restrict what applications can do inside containers. Currently, they work only for Linux containers, but they are worth understanding if you need to deal with mixed workloads, and support for Windows may be coming in future versions.

Linux containers can be run with the read-only flag, which creates the container with a read-only filesystem. The option can be used with any image, and it will start a container with the same entry process as usual. The difference is that the container does not have a writeable filesystem layer, so no files can be added or changed, the container cannot modify the contents of the image.

This is a useful security feature. A web application could have a vulnerability that allows attackers to execute code on the server, but a read-only container severely limits what the attacker can do. They cannot change app configuration files, alter access permissions, download new malware, or replace application binaries.

Read-only containers can be combined with Docker volumes, so applications can write to known locations for logging or caching data. If you have an application that writes to the filesytem, that's how you can run it in a read-only container without changing functionality. You need to be aware that if you write logs to a file in a volume and an attacker gained access to the filesystem, they could read historical logs which they can't do if logs are written to standard output and consumed by the Docker platform.

When you run Linux containers, you can also explicitly add or drop the system capabilities that are available to the container. You can start a container without the chown capability, so no process inside the container can change file access permissions. Similarly, you can restrict binding to network ports or write access to kernel logs.

The read-only, cap-add, and cap-drop options have no effect on Windows containers, but support may come in future versions of Docker on Windows.

 One great thing about Docker is that the free CE feeds into the supported EE. You can make feature requests and track bugs on GitHub in the moby/moby repository, which is the source code for Docker CE. When features are implemented in Docker CE, they become available in the subsequent EE release.

Isolation in Hyper-V containers

Docker on Windows has one big security feature that Docker on Linux does not have, extended isolation with Hyper-V containers. Containers running on Windows Server 2016 use the host's operating system kernel. You can see this when you run a container, and the process inside the container is listed on **Task Manager** on the host.

On Windows 10, the behavior is different. Windows 10 does not have the exact same kernel as Windows Server, so when you run Docker containers on Windows 10, each one is created with its own Windows Server kernel.

Containers with their own kernel are called **Hyper-V** containers. They are implemented with a lightweight virtual machine that provides the server kernel, but this is not a full VM and doesn't have the typical overhead of a VM. Hyper-V containers use normal Docker images and the normal Docker engine, they don't show in the Hyper-V management tool because they are not full virtual machines.

Hyper-V containers can also be run on Windows Server using the `isolation` option. This command runs the IIS image as a Hyper-V container, publishing port `80`:

```
docker container run -d -p 80 --isolation=hyperv microsoft/iis:nanoserver
```

The container behaves in the same way. External users can browse to port `80` on the host and the traffic is handled by the container. On the host, you can run `docker container inspect` to see the IP address and go to the container directly. Features such as Docker networking, volumes, and swarm mode work in the same way for Hyper-V containers.

The extended isolation of Hyper-V containers offers additional security. There is no shared kernel, so even if a kernel vulnerability allowed the container application to access the host, the host is just a thin VM layer running in its own kernel. There are no other processes or containers running on that kernel, so there is no ability for attackers to compromise other workloads.

Hyper-V containers have additional overheads because of the separate kernels. They typically have a slower start up time, and by default, they impose memory limits, restricting memory at the kernel level that the container can't exceed. In some scenarios, the trade-off is worthwhile. In multi-tenant situations where you assume zero trust for every workload, extended isolation can be a useful defense.

Licensing is different for Hyper-V containers. Normal Windows Server containers are licensed at the host level, so you need licenses for your servers, but then you can run as many containers as you like. Hyper-V containers each have their own kernel, and there are licensing levels that restrict the number of containers you can run on each host.

Securing applications with secure Docker images

I've covered many aspects of securing containers at runtime, but the Docker platform provides security in depth that starts before any containers are run. You start securing your application by securing the image that packages your application.

Building minimal images

It's unlikely that an attacker can compromise your application and gain access to the container, but you should build your image to mitigate the damage if that happened. Building a minimal image is key. The ideal Docker image should contain nothing more than the application and the dependencies it needs to run.

This is more difficult to achieve for Windows applications than Linux apps. A Docker image for a Linux app can use a minimal distribution as the base, packaging just the application binaries on top. The attack surface for that image is very small even if an attacker gained access to the container, they would find themselves in an operating system with very few features.

In contrast, Docker images using Windows Server Core have a fully featured operating system at the base. The minimal alternative is Nano Server, which has a significantly reduced API but still has PowerShell installed, which has a large feature set that could be exploited. In theory, you can remove features, disable Windows Services, and even delete Windows binaries in your Dockerfile in order to limit the capabilities of the final image. That's not a well-explored option at the moment.

Docker's recognition for experts and community leaders is the Captain's program. Docker Captains are like Microsoft MVPs, and Stefan Scherer is both a Captain and an MVP. Stefan has done some promising work by looking at reducing Windows image size by creating images with an empty filesystem and adding a minimal set of Windows binaries.

You can't easily limit the features of the base Windows image, but you can limit what you add on top. Wherever possible, you should add just your application content and the minimal application runtime so an attacker can't modify the app. Some programming languages have better support for this than others, for example, the following:

- Go applications can be compiled to native binaries, so you only need to package the executable in your Docker image, not the Go runtime.
- .NET Core apps can be published as assemblies, so you only need to package the .NET Core runtime to execute them, not the full .NET Core SDK.
- .NET Framework apps need the matching .NET Framework installed in the container image, but you can still minimize the app content that you package. You should compile the app in release mode and ensure you don't package debug files.
- Node.js uses V8 as an interpreter and compiler, so to run apps in Docker, the image needs to have the full Node.js runtime installed, and the full source code for the app needs to be packaged.

You will be limited by what your application stack supports, but a minimal image is the goal. If your application will run on Nano Server, it's definitely preferable to Windows Server Core. Full .NET apps don't run on Nano Server, but .NET Standard is advancing rapidly, so it could be a viable option to port your app to .NET Core, which can then run on Nano Server.

When you run your application in Docker, the unit you work with is the container, and you administer and monitor it using Docker. The underlying operating system doesn't affect how you interact with the container, so having a minimal OS doesn't limit what you can do with your application.

Docker Security Scanning

A minimal Docker image could still contain software with known vulnerabilities. Docker images use a standard, open format, which means tools can be reliably built to navigate and inspect image layers. One tool is Docker Security Scanning, which examines the software inside Docker images for vulnerabilities.

Docker Security Scanning looks at all the binary files in the image, in your application dependencies, the application framework, and even the operating system. Every binary is checked against multiple **Common Vulnerability and Exploit (CVE)** databases, looking for known vulnerabilities. If any issues are found, Docker reports the details.

Docker Security Scanning is available on Docker Hub for official repositories, on Docker Cloud for your private repositories, and on DTR for your own private registry. The web interface of those systems shows the output of each scan. Minimal images such as Alpine Linux can be completely free of vulnerabilities:

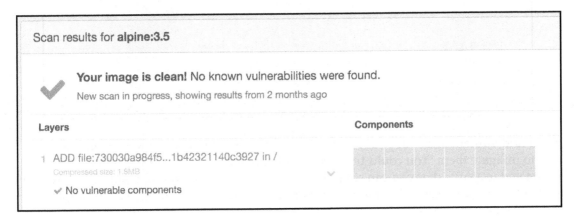

The official nats image has a Nano Server variant, and you can see that there is a vulnerability in that image:

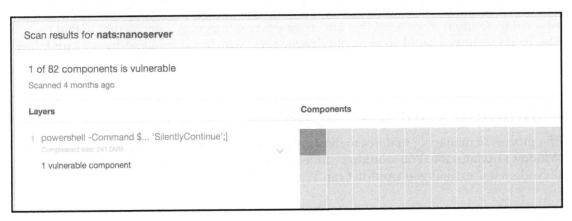

Where there are vulnerabilities, you can drill down to see exactly which binaries are flagged, and that links off to the CVE database, describing the vulnerability. In the case of the `nats:nanoserver` image, the vulnerability is in the version of SQLite that is packaged in the Nano Server base image:

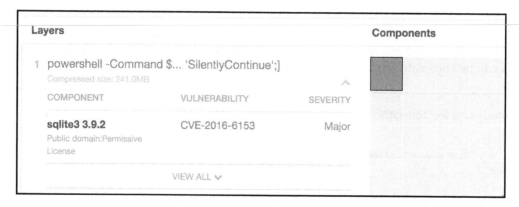

If you find vulnerabilities in your images, you can see exactly where they are and decide how to mitigate them. You could try removing the binaries altogether if you have an automated test suite that you can confidently use to verify that your app still works without them. Or, you may decide that there's no path to the vulnerable code from your application and leave the image as it is.

However you manage it, knowing that there are vulnerabilities in your application stack is extremely useful. Docker Security Scanning can work on each push, so you get immediate feedback if a new version introduces a vulnerability. It can also work on a schedule, so if a new vulnerability is discovered that affects an existing image, you get alerted to that too. This could identify a problem in an old dependency, which you could address by updating package versions in your Dockerfile.

Managing Windows updates

The process of managing updates to the application stack for your Docker image applies to Windows updates too. You wouldn't connect to a running container to update the version of Node.js it uses, and you wouldn't run Windows Update either.

Microsoft released a combined set of security patches and other hotfixes for Windows, typically on a monthly basis as a Windows update. At the same time, they published new versions of the Windows Server Core and Nano Server base images and any dependent images on Docker Hub. The version number in the image tag matches the version number of the Windows release.

It's a good practice to explicitly state the Windows version to use in the FROM instruction in your Dockerfile and use specific versions of any dependencies you install. This makes your Dockerfile deterministic any time you build it in future, you will get the same image as a result.

Specifying the Windows version also makes it clear how you manage Windows updates for your dockerized applications. The Dockerfile for an ASP.NET application may start like this:

```
FROM microsoft/aspnet:windowsservercore-10.0.14393.1066
```

This pins the image to Windows Server 2016 release 1066. With the release of the new base image, you update your application by changing the tag in the FROM instruction, in this case, to release 1198 and rebuilding your image:

```
FROM microsoft/aspnet:windowsservercore-10.0.14393.1198
```

I'll cover automated build and deployment in this chapter. With a good CI/CD pipeline, you can rebuild your images with a new Windows version and run all your tests to confirm that the update doesn't impact any features. Then, you can roll out the update to all your running applications, with no downtime, using docker stack deploy or docker service update, specifying the new versions of your application images. The whole process can be automated, so the IT Admin's pain on *Patch Tuesday* disappears with Docker.

Securing the software supply chain with DTR

DTR is the second part of Docker's extended EE offering (I covered **Universal Control Plane (UCP)** in Chapter 8, *Administering and Monitoring Dockerized Solutions*). DTR is a private Docker registry, which adds an important piece to the overall security story of the Docker platform: a secure software supply chain.

You can digitally sign Docker images with DTR, and DTR lets you configure who can push and pull images, securely storing all the digital signatures users have applied to an image. It also works in conjunction with UCP to enforce content trust. With Docker Content Trust, you can set up your cluster so it will only run containers from images that have been signed by specific users or teams.

This is a powerful feature that meets the audit requirements for a lot of regulated industries. There may be requirements for a company to prove that the software running in production is actually built from the code in the repository. This is very difficult to do without a software supply chain; you have to rely on manual processes and a document trail. With Docker, you can enforce it at the platform and meet the audit requirements with automated processes.

Repositories and users

DTR uses the same authentication model as UCP, so you can use either your **Active Directory** (**AD**) account to log in, or you can use an account created in UCP. But DTR has a separate authorization model. Users can have completely different access rights to image repositories in DTR and the services that are running from those images in UCP.

Some parts of the DTR authorization model are familiar to Docker Hub and Docker Cloud. Users can own public or private repositories, which are prefixed with their username. Administrators can create organizations, and organization repositories can set user access with a fine level of control.

I covered image registries and repositories in Chapter 4, *Pushing and Pulling Images from Docker Registries*. The full name for a repository contains the registry host, the owner, and the repository name. I've set up Docker Datacenter in Azure using the Azure Marketplace. In my DTR instance, I've created a user called **elton**. The user has one private repository that they can push and pull from:

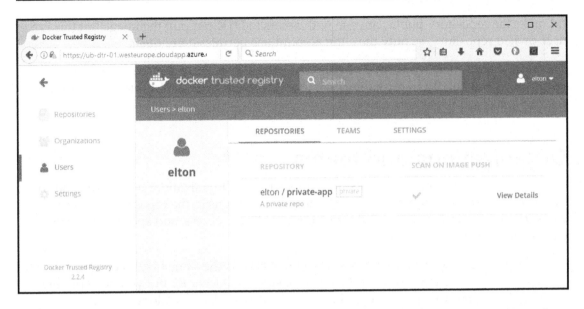

To push and pull the image in the repository called **private-app** for the user elton, I need to tag it with the full DTR domain in the repository name. My DTR instance is running at ub-dtr-01.westeurope.cloudapp.azure.com, so the full image name is ub-dtr-01.westeurope.cloudapp.azure.com/elton/private-app:

```
docker image tag microsoft/iis:nanoserver `
  ub-dtr-01.westeurope.cloudapp.azure.com/elton/private-app
```

This is a private repository, so it can be accessed only by the elton user. DTR presents the same API as any other Docker registry, so I log in with the docker login command, specifying the DTR domain as the registry address:

```
> docker login ub-dtr-01.westeurope.cloudapp.azure.com/elton/private-app
Username: elton
Password:
Login Succeeded

> docker image push ub-dtr-01.westeurope.cloudapp.azure.com/elton/private-app
The push refers to a repository [ub-dtr-01.westeurope.cloudapp.azure.com/elton/private-app]
. . .
```

If I make the repository public, anyone with access to DTR can pull the image but this is a user-owned repository, so only the elton account has permission to push.

This is the same as Docker Hub, where anyone can pull an image from my sixeyed user repositories, but only I can push them. For shared projects where multiple users need access to push images, you use organizations.

Organizations and teams

Organizations are for shared ownership of repositories. Organizations and the repositories they own are separate from the users who have permissions to the repositories, specific users may have admin access, others may have read-only access, and specific teams may have read-write access.

> The user and organization model of DTR is the same in Docker Cloud. If you don't need the full enterprise suite of Docker EE but you need private repositories with shared access, you can use Docker Cloud.

Here, I have an organization set up called **nerd-dinner**, which has repositories for all the images I've been using in the sample application so far. The organization represents a project with multiple components, and the members of the project team can have different access levels for each component:

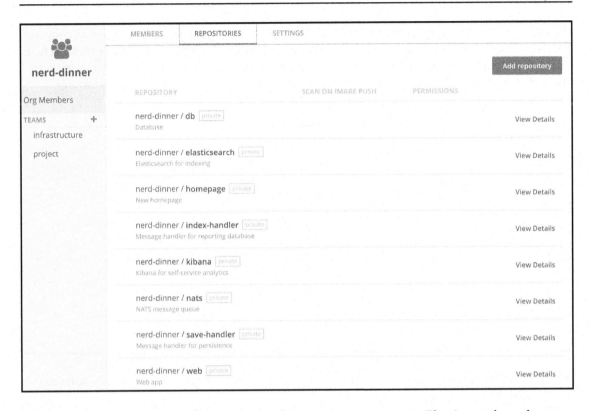

There are different types of images there. The nats message queue, Elasticsearch, and Kibana are infrastructure components, they're stock images that aren't modified for the NerdDinner project. They originally came from Docker Hub, but I have re-tagged them and pushed to DTR, which gives me the benefits of image signing, scanning, and content trust.

Access to the stock components is different from the custom application images, as they are managed by different groups of users. In the organization, I have two teams: **infrastructure** and **project**. In this scenario, members of the infrastructure team have read-write access to the nats, Elasticsearch, and Kibana images, so team members can pull and push image versions:

Members of the project team have only read-access to infrastructure repositories such as Elasticsearch:

This means shared components can be managed by a dedicated team, and an update to nats or Elasticsearch has to be approved by an infrastructure team member. NerdDinner project members have read access, so they can always pull the latest infrastructure images and run the full application, but they can't push updates.

Conversely, the project team members have read-write access to the web application image, where the infrastructure team has only read access. This means only members of the project team can push app updates, but members of the infrastructure team can pull them, so they could run the whole stack if they needed to test a new version of nats.

DTR has permission levels of none, read, read-write, and admin. They can be applied at the repository level to teams or individual users. The consistent authentication but separate authorization models of DTR and UCP mean a developer can have full access to pull and push images in DTR but may have only read access to view running containers in UCP.

Image Signing and Content Trust

DTR also makes use of the client certificates managed by UCP to sign images with a digital signature that can be tracked to a known user account. Users download a client bundle from UCP, which contains a public and private key for their client certificate, which is used by the Docker command-line.

You can switch Docker Content Trust on with an environment variable, and when you push images to a registry, Docker will sign them using the key from your client bundle. Content trust will work only for specific image tags and not the default `latest` tag, as the signatures are stored against the tag.

I can add the `vNext` tag to my image, enable content trust in the PowerShell session, and push the tagged image to DTR:

```
> docker image tag ub-dtr-01.westeurope.cloudapp.azure.com/nerd-
dinner/index-handler `
                  ub-dtr-01.westeurope.cloudapp.azure.com/nerd-
dinner/index-handler:vNext

> $env:DOCKER_CONTENT_TRUST=1

> docker image push ub-dtr-01.westeurope.cloudapp.azure.com/nerd-
dinner/index-handler:vNext
```

The act of pushing the image adds the digital signature, in this case, using the certificate for the elton account. DTR records the signatures for each image tag, and users can push images to add their own signature. This enables an approval pipeline, where authorized users pull an image, run whatever tests they need to, and then push it again to confirm their approval.

 DTR uses Notary to manage access keys and signatures. Like SwarmKit and LinuxKit, Notary is an open source project that Docker integrates into a commercial product, adding features and providing support. To see image signing and content trust in action, check out my Pluralsight course *Getting Started with Docker Datacenter*.

UCP integrates with DTR to verify image signatures. In the Admin Setting, you can configure UCP so it will run containers from only those images that have been signed by a known group of users:

I've configured Docker Content Trust so UCP will only run containers that have been signed by members of the Sys Admins, UAT, and release managers teams. This explicitly captures the release approval workflow, and the platform enforces it. Not even administrators can run containers from images that have not been signed by users from the required set of teams.

Golden images

One final security consideration for images and registries is the source of the base images used for application images. Companies running Docker in production typically restrict the base images developers can use to a set that has been approved by infrastructure or security stakeholders. This set of Golden images available to use may just be captured in documentation, but it is easier to enforce with a private registry.

Golden images in a Windows environment may be limited to two options: a version of Windows Server Core and a version of Nano Server. Instead of allowing users to use the public Microsoft images, the Ops team may build custom images from Microsoft's base images. The custom images may add security or performance tweaks or set some defaults that apply to all applications, such as packaging the company's Certificate Authority certs.

Using DTR, you can create an organization called **base-images**, where the Ops team has read-write access to the repositories, while all other users have read access. Checking that images are using a valid base just means checking that the Dockerfile is using an image from the base-images organization, which is an easy test to automate in your CI/CD process.

This feature may soon be available in Docker EE. Docker demonstrated a new policy engine at DockerCon that works across UCP and DTR. A policy could state that images need to have zero security vulnerabilities. The engine would then automatically promote images from a testing repository to a production repository if they met the policy and then deploy an update to a running service. As this functionality matures, policies may be configurable to include checks on the source image.

 DockerCon is the container conference organized by Docker. It runs in America and Europe every year and is packed with workshops and sessions ranging from black-belt Docker internals to production use cases from global enterprises. The Docker ecosystem is out in force at DockerCon too, and it's one of the most educational, fun, and inspiring conferences you can go to.

Understanding security in swarm mode

Docker's security-in-depth approach covers the whole software life cycle, from image signing and scanning at build time through to container isolation and management at runtime. I'll end this chapter with an overview of the security features implemented in swarm mode.

Distributed software offers a lot of attractive attack vectors. Communication between components can be intercepted and modified. Rogue agents can join the network and gain access to data or run workloads. Distributed data stores can be compromised. Docker swarm mode, built on top of the open source SwarmKit project, addresses these vectors at a platform level so your application is running on a secure base by default.

Nodes and join tokens

You switch to swarm mode by running `docker swarm init`. The output of this command gives you a token to use for other nodes to join the swarm. There are separate tokens for workers and managers. Nodes cannot join a swarm without the token, so you need to keep the token protected like any other secret.

 The join tokens are comprised of the prefix, the format version, the hash of the root key, and a cryptographically strong random string.

Docker uses a fixed `SWMTKN` prefix for tokens, so you can run automated checks to see whether a token has been accidentally shared in the source code or on another public location. If the token is compromised, rogue nodes could join the swarm if they had access to your network. Swarm mode can use a specific network for node traffic, so you should use a network that is not publicly accessible.

Join tokens can be rotated with the `join-token rotate` command, which can target either the worker token or the manager token:

```
> docker swarm join-token --rotate worker
Successfully rotated worker join token.

To add a worker to this swarm, run the following command:

    docker swarm join --token SWMTKN-1-0ngmvmnpz0twctlya5ifu3ajy3pv8420st...
10.211.55.7:2377
```

Token rotation is a fully managed operation by the swarm, existing nodes are all updated, and any error conditions, such as nodes going offline or joining mid-rotation are gracefully handled.

Encryption and secrets

Communication between swarm nodes is encrypted using **Transport Layer Security (TLS)**. The swarm manager configures itself as a certification authority when you create the swarm, and the manager generates certificates for each node when they join. Communication between nodes in the swarm is encrypted using mutual TLS.

Mutual TLS means that the nodes can securely communicate and trust each other, as every node has a trusted certificate to identify itself. Nodes are assigned a random ID that is used in the certificate, so the swarm doesn't rely on attributes such as the hostname, which could potentially be faked.

Trusted communication between nodes is the foundation for Docker Secrets in swarm mode. Secrets are stored and encrypted in the Raft log on the managers, and a secret is sent to the worker only if that worker is going to run a container that uses the secret. The secret is always encrypted in transit, using mutual TLS. On the worker node, the secret is made available in plain text on a temporary RAM drive that is surfaced to the container as a volume mount. The data is never persisted in plain text.

 Windows doesn't have a native RAM drive, so the secrets implementation currently stores the secret data on the disk on the worker nodes, with the recommendation that BitLocker is used for the system drive. This limitation will be addressed in a future release of Docker, which will store secrets in a RAM drive on Windows too.

Inside the container, access to secret files is restricted to certain user accounts. The accounts with access can be specified in Linux, but in Windows, there's currently a fixed list. I use secrets in the ASP.NET web application in Chapter 7, *Orchestrating Distributed Solutions with Docker Swarm* and you can see there that I configure the IIS application pool to use an account with access.

When containers are stopped, paused, or removed, the secrets that were available to the container are removed from the host. On Windows, where secrets are currently persisted to disk, if the host is forcefully shut down, then secrets are removed when the host restarts.

Node labels and external access

Once a node has been added to a swarm, it is a candidate for container workloads to be scheduled. Many production deployments will use constraints to ensure applications run on the correct type of node, Docker will try to match the requested constraints to labels on the nodes.

In a regulated environment, you may have requirements to ensure applications run only on those servers that have met required audit levels, such as PCI compliance for credit card processing. You can identify compliant nodes with labels and use constraints to ensure the applications run only on those nodes. Swarm mode helps ensure that these constraints are properly enforced.

There are two types of labels in swarm mode. Engine labels are set by the machine, in the Docker service configuration, so if a worker was compromised, an attacker could add labels and make a restricted machine appear to be compliant. Node labels are set by the swarm, so they can only be created by a user with access to a swarm manager. Node labels mean you don't have to rely on claims made by individual nodes, so if they are compromised, the impact can be limited.

Node labels are also useful in segregating access to applications. You may have Docker hosts that are accessible only on your internal network and others that have access to the public internet. With labels, you can explicitly record that it is a distinction and run containers with constraints based on the labels. You could have a content management system in a container that is only available internally but a web proxy that is available publicly.

Summary

This chapter looked at the security considerations of Docker and Windows containers. You learned that the Docker platform is built for security in depth, and the runtime security of containers is only one part of the story. Security scanning, image signing, content trust, and secure distributed communication combine to give you a secure software supply chain.

You looked at the practical security aspects of running apps in Docker and learned how processes in Windows container run in a context that makes it difficult for attackers to escape from containers and invade other processes. Container processes will use all the compute resources they need, but I also demonstrated how to limit CPU and memory usage, which can prevent rogue containers starving the host's compute resources.

In a dockerized application, you have much more scope to enforce security in depth. I explained why minimal images help keep applications safe and how you can use Docker Security Scanning to be alerted if there are vulnerabilities in any of the dependencies your application uses. You can enforce good practices by digitally signing images and configuring Docker, so it will run containers only from images that have been signed by approved users.

Lastly, I looked at the security implementation in the Docker swarm mode. Swarm mode has the most in-depth security of all the orchestration layers, and it provides a solid foundation for you to run your apps securely. Using secrets to store sensitive application data and node labels to identify host compliance makes it very easy for you to run a secure solution.

In the next chapter, we'll work with a distributed application and look at building a pipeline for CI/CD. The Docker service can be configured to provide remote access to the API, so it's easy to integrate Docker deployments with any build system. The CI server can even run inside a Docker container and you can use Docker for the build agents, so you don't need any complex configuration for CI/CD.

10

Powering a Continuous Deployment Pipeline with Docker

Docker supports building and running software in components that can be easily distributed and managed. The platform also lends itself to development environments, where source control, build servers, build agents, and test agents can all be run in Docker containers from standard images.

Using Docker for development lets you consolidate many projects onto a single set of hardware while maintaining isolation. You could have services for Git and the image registry, running in highly available configurations in a Docker swarm, shared by many projects. Each project could have a dedicated build server configured with their own pipeline and their own build setup, running in a lightweight Docker container.

Setting up a new project in this environment is simply a case of creating a source control repository and a registry account and running new containers for the build process. These steps can all be automated, so project on-boarding becomes a simple process that takes minutes and uses existing hardware.

In this chapter, I'll walk you through the setup of a **continuous integration and continuous delivery (CI/CD)** pipeline using Docker, including the following:

- Running shared services, such as a Git server and an automation server in Docker containers
- Using multi-stage builds to compile and package .NET applications without MSBuild or Visual Studio

- End-to-end testing of distributed solutions, with the application and the test agents running in containers
- Publishing to local and external Docker Registries and deploying to a remote Docker swarm

Designing CI/CD with Docker

The pipeline will support full continuous integration—when developers push code to the shared source repository, which will trigger a build that produces a release candidate. The release candidates will be tagged Docker images stored in a local registry. The CI workflow deploys the solution from the built images as containers and runs an end-to-end test pack.

My sample pipeline has a manual quality gate. If the tests pass, the image versions are made publicly available on Docker Hub, and the pipeline can start a rolling upgrade in the public QA environment.

The stages of the pipeline will all be powered by software running in Docker containers:

- **Source control**: Bonobo, a simple open source Git server written in ASP.NET
- **Build server**: Jenkins, a Java-based automation tool using plugins to support many workflows
- **Build agent**: MSBuild packaged into a Docker image to compile code in a container
- **Test agent**: NUnit packaged into a Docker image to run integration or end-to-end tests against deployed code

Bonobo and Jenkins can run in long-running containers on a Docker swarm or an individual Docker host. The build and test agents are task containers that will be run by Jenkins to perform the pipeline steps and then end. The release candidate will be deployed as a set of containers that are removed when the tests are completed.

The only requirement to set this up is to have remote access to the Docker API—both in the development and QA environments. I covered remote API access in Chapter 1, *Getting Started with Docker on Windows*, using the `stefanscherer/dockertls-windows` image to generate certificates so the API is secured. You need to have remote access configured so the Jenkins container can create containers in development and start the rolling upgrade in QA.

The workflow for this pipeline starts when a developer pushes code to the Git server, which is running Bonobo in a Docker container. Jenkins is configured to poll the Bonobo repository, and it will start a build if there are any changes. All the custom components in the solution use multi-stage Dockerfiles, which are stored in the Git repository for the project. Jenkins runs `docker image build` commands for each Dockerfile, building the image on the Docker host where Jenkins itself is running as a container.

When the builds complete, Jenkins deploys the solution locally as containers on the same Docker host. Then, it runs end-to-end tests, which are packaged in a Docker image and run as a container in the same Docker network as the solution under test. If all the tests pass, then the final pipeline step pushes these images as release candidates to the local registry, also running in a Docker container.

When you run your development tools in Docker, you get the same benefits as when you run production workloads in Docker. The whole tool chain becomes portable, and you can run it wherever you like with minimal compute requirements.

Running shared development services in Docker

Services such as source control and the image registry are good candidates to be shared between many projects. They have similar requirements for high availability and reliable storage, so they can be deployed across a cluster that has enough capacity for many projects. The CI server can be run as a shared service or as a separate instance for each team or project.

I covered running a private registry in a Docker container in `Chapter 4`, *Pushing and Pulling Images from Docker Registries*. Here, I'll look at running a Git server and a CI server in Docker.

Packaging a Git server into a Windows Docker image

Bonobo is a popular open source Git server. It's written in ASP.NET using the full .NET Framework, and you can easily package it as a Docker image based on Windows Server Core. Bonobo is a simple Git server; it provides remote repository access over HTTP and HTTPS, and it has a web UI. It supports integrated Windows authentication, but I won't cover that here.

Windows containers are not domain-joined, but you can make use of Windows authentication in Docker containers. You need to create a **group Managed Service Account (gMSA)** in Active Directory and give the Docker host access to the gMSA. Then, you run containers with an additional security option, and any processes in the container running as the Local System or Network Service account will actually use the gMSA.

Packaging Bonobo in a Docker image is straightforward. It's a full .NET Framework application, so my Docker image is based on `microsoft/aspnet:windowsservercore`. There are no additional dependencies to install. In the Dockerfile for `dockeronwindows/ch10-bonobo`, I download the packaged ZIP file, expand it, and remove the ZIP file using the normal pattern (with the set the Bonobo version as an environment variable):

```
RUN Invoke-WebRequest
"https://bonobogitserver.com/resources/releases/$($env:BONOBO_VERSION).zip"
`

    -OutFile 'bonobo.zip' -UseBasicParsing; `
    Expand-Archive bonobo.zip; `
    Remove-Item bonobo.zip
```

Inside the ZIP file is the `Web.config` file for the app, which is set with the default configuration values. The default values save the state to the local `C` drive, which I want to change so I can store the repository database and the repository content in a Docker volume. You can change the settings in the UI, but I want a fully configured Docker image so that in my Dockerfile, I update the values in `Web.config`.

This is a useful approach when you want to change a subset of configuration values in a packaged application, but you don't want to maintain a separate config file. Copying my own config file over the packaged one would be easier initially, but I would need to keep my copy up to date with every new version of the application. By overwriting specific values, I can leave the rest of the defaults in place. I read the config file as XML in a PowerShell using `RUN` instruction and update the element values:

```
RUN $file = $env:BONOBO_PATH + '\Web.config'; `
    [xml]$config = Get-Content $file; `
    $repo = $config.configuration.appSettings.add | where {$_.key -eq
'DefaultRepositoriesDirectory'}; `
    $repo.value = 'G:\repositories'; `
    $db = $config.configuration.connectionStrings.add | where {$_.name -eq
'BonoboGitServerContext'}; `
    $db.connectionString = 'Data
Source=G:\Bonobo.Git.Server.db;BinaryGUID=False;'; `
    $config.Save($file)
```

I set the database file path and the repositories directory to use the G drive. There is no G drive in the container, but this is a neat way of getting around any problems with **symbolic link (symlink)**.

Docker volumes are exposed in the container as a symlink directory, with a value like `\\?\ContainerMappedDirectories\01BA2580-95DA-48B9-94F2-B397D00CD0A1`. If applications try to resolve this path (which actually points to a location on the host), the resolution can fail. The workaround is to create the Docker volume and then map the volume location as a drive letter with a registry entry:

```
ENV DATA_PATH="C:\data"
VOLUME C:\data
RUN Set-ItemProperty -Path 'HKLM:\SYSTEM\CurrentControlSet\Control\Session
Manager\DOS Devices' `
    -Name 'G:' -Value "\??\$($env:DATA_PATH)" -Type String
```

The G drive mapping isn't a symlink, so the application writes to it without resolving the path. The Windows filesystem uses `C:\data` instead of G, and the filesystem calls work correctly with symlink directories. Bonobo will write data to directories on the G drive, which is actually a Docker volume stored on the host.

One final piece of setup work is needed. Bonobo writes temporary files to the `App_Data` folder, as many ASP.NET apps do. The Dockerfile commands execute as the container administrator account, so that account will be the owner of the `App_Data` directory when it is created from the ZIP file. Bonobo runs as a website in **Internet Information Services (IIS)**, so the IIS user account needs to be given permission to write to that folder. I do this with a simple PowerShell script called `Set-OwnerAcl.ps1` to set the **access control list (ACL)**:

```
$acl = Get-Acl $path; `
$newOwner = [System.Security.Principal.NTAccount]($owner); `
$acl.SetOwner($newOwner); `
Set-Acl -Path $path -AclObject $acl; `
Get-ChildItem -Path $path -Recurse | Set-Acl -AclObject $acl
```

In the Dockerfile, I call that script to set the IIS user group as the owner of `App_Data`:

```
RUN $path = $env:BONOBO_PATH + '\App_Data'; `
    .\Set-OwnerAcl.ps1 -Path $path -Owner 'BUILTIN\IIS_IUSRS'
```

Building this image gives me a Git server that I can run in a Windows container.

Running the Bonobo Git server in Docker

Run Bonobo just like any other detached container, mapping the HTTP port and using a host mount to store the data outside of the container:

```
docker run -d -p 80:80 `
  -v C:\bonobo:C:\data `
  dockeronwindows/ch10-bonobo
```

Browse /Bonobo.Git.Server in the container's IP address (or the Docker host's IP address if you're accessing externally), and you'll see the logon page. The default username is admin and the password is admin, which will take you to the home page:

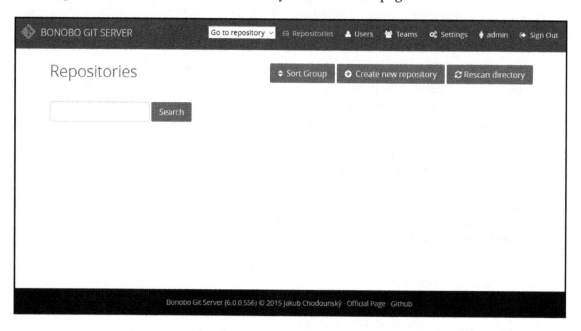

Your first step should be to create a new user account with a secure password, log in as that user, and delete the default admin account. Then, you can customize Bonobo in the settings page and create repositories. Bonobo stores all repositories at the root level, but you can assign a group tag to a repository, which is used to arrange repositories in the home display:

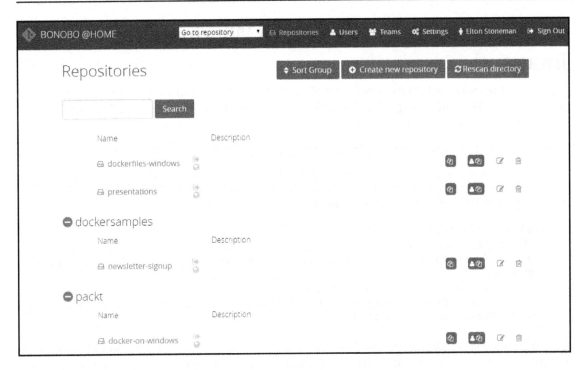

Now you can use Bonobo running in your Docker container just like any other remote Git server—such as GitHub or GitLab. The Windows server address on my home network is 192.168.2.160, so I can add Bonobo as a remote to my Git repository like this:

```
git remote add bonobo
http://192.168.2.160/Bonobo.Git.Server/docker-on-windows.git
```

And then, we can use `git push bonobo` and `git pull bonobo` to work with the remote repository. Bonobo is stable and lightweight when running in a Docker container. My instance typically uses 200 MB of memory and less than 1% CPU at idle.

> Running a local Git server is a good idea even if you use a hosted service such as GitHub or GitLab. Hosted services have outages, and although rare, they can have a significant impact. Having a local secondary running with very little cost can protect you from being impacted when the next outage occurs.

The next step is to run a CI server in Docker.

Packaging a CI server into a Windows Docker image

Jenkins is a popular automation server that is used for CI/CD and that supports custom workflows with multiple trigger types. It's a Java application that's straightforward to package in Docker—although it's not so simple to fully automate the Jenkins setup.

In the source code for this chapter, I have a Dockerfile for the image `dockersamples/ch10-jenkins-base`. This Dockerfile packages a clean installation of Jenkins, using the official OpenJDK image as the base and downloading the Jenkins web archive (using environment variables for the Jenkins version and SHA hash):

```
WORKDIR C:\jenkins
RUN Invoke-WebRequest
"https://repo.jenkins-ci.org/.../$($env:JENKINS_VERSION)/jenkins-war-$($env
:JENKINS_VERSION).war" `
 -OutFile 'jenkins.war' -UseBasicParsing; `
 if ((Get-FileHash jenkins.war -Algorithm sha256).Hash.ToLower() -ne
$env:JENKINS_SHA256) {exit 1}
```

Like the Bonobo image, I create a Docker volume at `C:\data` and use the Windows registry setting to map that path to the `G` drive. Jenkins is simple to configure when it comes to the main storage location; you just set the value of the `JENKINS_HOME` environment variable in the Dockerfile:

```
ENV JENKINS_HOME="G:\jenkins"
```

A clean Jenkins installation doesn't have many useful features; almost all functionality is provided by plugins that you install after Jenkins is set up. Some of these plugins also install the dependencies they need, but others don't. For my CI/CD pipeline, I need a Git client in Jenkins, so it can connect to the Git server running in Bonobo, and I also want the Docker CLI so I can use Docker commands in my builds.

I can install these dependencies in the Jenkins Dockerfile, but that would make it large and difficult to manage. Instead, I can split these tools into their own Docker images and combine them using multi-stage builds. The `dockeronwindows/ch10-git` packages the Git client into a Windows Docker image, and `dockeronwindows/ch10-docker` packages the Docker and Docker Compose clients into a second image.

I can use both of these, along with the Jenkins base image, to build my final Jenkins image. The Dockerfile for `dockeronwindows/ch10-jenkins` starts with multiple FROM instructions:

```
FROM dockeronwindows/ch10-git AS git
FROM dockeronwindows/ch10-docker AS docker
FROM dockeronwindows/ch10-jenkins-base
```

To add the Git client to the final Jenkins image, I set up a directory, add it to the path, and then copy the content from the Git image:

```
RUN New-Item -Type Directory 'C:\git'; `
    $env:PATH = 'C:\git\cmd;C:\git\mingw64\bin;C:\git\usr\bin;' +
$env:PATH; `
    [Environment]::SetEnvironmentVariable('PATH', $env:PATH,
[EnvironmentVariableTarget]::Machine)

COPY --from=git C:\git C:\git
```

The process is the same for the Docker command-line tools, copied from the Docker image into the Jenkins image:

```
RUN New-Item -Type Directory 'C:\docker'; `
  $env:PATH = 'C:\docker;' + $env:PATH; `
  [Environment]::SetEnvironmentVariable('PATH', $env:PATH,
[EnvironmentVariableTarget]::Machine)

COPY --from=docker C:\docker\docker.exe C:\docker
COPY --from=docker C:\docker\docker-compose.exe C:\docker
```

Using different Dockerfiles for the dependencies gives me a final Docker image with all the components I need but with a manageable Dockerfile and a set of reusable source images. Now I can run Jenkins in a container and finish the setup by installing plugins.

Running the Jenkins automation server in Docker

Jenkins uses port 8080 for the Web UI, so you can run it from the sample image using this command—which maps the port and mounts a local folder for the Jenkins root directory:

```
docker run -d -p 8080:8080 -v C:\jenkins:C:\data --name jenkins
dockeronwindows/ch10-jenkins
```

Before you browse to the web interface, check the logs of your Jenkins container to find the administrator password that Jenkins generates for each new deployment:

```
> docker logs jenkins
...
**************************************************************
Jenkins initial setup is required. An admin user has been created and a
password generated.
Please use the following password to proceed to installation:
969fe9f8b2894d75b5950e267564fcf2
This may also be found at: G:\jenkins\secrets\initialAdminPassword
**************************************************************
```

Now you can browse to port 8080 on the container IP address or the Docker host's IP address; enter the generated password and add the Jenkins plugins you need. As a bare minimum example, I've chosen to customize the plugin installation and chosen only **Folders Plugin** and **Git plugin** from the recommended options:

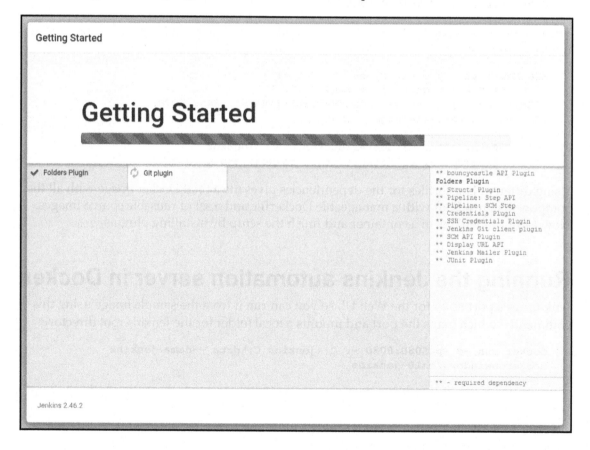

I need one more plugin to run PowerShell scripts in build jobs. This isn't a recommended plugin, so once Jenkins starts, I go to *Manage Jenkins...Manage Plugins*, and from the **Available** list, I choose **PowerShell plugin** and click on **Install without restart**:

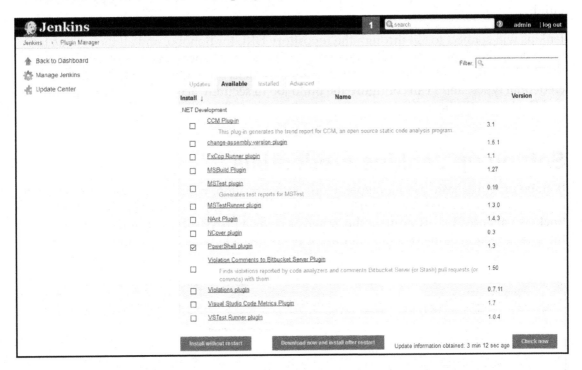

You can automate the plugin installation with Jenkins, but it requires an additional download and some scripting of the Jenkins API. Plugin dependencies are not always resolved when you install that way, so it can be safer to manually set up the plugins and your user accounts and then export the container to a custom image with docker container commit.

When this is complete, I have all the infrastructure services I need to run my CI/CD pipeline.

For my setup, I use a Docker Compose file to configure Jenkins, Bonobo, and the Docker Registry on my server rather than running individual containers. This isn't a distributed solution where the containers access each other directly, but these services all have the same SLA, so defining them in a compose file lets me capture that and start all the services together.

Configuring CI/CD using Jenkins in Docker

I'll configure my build to poll a Git repository and use Git pushes as the trigger for a new build.

Jenkins will connect to Git through the repository URL for Bonobo, and all the actions to build, test, and deploy the solution will run as Docker containers. The Bonobo server and the Docker engine have different authentication models, but Jenkins supports many credential types, and I can configure the build job to securely access the source repository and Docker on the host.

Setting up Jenkins credentials

Bonobo provides basic username/password authentication, which I'm using in my setup. In a business environment, I would use HTTPS for Bonobo, either by packaging a **Secure Sockets Layer (SSL)** certificate in the image or using a proxy server in front of Bonobo. In the Users section of the Bonobo interface, I've created a Jenkins CI user and given it read access to the docker-on-windows Git repository, which I'll use for my sample CI/CD job:

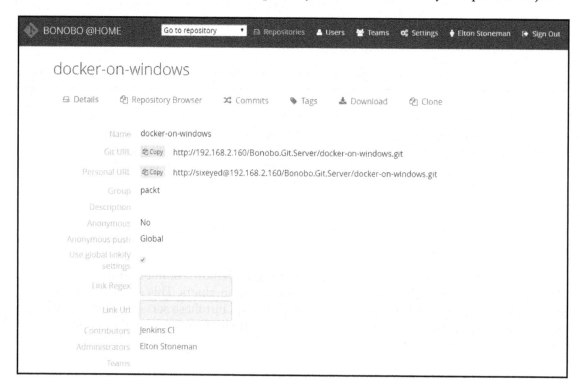

I've added the username and password to Jenkins as global credentials:

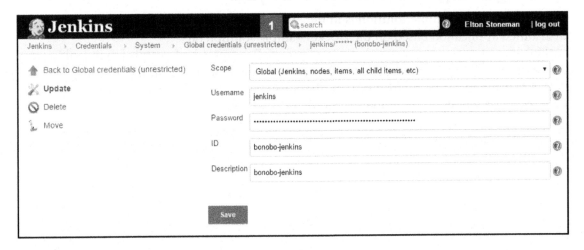

Jenkins doesn't display the password once entered, and it records an audit trail for all the jobs that use the credential, so this is a secure way of authenticating.

To authenticate with Docker, I'll use the **Transport Layer Security** (**TLS**) certificates I generated when securing the Docker engine. There are three certificates—the **Certificate Authority** (**CA**), the server certificate, and the key. They need to be passed to the Docker CLI as file paths, and Jenkins supports this with credentials that can be saved as secret files. I've uploaded the PEM files containing the certificates as global credentials, so my Jenkins instance has credentials for Git and Docker:

Configuring the Jenkins CI job

In this chapter, the sample solution is in the `ch10-newsletter` folder. It's a simple distributed application based on the Docker sample solution on GitHub—`dockersamples/newsletter-signup`. I've created a freestyle job in Jenkins to run the build and configured Git for source code management. It's simple to configure Git—I'm using the same repository URL that I use for the Git repository on my laptop, and I've selected the Bonobo credentials for Jenkins to access:

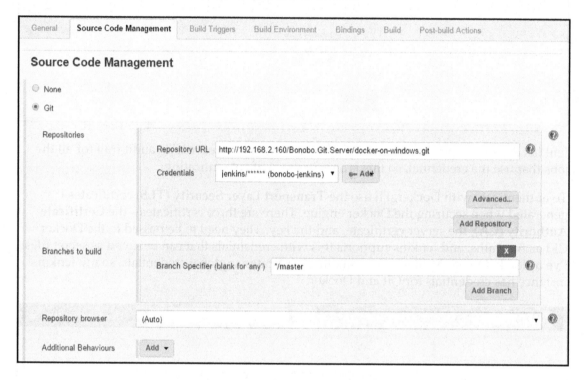

Jenkins is running in a Docker container, and Bonobo is running in a container on the same Docker network. I could use the container name instead of the host IP address and Docker would resolve the service. But that would restrict me to running the containers in the same Docker network, and it also means I'm using different repository URLs on the CI server and the client, so it's preferable to use the full URL.

Jenkins supports multiple types of build triggers. In this case, I'm going to poll the Git server on a set schedule. I'm using `H/5 * * * *` as the schedule frequency, which means Jenkins will check the Bonobo repository every five minutes. If there are any new commits since the last build, Jenkins will run the job.

I need to give the job explicit access to the secret files where the Docker TLS certificates are stored in Jenkins. On the **Build Environment** page, I specify that secret files are to be made available, and then for each certificate file, I create a binding, selecting the certificate file and giving it a variable name:

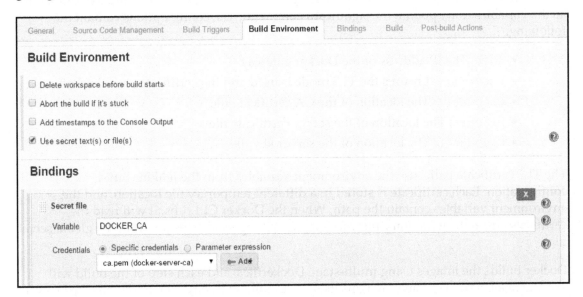

The certificates are surfaced to the job steps as temporary files, and the variable name contains the path to the temporary file. In this example, the DOCKER_CA environment variable contains the path to the CA certificate for the Docker engine. That's all the job configuration I need, and all the build steps will now run using Docker containers.

Building the solution using Docker Compose in Jenkins

All the build steps will use PowerShell, running as simple scripts so there's no dependency on more complex Jenkins plugins. There are plugins specific to Docker that wrap up several tasks, such as building images and pushing them to a registry, but I can do everything I need with basic PowerShell steps. The first step builds the solution using Docker Compose:

```
cd source\ch10\ch10-newsletter

$config = '--host', 'tcp://192.168.160.1:2376', '--tlsverify', `
  '--tlscacert', $env:DOCKER_CA,'--tlscert', $env:DOCKER_CERT, '--tlskey', `
$env:DOCKER_KEY
```

```
& docker-compose $config `
 -f .\app\docker-compose.yml -f .\app\docker-compose.build.yml build
```

There are several configuration settings needed to connect securely to the remote Docker engine. I capture them in a PowerShell array and pass it to the Docker Compose command, so the variables don't pollute the significant command. The config options contain the following:

- `host`: The IP address of the Docker gateway
- `tlsverify`: Ensures the TLS mode is used and the certificates are checked
- `tlscacert`: The location of the CA certificate file
- `tlscert`: The location of the server certificate file
- `tlscacert`: The location of the server key file

The TLS certificate paths use the environment variables from the Jenkins build configuration. Each certificate is stored in a different temporary file location, and the environment variables contain the path. When the Docker CLI runs, it will read the certificates from the temporary files, which Jenkins copies into the job from the global secret files.

Docker builds the images using multi-stage Dockerfiles, and each step of the build will execute in a Docker container. Jenkins itself is running in a container, and it has the Docker and Docker Compose CLIs available in the image. To connect the CLI inside the container to the Docker engine running on the host, I need to pass the host's address—but this is not the external IP address of the host.

My server runs on `192.168.2.160`, but inside the container, Docker can't access that address. Instead, you need to use the gateway address, which is how the container resolves access to the host. There are two ways to find the gateway address. On the host, you can get the IP address of the `vEthernet` adapter using PowerShell:

```
> Get-NetIPAddress | `
 Where {$_.InterfaceAlias -Like 'vEthernet*' -and $_.AddressFamily -eq
'IPv4'} | `
 Select IPAddress

IPAddress
---------
192.168.160.1
```

Or, you can get the default gateway from the container using `Get-NetRoute`:

```
> docker exec -it jenkins powershell "Get-NetRoute -DestinationPrefix
'0.0.0.0/0' | Select NextHop"

NextHop
-------
192.168.160.1
```

Both values should be the same, in my case, it's `192.168.160.1`. This is the address that is used for the Docker host.

I'm using Docker Compose for the build, so I can build every component with a single command. I use overrides in Docker Compose (which I covered in `Chapter 6`, *Organizing Distributed Solutions with Docker Compose*) to separate the concerns. The basic `docker-compose.yml` file specifies the services and their configuration. This describes the solution architecture that is applicable for every environment. I also have an override file called `docker-compose.build.yml`, which adds the build configuration for my images:

```
version: '3.3'
services:

  signup-app:
    build:
      context: ../
      dockerfile: ./docker/web/Dockerfile

  signup-save-handler:
    build:
      context: ../
      dockerfile: ./docker/save-handler/Dockerfile

  signup-index-handler:
    build:
      context: ../
      dockerfile: ./docker/index-handler/Dockerfile
```

Each of these Dockerfiles contains a multi-stage build, where the first stage compiles the application in a container using MSBuild, and the second stage copies the compiled application into the final Docker image.

Multi-stage builds in CI pipelines

When I configured Jenkins, I didn't add any build agents; there's no MSBuild, NuGet, or Visual Studio components in the Jenkins Docker container. Everything needed to build the application is configured in Docker. This is how the Dockerfile starts for the `dockeronwindows/ch10-newsletter-save-handler` image, which is a simple .NET console app:

```
# escape=`
FROM sixeyed/msbuild:netfx-4.5.2 AS builder

WORKDIR C:\src\SignUp.MessageHandlers.SaveProspect
COPY src\SignUp\SignUp.MessageHandlers.SaveProspect\packages.config .
RUN nuget restore packages.config –PackagesDirectory ..\packages

COPY src\SignUp C:\src
RUN msbuild SignUp.MessageHandlers.SaveProspect.csproj `
    /p:OutputPath=c:\out\save-prospect\SaveProspectHandler
```

This is the first stage of the build. It uses `sixeyed/msbuild` as the `FROM` image, and it gives this stage the name `builder`. The base image is a public image on Docker Hub, which packages MSBuild with the .NET Framework 4.5.2 Developer Pack and NuGet. This image has all the requirements to build .NET Framework apps in a Docker container.

In the Dockerfile, I use NuGet first—copying in the package configuration and running `nuget restore` (the base image sets up all the paths for the command-line tools). Then, I copy in the rest of the source code and run `msbuild` to compile the project.

I split the NuGet part from the MSBuild part so I can take advantage of Docker's image layer caching. Restoring packages from NuGet can be time consuming, so I don't want to do that for every build. By copying just the `packages.config` file and running `nuget restore`, I'm building image layers that will be cached until the `packages.config` file changes. Unless I change the package configuration in the project, the layers containing the restored NuGet packages will be used from the cache.

The MSBuild layers will also be cached unless any of the source code files change. You can run the build repeatedly, and if there are no code changes, it will finish in seconds. Fast builds are especially important in a CI process, where many developers can be pushing changes. You want the build process to do as little work as possible in order to generate the latest artifacts in the shortest time and the Docker image layer cache makes it easy to do that.

The Dockerfile for the image continues, with another `FROM` instruction delineating a new stage in the build. This is the final stage, so this will be my application image:

```
FROM microsoft/windowsservercore
SHELL ["powershell", "-Command", "$ErrorActionPreference = 'Stop';"]

RUN Set-ItemProperty -path
'HKLM:\SYSTEM\CurrentControlSet\Services\Dnscache\Parameters' -Name
ServerPriorityTimeLimit -Value 0 -Type DWord

WORKDIR /save-prospect-handler
CMD .\SignUp.MessageHandlers.SaveProspect.exe

ENV MESSAGE_QUEUE_URL="nats://message-queue:4222" `
  DB_MAX_RETRY_COUNT="5" `
  DB_MAX_DELAY_SECONDS="10"

COPY --from=builder C:\out\save-prospect\SaveProspectHandler .
```

This component is a message handler running as a .NET Framework console application. It's packaged into a Windows Server Core image, with the usual Dockerfile instructions to switch to PowerShell and turn off the Windows DNS cache. The `CMD` instruction runs the console app, and the `ENV` instructions specify default environment variables used for the message queue and the SQL Server connection.

This is the final line in the Dockerfile that connects the two stages. `COPY --from=builder` ... instructs Docker to copy content into the image, from the previous part of the build, the stage called `builder`. The compiled application is copied from the known location in the builder stage into the desired location in the final application image.

In the sample solution, the other custom images—`dockeronwindows/ch10-newsletter-index-handler` and `dockeronwindows/ch10-newsletter-web`, follow exactly the same pattern. They use the relevant MSBuild image as the base in the builder stage and package the full application in the final stage. This gives me a set of nice, efficient, repeatable builds. The application images don't have any unnecessary components because the build tools are all isolated in the builder stage. Anyone can build this app if they have Docker on Windows; there are no other dependencies.

> The `sixeyed/msbuild` images have multiple variants, supporting different project types. The basic image supports the .NET Framework app, and there are variants to build Visual Studio web projects and SQL Server database projects.

It takes only a single `docker-compose` command to build the entire solution, and it's straightforward to deploy and verify the solution as the next step in the Jenkins build.

Running and verifying the solution

The next build step in Jenkins will deploy the solution locally on the build server, running in Docker containers, and verify that the build is working correctly. This step is another PowerShell script, which starts by deploying the application with Docker Compose:

```
cd source\ch10\ch10-newsletter

$config = '--host', 'tcp://192.168.160.1:2376', '--tlsverify', `
 '--tlscacert', $env:DOCKER_CA,'--tlscert', $env:DOCKER_CERT, '--tlskey',
 $env:DOCKER_KEY

& docker-compose $config `
 -f .\app\docker-compose.yml -f .\app\docker-compose.local.yml up -d
```

As before, I pass the remote connection details for the Docker host, including the gateway IP address and the TLS certificate paths as a configuration array. Each step in the Jenkins job executes in a separate PowerShell session, so I need to set the values each time. In addition to the base compose file, I use the `docker-compose.local.yml` override file that publishes the ports and specifies the network configuration to run locally:

```
version: '3.3'
services:

  signup-app:
    ports:
      - 80

  kibana:
    ports:
      - 5601

...

networks:
  app-net:
    external:
      name: nat
```

I'm not specifying host ports to publish, so Docker will use random ports (port 80 on the application container may be published to port 33504). This is important because ports are scarce resources. If you publish to known ports, then you limit the scalability of your build server with my app server publishing to port 80, I couldn't run any other projects that also tried to use port 80. Random ports mean I can run as many containers as the host can manage.

The `docker-compose` command starts the whole solution in detached containers. The web application uses Entity Framework Code-First to deploy the database schema, so when the containers are started, there is still setup work to be done. In the web application Dockerfile, there is a HEALTHCHECK instruction, so the container will start the setup work but I don't want to run automated tests until that is complete; otherwise, the build could fail on a timing issue.

In the deployment step, I continue with a short sleep to give the setup time to finish, and then I get the IP address of the web container and make a verification call to check whether the website is available:

```
Start-Sleep -Seconds 20

$ip = & docker $config inspect --format '{{
.NetworkSettings.Networks.nat.IPAddress }}' app_signup-app_1

Invoke-WebRequest -UseBasicParsing "http://$ip/SignUp"
```

At this point, the application is up and running and I've verified that the home page is accessible. The build steps are all console commands, so the output will be written to the job log in Jenkins. For a fresh build, you will see the all the output, including the following:

- Docker pulling the `sixeyed/msbuild` images
- NuGet and MSBuild steps compiling the application
- Docker building the application images
- Docker Compose starting the application containers
- PowerShell making the web request to the application

The `Invoke-WebRequest` cmdlet is a simple build verification test. If it gives an error, the build will fail, but if it succeeds, that does not mean the application is working correctly. For greater confidence in the build, I run end-to-end integration tests in the next build step.

Running end-to-end tests in Docker

There's one more component to my sample solution, it's a test project that uses a simulated browser to interact with the web application and which then checks for the expected output in SQL Server.

The `SignUp.EndToEndTests` project uses SpecFlow to define feature tests, stating the expected behavior of the solution. The SpecFlow tests are executed using selenium, which automates browser testing, and SimpleBrowser, which presents a headless browser. These are web tests that can be run from the console, so no UI components are needed and the tests can be executed in a Docker container.

I have a Dockerfile to build the `dockeronwindows/ch10-newsletter-e2e-tests` image, which uses a multi-stage build to compile the test project and then package the test assembly. The final stage of the build configures NUnit with the compiled test assembly, copying the output from the builder stage:

```
FROM sixeyed/nunit:3.6.1
SHELL ["powershell", "-Command", "$ErrorActionPreference = 'Stop';"]

RUN Set-ItemProperty -path
'HKLM:\SYSTEM\CurrentControlSet\Services\Dnscache\Parameters' -Name
ServerPriorityTimeLimit -Value 0 -Type DWord

WORKDIR /e2e-tests
CMD nunit3-console SignUp.EndToEndTests.dll

COPY --from=builder C:\out\tests\EndToEndTests .
```

The next step of the Jenkins build runs these end-to-end tests. It's a simple PowerShell script again, building the Docker image and then running a container. The test container will execute in the same Docker network as the application, so the test browser can reach the web application using the container name in the URL.

```
cd source\ch10\ch10-newsletter

$config = '--host', 'tcp://192.168.160.1:2376', '--tlsverify', `
 '--tlscacert', $env:DOCKER_CA, '--tlscert', $env:DOCKER_CERT, '--tlskey',
$env:DOCKER_KEY

& docker $config build -t dockeronwindows/ch10-newsletter-e2e-tests -f
docker\e2e-tests\Dockerfile .

& docker $config run --env-file app\db-credentials.env
dockeronwindows/ch10-newsletter-e2e-tests
```

Each build step runs in a separate PowerShell session, which is why the steps start by switching to the source directory and setting up the config array. Every `docker` and `docker-compose` command needs the TLS and host settings from the array, which is expanded with the PowerShell `&` syntax.

When this step runs, it will execute a suite of 26 tests against the application. Each test uses a simulated browser to enter details into a web form and then queries SQL Server to verify that the data has been saved. In the Jenkins build output, you will see the results of the test run like this:

```
Run Settings
  DisposeRunners: True
  WorkDirectory: C:\e2e-tests
  ImageRuntimeVersion: 4.0.30319
  ImageTargetFrameworkName: .NETFramework,Version=v4.5.2
  ImageRequiresX86: False
  ImageRequiresDefaultAppDomainAssemblyResolver: False
  NumberOfTestWorkers: 2

Test Run Summary
  Overall result: Passed
  Test Count: 26, Passed: 26, Failed: 0, Warnings: 0, Inconclusive: 0,
Skipped: 0
  Start time: 2017-05-30 22:41:37Z
  End time: 2017-05-30 22:41:58Z
  Duration: 20.622 seconds

Results (nunit3) saved as TestResult.xml
```

The test suite uses a fixed set of data. Ordinarily, this is one of the problems of integration tests, the database needs to be in a known state before running the tests to be sure that you're verifying the output of this test run and not some previous test run. With Docker, this is not an issue because each test run uses a new SQL Server database running in a container. When the tests complete, the database container and all the other application containers are removed in the last part of the test step:

```
& docker-compose $config -f .\app\docker-compose.yml -f .\app\docker-
compose.local.yml down
```

Now I have a set of application images that are tested and known to be good. The images exist only on the build server, so the next step is to push them to the local registry.

Tagging and pushing Docker images in Jenkins

How you push images to your registry during the build process is your choice. You might start by tagging every image with the build number and pushing every image version to the registry as part of the CI build. Projects using efficient Dockerfiles will have minimal differences between builds, so you benefit from cached layers, and the amount of storage you use in your registry shouldn't be excessive.

If you have larger projects with a lot of development churn and a shorter release cadence, the storage requirements could grow so you might move to a scheduled push, tagging images daily, and pushing the latest build to the registry. Or, if you have a pipeline with a manual quality gate, the final release stage could push to the registry, so the only images you store are valid release candidates.

For my sample CI job, I'll push to the local registry with every successful build once the tests have passed using the Jenkins build number as the image tag. The build step to tag and push images is another PowerShell script that uses the built-in environment variables from Jenkins for tagging:

```
$config = '--host', 'tcp://192.168.160.1:2376', '--tlsverify', `
  '--tlscacert', $env:DOCKER_CA, '--tlscert', $env:DOCKER_CERT, '--tlskey',
$env:DOCKER_KEY

& docker $config `
  tag dockeronwindows/ch10-newsletter-web
"registry.sixeyed:5000/dockeronwindows/ch10-newsletter-
web:$($env:BUILD_TAG)"

& docker $config `
  push "registry.sixeyed:5000/dockeronwindows/ch10-newsletter-
web:$($env:BUILD_TAG)"
```

This snippet shows the web application image being pushed, and the same process is used for the message handler images.

> I use an alias in the host's file for my registry, using `registry.sixeyed` as the hostname. On the Docker server that runs the registry container, the `registry.sixeyed` name is set to resolve to the container's IP address. On remote machines, the `registry.sixeyed` name resolves to the Docker server. This way, I can use consistent image tags on every machine.

After a few builds have completed, I can make a REST call to the registry API from my development laptop to query the tags for the dockeronwindows/ch10-newsletter-web repository. The API will give me a list of all the tags for my web application image, so I can verify that they've been pushed by Jenkins:

```
> Invoke-RestMethod
http://registry.sixeyed:5000/v2/dockeronwindows/ch10-newsletter-web/tags/li
st |
Select tags

tags
----
{jenkins-docker-on-windows-ch10-ch10-newsletter-20,
 jenkins-docker-on-windows-ch10-ch10-newsletter-21,
 jenkins-docker-on-windows-ch10-ch10-newsletter-22}
```

The Jenkins build tag gives me the complete path to the job that created the images. I can use the GIT_COMMIT environment that Jenkins provides variable instead to tag images with the commit ID. This makes for a much shorter tag, but the Jenkins build tags include the incrementing build number, so I can always find the latest version by ordering the tags. The Jenkins web UI shows the Git commit ID for each build, so it's easy to track back from the job number to the exact source revision.

The CI part of the build is done now. For every new push to the Git server, Jenkins will compile, deploy, and test the application and then push good images to the local registry. The next part is deploying the solution to the QA environment.

Deploying to a remote Docker swarm using Jenkins

The workflow for my sample application uses a manual quality gate and separates the concerns for local and external artifacts. On every source code push, the solution is deployed locally and tests are run. If they pass, images are saved to the local registry. The final deployment stage is to push these images to an external registry and deploy the application to the public QA environment. This simulates a project approach where builds happen internally, and approved releases are then pushed externally.

In this example, I'll use public repositories on Docker Hub and deploy to a Windows VM in Microsoft Azure running as a single-node Docker swarm. I'll continue to use PowerShell scripts and run basic `docker` and `docker-compose` commands. The principles are exactly the same to push images to other registries and deploy to larger Docker swarms or to **Universal Control Plane (UCP)** running on **Docker Enterprise Edition (Docker EE)**.

I've created a new Jenkins job for the deployment step, which is parameterized to take the version number to deploy. The version number is the job number from the CI build, so I can deploy a known version at any time. In the new job, I need some additional credentials. I've added secret files for the swarm manager's TLS certificates, which will allow me to connect to the manager node of the Docker swarm running in Azure.

I'm also going to push images to Docker Hub as part of the release step, so I've added a username and password credential in Jenkins in order to authenticate to Docker Hub. To authenticate in the job step, I've added a binding for the credentials in the deployment job, which exposes the username and password as environment variables:

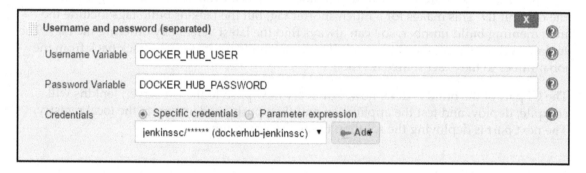

Then, I set up the command configuration and use `docker login` in the PowerShell build step, specifying the credentials from the environment variables:

```
$config = '--host', 'tcp://192.168.160.1:2376', '--tlsverify', `
 '--tlscacert', $env:DOCKER_CA,'--tlscert', $env:DOCKER_CERT, '--tlskey',
$env:DOCKER_KEY

& docker $config `
 login --username $env:DOCKER_HUB_USER --password
"$env:DOCKER_HUB_PASSWORD"
```

I'm still using my local Docker server here, connecting to the gateway IP address. That's my internal environment, which is the source for pushing to the external repositories on Docker Hub.

Now for each of the custom images, I pull them from the local registry, tag them for Docker Hub, and then push them to Hub. The initial pull is there in case I want to deploy a previous build, and the local server cache has been cleaned since the build, it ensures the correct image is present from the local registry. For Docker Hub, I use a simpler tagging format, just applying the version number.

This example is for the web image, and the pattern is repeated for the message handlers:

```
& docker $config `
  pull "registry.sixeyed:5000/dockeronwindows/ch10-newsletter-web:jenkins-
docker-on-windows-ch10-ch10-newsletter-$($env:VERSION_NUMBER)"

& docker $config `
  tag "registry.sixeyed:5000/dockeronwindows/ch10-newsletter-web:jenkins-
docker-on-windows-ch10-ch10-newsletter-$($env:VERSION_NUMBER)" `
  "dockeronwindows/ch10-newsletter-web:$($env:VERSION_NUMBER)"

& docker $config `
  push "dockeronwindows/ch10-newsletter-web:$($env:VERSION_NUMBER)"
```

When this step completes, the images are publicly available on Docker Hub. Now the last step in the deployment job deploys the latest application version on the remote Docker swarm using these public images. I use Docker Compose to pull the latest images and to compile the stack deploy file for the QA environment. Then, I deploy to the swarm using `docker stack deploy`:

```
cd source\ch10\ch10-newsletter

$config = '--host', 'tcp://dockerwin-
test.westeurope.cloudapp.azure.com:2376', '--tlsverify', `
  '--tlscacert', $env:DOCKER_QA_CA, '--tlscert', $env:DOCKER_QA_CERT, '--
tlskey', $env:DOCKER_QA_KEY

& docker-compose $config `
  -f .\app\docker-compose.yml -f .\app\docker-compose.qa.yml pull

& docker-compose $config `
  -f .\app\docker-compose.yml -f .\app\docker-compose.qa.yml config >
docker-compose.stack.yml

& docker $config `
  stack deploy -c docker-compose.stack.yml newsletter
```

In this step, the configuration is set up to use the remote Docker server, the hostname is the Azure VM, and the credential files are the certificates for that QA server. Pulling the images means the latest versions are available when the application is upgraded, as this is just a single-node swarm. The override file specifies the extra settings needed for the QA environment.

 Remember that Docker stacks use the Docker Compose file format, but multiple file overrides are not supported in `docker stack deploy`. I use `docker-compose config` to compile the basic compose file and the QA override file into a single output file. This consolidated file is used to deploy the stack.

The QA override file specifies the DNS round-robin endpoint mode for all services, which is required for Windows containers to communicate in an overlay network:

```
version: '3.2'
services:

  signup-db:
    deploy:
      endpoint_mode: dnsrr

  message-queue:
    deploy:
      endpoint_mode: dnsrr

...
```

The public-facing services need to be configured in the override file with host port publishing. As an example, the Kibana override publishes port `5601`:

```
kibana:
  ports:
    - mode: host
      target: 5601
      published: 5601
  deploy:
    endpoint_mode: dnsrr
```

The services from my custom images need to use the same network configuration and specify the version number in the image tag. Docker Compose supports environment variable expansion, so I use the VERSION_NUMBER environment variable as the image tag. This is the version number that was generated in the build job and passed into Jenkins as a parameter for the deploy job:

```
signup-app:
  image: dockeronwindows/ch10-newsletter-web:${VERSION_NUMBER}
  ports:
    - mode: host
      target: 80
      published: 80
  deploy:
    endpoint_mode: dnsrr

signup-save-handler:
  image: dockeronwindows/ch10-newsletter-save-handler:${VERSION_NUMBER}
  deploy:
    endpoint_mode: dnsrr

signup-index-handler:
  image: dockeronwindows/ch10-newsletter-index-handler:${VERSION_NUMBER}
  deploy:
    endpoint_mode: dnsrr
```

Lastly, the QA override contains a basic entry for the application network. This means Docker will create the network using the default driver and scope. As the target is a Docker swarm, it will create an overlay network:

```
networks:
  app-net:
```

When this job completes, the updated services are deployed. Docker compares stack definitions against running services in the same way that Docker Compose does for containers, so services are updated only if the definition has changed. After the deployment job is complete, I can go to the Azure VM and see the application:

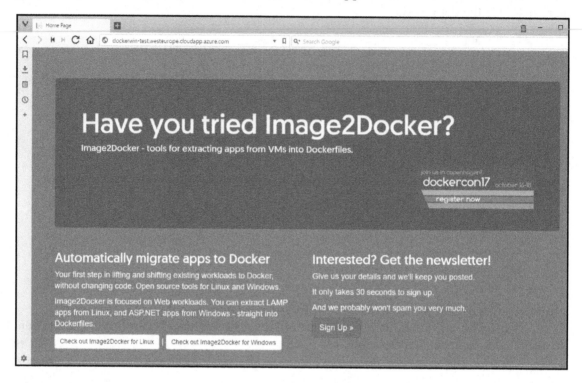

My workflow uses two jobs so I can manually control the release to the QA environment. This can be automated instead for a full CD setup, and you can easily build on your Jenkins jobs to add more functionalities, such as displaying the test output and coverage, joining the builds into a pipeline, and breaking jobs up into reusable parts.

Summary

This chapter covered CI/CD in Docker, with a sample deployment workflow configured in Jenkins. Every part of the process I demonstrated ran in Docker containers, the Git server, Jenkins, the build agents, the test agents, and the local registry.

You saw that it is straightforward to run your own development infrastructure with Docker, giving you an alternative to hosted services. It's also straightforward to use these services for your own deployment workflow, whether it's full CI/CD or separate workflows with a gated manual step.

You saw how to configure and run the Bonobo Git server and the Jenkins automation server in Docker to power the workflow. I used multi-stage builds for all the images in my application, which means I can have a very simple Jenkins setup with no need to deploy any toolchains or SDKs.

My CI pipeline was triggered from a developer pushing changes to Git, and the build job pulled the source, compiled the application components, built them into Docker images, and ran a local deployment of the app in Docker. I run end-to-end tests in another container, and if they pass, I tag and push all the images to the local registry.

I demonstrated a manual deployment step, with a job that the user initiates, specifying the built version to be deployed. This job pushes the built images to the public Docker Hub and deploys an update to the QA environment by deploying the stack on a Docker swarm running in Azure.

There are no hard dependencies on any of the technologies I used in this chapter. The process I implemented with Bonobo, Jenkins, and the open source registry can just as easily be implemented with hosted services such as GitHub, AppVeyor, and Docker Cloud. All the steps of the process use simple PowerShell scripts and can be run on any stack that supports Docker.

In the next chapter, I'll step back to the developer experience and look at the practicalities of running, debugging, and troubleshooting applications in containers.

11

Debugging and Instrumenting Application Containers

Docker can remove a lot of the friction in the typical developer workflow process and significantly reduce the time spent on overhead tasks, such as dependency management and environment configuration. When developers run the changes they're working on using the exact same application platform where the final product will run, there are far fewer opportunities for deployment mistakes, and the upgrade path is straightforward and well understood.

Running your application in a container during development adds another layer to your development environment. You'll be working with different types of assets such as Dockerfiles and Compose files and that experience is much improved if your IDE supports these file types. Also there's a new runtime between the IDE and your app, so the debugging experience will be different. You may need to change your workflow to make the most of the platform benefits.

In this chapter, I'll look at the development process with Docker, covering IDE integration and debugging and how to add instrumentation to your Dockerized applications. You'll learn:

- How Visual Studio 2017, 2015, and Visual Studio Code provide Docker support
- How to debug your application when it's running in a container
- How to instrument your code in a Docker-friendly way
- How to add runtime metrics to existing projects without changing code
- What the bug fixing workflow looks like with Docker

Working with Docker in integrated development environments

In the previous chapter, I demonstrated a containerized outer loop, the compilation and packaging CI process that is triggered from central source control, when developers push changes. The **integrated development environments (IDEs)** are beginning to support containerized workflows for the inner loop, the developer process of writing, running, and debugging applications before pushing changes to central source control.

Visual Studio 2017 has native support for Docker artifacts, including IntelliSense and code completion for Dockerfiles. There is also runtime support for ASP.NET projects running in containers, both .NET Framework and .NET Core. In Visual Studio 2017, you can hit the *F5* key and your web app launches inside a container, running in Docker for Windows. The application uses the same base image and Docker runtime that you will use in all other environments.

Visual Studio 2015 has a plugin that provides support for Docker artifacts, and Visual Studio Code has a very useful Docker extension. Visual Studio 2015 and Visual Studio Code don't provide an integrated *F5* debugging experience for .NET apps running in Windows containers, but you can configure this manually, and I will demonstrate that in this chapter.

There's a compromise when you debug inside a container, it means creating a disconnect between the inner loop and the outer loop. Your development process uses a different set of Docker artifacts from your **continuous integration (CI)** process in order to make the debugger available to the container and to map the application assemblies to the source code. The benefit is that you can run in a container in development but with the same developer build and debug experience that you're used to. The downside is that your development Docker image is not the exact same image you'll be promoting to test.

A good way to mitigate that is to use the local Docker artifacts for development when you're iterating rapidly over a feature. And then, use the CI Docker artifacts, still running locally for the final build and end-to-end tests before pushing your changes.

Docker in Visual Studio 2017

Visual Studio 2017 has the most complete Docker support of all the .NET IDEs. You can open an ASP.NET Web project in Visual Studio 2017 which is full ASP.NET, right-click on the project and select **Add** | **Docker Support**:

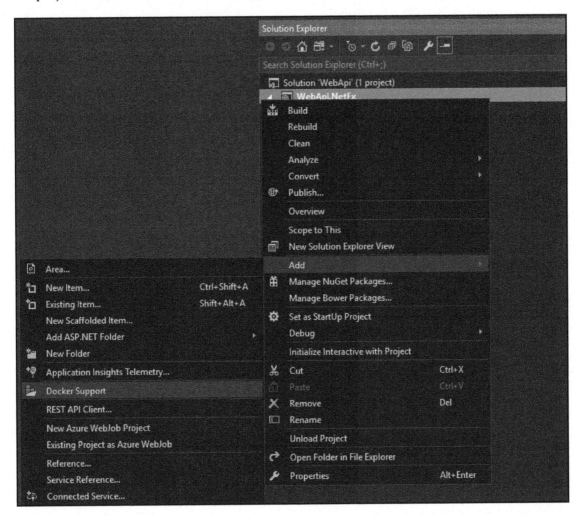

Visual Studio then generates a set of Docker artifacts. In the Web project, it creates a Dockerfile that looks like this:

```
FROM microsoft/aspnet
ARG source
WORKDIR /inetpub/wwwroot
COPY ${source:-obj/Docker/publish} .
```

There's full IntelliSense support for the Dockerfile syntax, so you can hover over instructions and see information about them and use *Ctrl* + spacebar to open a prompt for all Dockerfile instructions.

The generated Dockerfile uses the `microsoft/aspnet` base image, which comes with ASP.NET 4.6 installed and configured. It uses a build argument to specify the location of the source folder, and then it copies the content of that folder to the web root directory `C:\inetpub\wwwroot`.

In the solution root, Visual Studio creates a set of Docker Compose files. There are multiple files, and Visual Studio uses them with the Docker Compose `build` and `up` commands to package and run the application. This works behind the scenes when you run the app with the *F5* key , but it's worth looking at how Visual Studio uses them; it shows you how you can add this level of support to different IDEs.

Debugging with Docker Compose in Visual Studio 2017

You'll need to select **Show all** files at the solution level to see all the Docker Compose files generated by Visual Studio 2017. There's a basic `docker-compose.yml` with the web application defined as a service, complete with build details for the Dockerfile:

```
services:
  webapi.netfx:
    image: webapi.netfx
    build:
      context: .\WebApi.NetFx
      dockerfile: Dockerfile
```

There's also a `docker-compose.vs.debug.yml`, which makes use of Docker volumes to provide the Visual Studio debugger experience:

```
services:
  webapi.netfx:
  image: webapi.netfx:dev
  build:
    args:
      source: ${DOCKER_BUILD_SOURCE}
  volumes:
    - .\WebApi.NetFx:C:\inetpub\wwwroot
    - ~\msvsmon:C:\msvsmon:ro
  labels:
    - "com.microsoft.visualstudio.targetoperatingsystem=windows"
```

There are a few things to note here:

- The Docker image uses the `dev` tag to distinguish it from the release build
- The build argument for the source location uses the environment variable `DOCKER_BUILD_SOURCE`
- A volume is used to map the web root in the container to the project folder on the host
- A second volume is used to map the Visual Studio remote debugger (called `msvsmon`) to the container from the host

In debug mode, the argument for the source code environment variable is an empty directory. Visual Studio builds a Docker image with an empty `web` directory and then mounts the source code folder from the host into the web root in the container in order to populate that folder at runtime.

You can hit *F5* now, and Visual Studio will build the app, run it in a Windows Docker container, and attach the debugger.

 At the time of writing, the generated Docker artifacts in Visual Studio 2017 do not include the port mappings you need for the debugger. In the source code for this chapter, in the folder `ch11-webapi-vs2017`, you will see that I've exposed ports `3072` and `4022` in the Dockerfile and published them in the Docker Compose file.

With the remote debugging ports published, you can add a breakpoint and debug directly in the container with the *F5* experience:

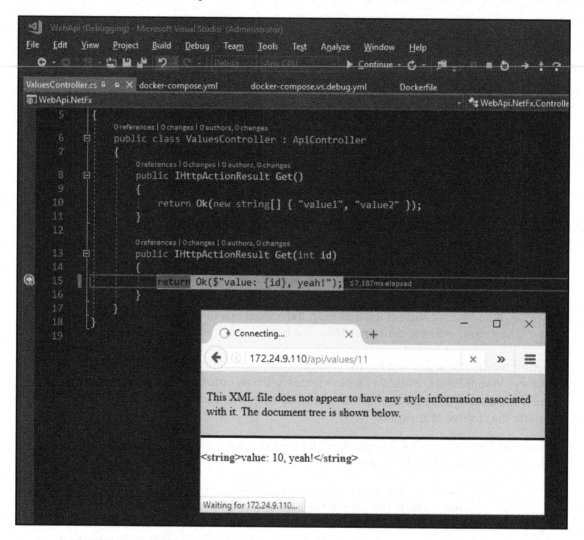

Visual Studio 2017 keeps the container running in the background when you stop debugging. If you make a change to the program and rebuild, the same container is used, so there's no startup lag. By mounting the project location into the container, any changes in content or binaries are reflected when you rebuild. By mounting the remote debugger from the host, your image doesn't have any development tools baked into it; they stay on the host.

This is the inner loop process, where you get fast feedback. Whenever you change and rebuild your app, you see these changes in the container. However the Docker image from the debug mode is not usable for the outer loop CI process; the app is not copied into the image; it works only if you mount the app from your local source into a container.

To support the outer loop, there's also a Docker compose override file for release mode in `docker-compose.vs.release.yml`:

```
services:
  webapi.netfx:
  build:
    args:
      source: ${DOCKER_BUILD_SOURCE}
  volumes:
    - ~\msvsmon:C:\msvsmon:ro
  labels:
    - "com.microsoft.visualstudio.targetoperatingsystem=windows"
```

The only difference here is that there's no volume mapping the local source location to the web root in the container. When you compile in release mode, the value of the `DOCKER_BUILD_SOURCE` environment variable is a published location that contains the web app. Visual Studio builds the release image by packaging the published application into the container.

There's a Docker output window in Visual Studio 2017, where you can see all the commands Visual Studio executes. The *F5* workflow uses `docker-compose build` and `docker-compose run` to start the app and executes `msvsmon` inside the container to start the remote debugger. Then, it grabs the container IP address and launches the browser.

In Release mode, you can still run the application in a Docker container and you can still debug the application. But you lose the fast feedback loop because in order to change the app, Visual Studio needs to rebuild the Docker image and start a new container.

This is a good compromise, and the Docker tooling in Visual Studio 2017 gives you a seamless development experience, along with the basis for your CI build. One thing Visual Studio 2017 doesn't do right now is use multi-stage builds, so the project compilation still happens on the host rather than inside a container. This makes the generated Docker artifacts less portable, you need more than just Docker to build this app on a build agent.

Docker in Visual Studio 2015

Visual Studio 2015 has a plugin available from the Marketplace, called **Visual Studio Tools for Docker**. This gives you syntax highlighting for Dockerfiles, but it doesn't integrate Visual Studio with Docker for .NET Framework apps. With Visual Studio 2015, you can add Docker support to a .NET Core project, but you need to manually write your own Dockerfile and Docker Compose files for full .NET.

Also, there's also no integrated debugging for applications running in Windows containers. You can still debug code running in a container, but you need to manually configure the setup. I'll demonstrate how to do that now, using the same approach as Visual Studio 2017 and with some of the same compromises.

In Visual Studio 2017, you can mount the folder containing the remote debugger from the host into your container. When you run the project, Visual Studio starts a container and executes the `msvsmon.exe` from the host which is the remote debugger agent. You don't need to install anything in your image to provide the debugging experience.

The remote debugger in Visual Studio 2015 is not so portable. You can mount the debugger from the host in the container, but when you try to start the agent, you'll see errors about missing files. Instead, you need to install the remote debugger into your image.

I have this set up in the image `dockeronwindows/ch11-webapi-vs2015`. In the Dockerfile for this image, I use a build-time argument to conditionally install the debugger if the value `configuration` is set to `debug`. This means I can build locally with the debugger installed, but when I build for deployment, the image doesn't have the debugger:

```
ARG configuration

RUN if ($env:configuration -eq 'debug') `
  { Invoke-WebRequest -OutFile c:\rtools_setup_x64.exe -UseBasicParsing -Uri
http://download.microsoft.com/download/1/2/2/1225c23d-3599-48c9-a314-f7d631
f43241/rtools_setup_x64.exe; `
   Start-Process c:\rtools_setup_x64.exe -ArgumentList '/install', '/quiet' -
NoNewWindow -Wait }
```

I use the same approach as Visual Studio 2017 to mount the source directory on the host into the container when running in the debug mode, but I create a custom website rather than using the default one:

```
ARG source
WORKDIR C:\web-app
RUN Remove-Website -Name 'Default Web Site';`
    New-Website -Name 'web-app' -Port 80 -PhysicalPath 'C:\web-app'
COPY ${source:-.\Docker\publish} .
```

The :- syntax in the `COPY` instruction specifies a default value if the `source` argument is not provided. The default is to copy from the published web application unless it is specified in the `build` command. I have a core `docker-compose.yml` file with the basic service definition and a `docker-compose.debug.yml` file that mounts the host source location, maps the debugger ports, and specifies the `configuration` variable:

```
services:
  ch11-webapi-vs2015:
    build:
      context: ..\
      dockerfile: .\Docker\Dockerfile
      args:
        - source=.\Docker\empty
        - configuration=debug
    ports:
      - "3702/udp"
      - "4020"
      - "4021"
    environment:
      - configuration=debug
    labels:
      - "com.microsoft.visualstudio.targetoperatingsystem=windows"
    volumes:
      - ..\WebApi.NetFx:C:\web-app
```

 The label specified in the compose file attaches a key-value pair to the container. The value isn't visible inside the container, unlike an environment variable but it is visible to external processes on the host. In this case, it is used by Visual Studio to identify the operating system of the container.

To start the app in debug mode, I use both Compose files to start the application:

```
docker-compose -f docker-compose.yml -f docker-compose.debug.yml up -d
```

Now the container is running my web app using **Internet Information Services (IIS)** inside the container, and the Visual Studio remote debugger agent is running as well. I can connect to a remote process in Visual Studio 2017 and use the IP address of the container:

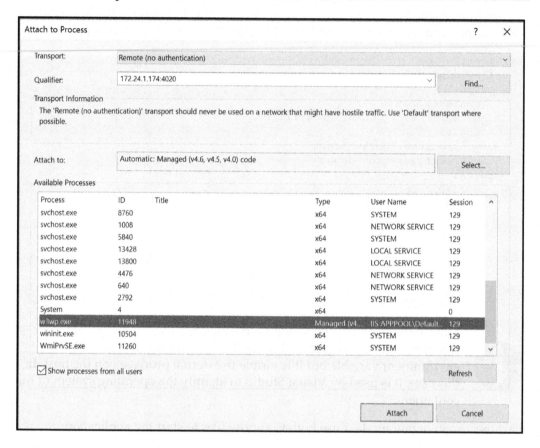

The debugger in Visual Studio attaches to the agent running in the container, and I can add breakpoints and view variables, just like debugging to a local process. In this approach, the container is using the host mount for the content of the web app. I can stop the debugger, make changes, rebuild the app and see the changes in the same container without having to start a new container.

This approach has the same benefits and drawbacks as the integrated Docker support in Visual Studio 2017. I'm running my app in a container for local debugging, so I get all the features of the Visual Studio debugger, and my app is running in the same platform I'll use in other environments. But I won't be using the same image, as the Dockerfile has conditional branches, so it produces different outputs for the debug and release modes.

There is an advantage to manually building debugger support in your Docker artifacts. You can construct your Dockerfile with conditioning so that the default `docker image build` command produces the production-ready image without requiring any additional artifacts. This example still does not use a multi-stage build, though, so the Dockerfile is not portable and the application needs to be compiled before it can be packaged.

In development, you build the image once in debug mode, run the container, and then attach the debugger whenever you need to. Your integration tests build and run the production image, so only the inner loop has the additional debugger components.

Docker in Visual Studio Code

Visual Studio Code is intended as a cross-platform IDE for cross-platform languages. The C# extension installs a debugger that can attach to .NET Core applications, but there's no support for debugging full .NET Framework apps.

The Docker extension adds some very useful features, including the ability to add Dockerfiles and Docker Compose files to existing projects, but the generated files do not currently provide debugging support for Windows containers. There is syntax highlighting for Dockerfiles and Docker Compose files and IntelliSense for Dockerfiles.

There are also integrations with the UI , you can right-click on a Dockerfile and have the option to build an image. You can hit *F1* key, type `Docker`, and see a list of useful options to run containers and manage services with compose files:

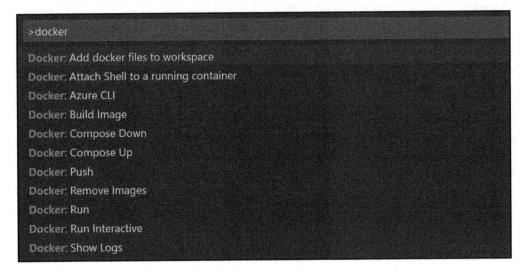

Visual Studio Code has a very flexible system for running and debugging your projects, so you can add your own configuration to provide debugging support for apps running in Windows containers. You can edit the `launch.json` file to add a new configuration for debugging in Docker.

In the `ch11-webapi-vscode` folder, I have a sample .NET Core project set up to run the application in Docker and attach a debugger. It uses the same approach as Visual Studio 2017. The debugger for .NET Core is called `vsdbg` and is installed with the C# extension in Visual Studio Code, so I mount the `vsdbg` folder from the host into the container, along with the source location, using a `docker-compose.debug.yml` file:

```
volumes:
 - .\bin\Debug\netcoreapp1.1\publish:C:\app
 - ~\.vscode\extensions\ms-vscode.csharp-1.10.0\.debugger:C:\vsdbg:ro
```

 This setup uses a specific version of the C# extension. That's 1.10 in my case, but you may have a later version, check for the location of `vsdbg.exe` in the `.vscode` folder in your user directory.

When you run the app through Docker Compose using the debug override file, it starts the .NET Core application and makes the debugger from the host available to run in the container. This is configured for a debugging experience in Visual Studio Code in the `launch.json` file. The `Debug Docker container` configuration specifies what type of application to debug and the name of the process to attach:

```
"name": "Debug Docker container",
"type": "coreclr",
"request": "attach",
"sourceFileMap": {
    "C:\\app": "${workspaceRoot}"
  },
"processName": "dotnet"
```

This configuration also maps the application root in the container to the source code location on the host, so the debugger can associate the correct source files with the debug files. In addition, the debugger configuration specifies how to launch the debugger by running a `docker container exec` command on the named container:

```
"pipeTransport": {
  "pipeCwd": "${workspaceRoot}",
  "pipeProgram": "docker",
  "pipeArgs": [
    "exec", "-i", "webapinetcore_webapi_1"
    ],
```

```
    "debuggerPath": "C:\\vsdbg\\vsdbg.exe",
    "quoteArgs": false
}
```

To debug my app, first, I start the container with the debug configuration using Docker Compose:

```
docker-compose -f .\docker-compose.yml -f .\docker-compose.debug.yml up
```

Then, I can activate the debugger using the Debug action and selecting **Debug Docker container**:

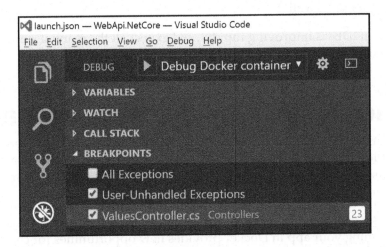

Visual Studio Code starts the .NET Core debugger vsdbg inside the container and attaches to the running **dotnet** process. You'll see the output from the .NET Core application redirected into the **DEBUG CONSOLE** window in Visual Studio Code:

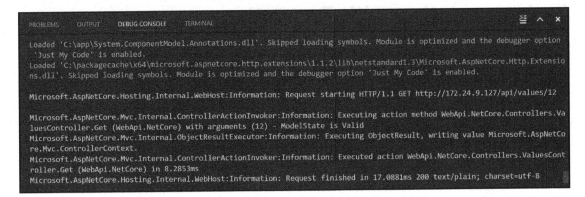

At the time of writing, Visual Studio Code doesn't fully integrate with the debugger running inside a Windows Docker container. You can place breakpoints in the code and the debugger will pause the process, but control does not pass to Visual Studio Code. Development is happening quickly in Visual Studio Code, so expect this to be fixed soon, check out my blog at `https://blog.sixeyed.com`for updates.

Running your application in a container and being able to debug from your normal IDE is a huge benefit. It means your app is running on the same platform and with the same deployment configuration it will use in all other environments, but you can step into code just as if it were running locally.

Docker support in IDEs is improving rapidly, so I expect all the manual steps I've detailed in this chapter to be built into products and extensions soon.

Instrumentation in Dockerized applications

Debugging your app is what you do when the logic doesn't work as expected and you're trying to track down what's going wrong. You don't debug in production, so you need your app to record its behavior in order to help you trace any problems that occur.

Instrumentation is often neglected, but it should be a crucial component of your development, as it's the best way to understand the health and activity of your app in production. Running your app in Docker provides new opportunities for centralized logging and instrumentation, so you can get a consistent view across the different parts of your application even if they use different languages and platforms.

Instrumentation with Prometheus

The ecosystem around Docker is very large and active, taking advantage of the open standards and extensibility of the platform. As the ecosystem has matured, a few technologies have emerged as strong candidates for inclusion in most Dockerized applications.

Prometheus is an open source instrumentation framework. It's a flexible component that you can use in different ways, but the typical implementation is to run a Prometheus server in a Docker container, configured to read instrumentation endpoints in your other Docker containers.

You configure Prometheus to poll all the container endpoints, and it stores the results in a time-series database. You can add a Prometheus endpoint to your application by simply adding a REST endpoint, which responds to GET requests from the Prometheus server with a list of the metrics you're interested in collecting.

For .NET projects, there is a NuGet package that does this for you, adding a Prometheus endpoint to your application. It exposes a useful set of metrics by default, including the values of key .NET statistics and Windows performance counters. You can add Prometheus support directly to your application, or you can run a Prometheus exporter alongside your app.

Adding a Prometheus endpoint to .NET projects

The prometheus-net NuGet package provides a set of default metric collectors and a MetricServer class that provides the instrumentation endpoint that Prometheus hooks into. This package is great for adding Prometheus support to any app, the metrics are provided by a self-hosted HTTP endpoint, and you can record provide custom metrics for your application.

In the dockeronwindows/ch11-api-with-metrics image, I've added Prometheus support into a Web API project. The code to configure and start the metrics endpoint is in the PrometheusServer class:

```
public static void Start()
{
  _Server = new MetricServer(50505, new IOnDemandCollector[] {
    new DotNetStatsCollector(), new PerfCounterCollector()
  });
  _Server.Start();
}
```

This starts a new MetricServer instance, listening on port 50505, and running the .NET statistics and performance counter collectors that the NuGet package provides. These are on-demand collectors, which means they provide metrics when the Prometheus server calls into the endpoint.

The `MetricServer` class will also return any custom metrics you set up in your application. In the `ValuesController` class, I have set up some simple counters to record requests and responses to the API:

```
private Counter _requestCounter =
    Metrics.CreateCounter("ValuesController_Requests", "Request count",
"method",
    "url");

private Counter _responseCounter =
    Metrics.CreateCounter("ValuesController_Responses", "Response count",
"code",
    "url");
```

When requests come into the controller, the controller action method increments the request count for the URL and increments the status count for the response code by calling the `Inc()` method on the counter objects:

```
public IHttpActionResult Get()
{
    _requestCounter.Labels("GET", "/").Inc();
    _responseCounter.Labels("200", "/").Inc();
    return Ok(new string[] { "value1", "value2" });
}
```

Prometheus has various types of metrics that you can use to record key information about your app. It also allows grouping by arbitrary labels, in this case, I add the URL and the HTTP method to the request count and the URL and status code to the response count.

The counters I set up in the Web API controller give me a set of custom metrics showing which endpoints are being used and the status of the responses. These are exposed by the server component in the `NuGet` package, along with the default metrics to record the system performance.

In the Dockerfile for this app, there are two additional lines needed for the Prometheus endpoint:

```
EXPOSE 50505
RUN netsh http add urlacl url=http://+:50505/metrics
user=BUILTIN\IIS_IUSRS; `
    net localgroup 'Performance Monitor Users' 'IIS APPPOOL\DefaultAppPool'
/add
```

The first line just exposes the custom port I'm using for the metrics endpoint. The second line sets up the permissions needed for that endpoint. In this case, the metrics endpoint is hosted inside the ASP.NET app, so the IIS user account needs permissions to listen on the custom port and to access the system performance counters.

You can build the Dockerfile and run a container from the image in the usual way, publishing all the ports with -P:

```
docker container run -d -P --name api dockeronwindows/ch11-api-with-metrics
```

To check whether the metrics are being recorded and exposed, I can run some PowerShell commands to grab the IP address of the container, make some calls to the API endpoint, and check the metrics:

```
$ip = docker inspect -f '{{.NetworkSettings.Networks.nat.IPAddress}}' api

for ($i=0; $i -lt 10; $i++) {
  iwr -useb "http://$($ip)/api/values"
}

(iwr -useb "http://$($ip):50505/metrics").Content
```

You'll see a plain text list of metrics, grouped by name and label. Each metric also contains the metadata for Prometheus, including the metric name, the type, and a friendly description:

```
# HELP process_windows_num_threads Total number of threads
# TYPE process_windows_num_threads GAUGE
process_windows_num_threads 32
# HELP dotnet_totalmemory Total known allocated memory
# TYPE dotnet_totalmemory GAUGE
dotnet_totalmemory 15225400
. . .
# HELP ValuesController_Requests Request count
# TYPE ValuesController_Requests COUNTER
ValuesController_Requests{method="GET",url="/"} 10
. . .
# HELP ValuesController_Responses Response count
# TYPE ValuesController_Responses COUNTER
ValuesController_Responses{code="200",url="/"} 10
```

The complete output is much larger. In this snippet, I've shown the total number of threads and the total allocated memory which comes from performance counters inside the container. I've also shown the custom HTTP request and response counters.

My custom counters in this application show the URL and the response code. In this case, I can see ten requests to the root URL of the value controller, and ten responses with status code 200. Later in the chapter, I'll show how to graph these statistics using Prometheus.

Adding the NuGet package to the project and running the MetricServer is a simple extension to the source code. It lets me record any kind of metric that is useful but it does mean changing the app.

In some cases, you may want to add monitoring without altering the application you want to instrument. In that case, you can run an **exporter** alongside your app. The exporter pulls metrics from your application process and exposes them to Prometheus.

Adding a Prometheus exporter alongside existing apps

In a Dockerized solution, Prometheus will make scheduled calls to the metrics endpoint exposed from a container and store the results. For an existing app, you don't need to add a metrics endpoint; you can run a console app alongside the current application and host the metrics in that console app.

I've added a Prometheus endpoint to the Bononbo Git server I set up in the previous chapter without changing any of the Bonobo code. In the dockeronwindows/ch11-bonobo-with-metrics image, I have a console app that provides the metrics endpoint, using the same NuGet package and MetricsServer class as the previous example. The console app is watching the w3wp process that hosts Bonobo, so it exposes Bonobo's metrics without altering the Bonobo app.

The **DotNetExporter** console application implements a custom counter collector, which reads the performance counter values for a named process running on the system. It uses the same set of counters as the default collector in the NuGet package, but by targeting a different process, I can monitor other processes running in the same container.

In the Program class, I use environment variables to configure the app and start counter collectors for each configured process:

```
var collectors = new List<IOnDemandCollector>();
foreach (var process in Config.MetricsTargets)
{
  WriteLine($"Adding collectors for process: {process}");
  collectors.Add(new ProcessPerfCounterCollector(process));
}
```

Then I create and start a `MetricServer` object, using the configured collectors and listening on the configured metrics endpoint:

```
var server = new MetricServer(Config.MetricsPort, collectors);
server.Start();
WriteLine($"Metrics server listening on port: {Config.MetricsPort}");
```

The console app is a lightweight component. It runs indefinitely and only uses compute resources when the metrics endpoint is called, so it has minimal impact when running on a Prometheus schedule. To provide metrics for Bonobo, I need to create a Dockerfile that packages the exporter app alongside Bonobo. I start with the Bonobo image from Chapter 10, *Powering a Continuous Deployment Pipeline with Docker* and set up the environment for the metrics exporter:

```
FROM dockeronwindows/ch10-bonobo
EXPOSE 50505
ENV METRICS_TARGETS="w3wp"
```

This exposes my default metrics port, `50505` and sets the exporter to monitor the `w3wp` process. Then, I copy the exporter console app, compiled in the builder stage in this Dockerfile, and set up the entry point to use a bootstrap PowerShell script:

```
WORKDIR C:\prometheus-exporter
COPY --from=builder C:\out\dotnet-exporter .

COPY bootstrap.ps1 /
ENTRYPOINT ["powershell", "C:\\bootstrap.ps1"]
```

In the bootstrap script, I start the IIS Windows service and make an HTTP call. This will launch the `w3wp` worker process to handle the request:

```
Start-Service W3SVC
Invoke-WebRequest http://localhost/Bonobo.Git.Server -UseBasicParsing |
Out-Null
```

Now that there's a process running, I start the exporter console app that will provide metrics from the `w3wp` process:

```
& C:\prometheus-exporter\DotNetExporter.Console.exe
```

When I build this image and run a container, I can use Bonobo in the normal way, with my additional exporter process running and providing access to metrics. I'll start the container and open the browser using PowerShell:

```
docker container run -d -P --name bonobo `
  dockeronwindows/ch11-bonobo-with-metrics
```

```
$ip = docker inspect -f '{{.NetworkSettings.Networks.nat.IPAddress}}'
bonobo

start "http://$($ip)/Bonobo.Git.Server"
```

I can use Bonobo in the browser, and the exporter will expose the metrics for the Bonobo worker process. I am using the same metrics endpoint as earlier, so I can see the statistics on port 50505:

```
> (iwr -useb "http://$($ip):50505/metrics").Content

# HELP process_pct_processor_time % Processor Time Perf Counter
# TYPE process_pct_processor_time GAUGE
process_pct_processor_time{process="w3wp"} 6.06265497207642
# HELP process_working_set Working Set Perf Counter
# TYPE process_working_set GAUGE
process_working_set{process="w3wp"} 329969664
. . .
```

In this case, there are no custom counters from the application, and all the metrics come from standard Windows and .NET performance counters. The exporter application can read these performance counter values for the running w3wp process, so the application doesn't need to change in order to provide basic information to Prometheus. To record custom metrics, you do need to instrument your code and explicitly record the data points you're interested in.

Adding instrumentation to your Dockerized application means providing the metrics endpoint that Prometheus can query. The Prometheus server itself runs in a Docker container, configured with the names of containers you want to monitor.

Running a Prometheus server in a Windows Docker container

Prometheus is a cross-platform application, written in Go, which can run on Nano Server. The installer for Prometheus comes as a GZipped Tar file, which you can't natively extract in Windows. To package Prometheus in Docker, I use a multi-stage build, where I download and extract the package in the first stage.

The best tool to extract a GZipped TAR file in Windows is 7-Zip, and I have a Docker image that installs 7-Zip called `dockeronwindows/ch11-7zip`. The Dockerfile for the Prometheus image `dockeronwindows/ch11-prometheus` starts using this image and then runs PowerShell cmdlets to download the package and extract it:

```
RUN Invoke-WebRequest
"https://github.com/prometheus/prometheus/releases/download/v$($env:PROMETH
EUS_VERSION)/prometheus-$($env:PROMETHEUS_VERSION).windows-amd64.tar.gz" `
 -OutFile 'prometheus.tar.gz' -UseBasicParsing; `
 & 'C:\Program Files\7-Zip\7z.exe' x prometheus.tar.gz; `
 & 'C:\Program Files\7-Zip\7z.exe' x prometheus.tar; `
 Rename-Item -Path "C:\prometheus-$($env:PROMETHEUS_VERSION).windows-amd64"
-NewName 'C:\prometheus'
```

The second (and final) stage of the Dockerfile starts from Nano Server and copies the extracted files from the installer stage. They are copied to specific locations, so the user of the container can override the contents with volume mounts to run Prometheus with a different configuration:

```
FROM microsoft/nanoserver:10.0.14393.1198

COPY --from=installer /prometheus/prometheus.exe /bin/prometheus.exe
COPY --from=installer /prometheus/promtool.exe /bin/promtool.exe
COPY --from=installer /prometheus/prometheus.yml
/etc/prometheus/prometheus.yml
COPY --from=installer /prometheus/console_libraries/ /etc/prometheus/
COPY --from=installer /prometheus/consoles/ /etc/prometheus/
```

There is much you can configure in Prometheus, but typically, you can get started just by specifying the JSON configuration file. My Dockerfile has an `ENTRYPOINT` with default values for all the settings and a `CMD` that lets the user override the config file location:

```
ENTRYPOINT ["C:\\bin\\prometheus.exe", `
 "-storage.local.path=/prometheus", `
 "-web.console.libraries=/etc/prometheus/console_libraries", `
 "-web.console.templates=/etc/prometheus/consoles" ]

CMD ["-config.file=/etc/prometheus/prometheus.yml"]
```

Docker Captain and Microsoft MVP Stefan Scherer have an alternative Dockerfile to package Prometheus, which has more flexibility in the startup command. It's on GitHub in the `stefanscherer/dockerfiles-windows` repository.

I have containers running from my instrumented API and Bonobo Git server images, which expose metrics endpoints for Prometheus to consume. To monitor them in Prometheus, I need to specify the metric locations in the configuration file. Prometheus will poll these endpoints on a configurable schedule, it calls this **scraping**, and I can add my container names and ports in the `scrape` configuration:

```
scrape_configs:
  - job_name: 'Api'
    static_configs:
      - targets: ['api:50505']
  - job_name: 'Bonobo'
    static_configs:
      - targets: ['bonobo:50505']
```

Each application to monitor is specified as a job, and each endpoint is listed as a target. Prometheus will be running in a container on the same Docker network, so I can refer to the targets by the container name. Now I can start the Prometheus server in a container, mounting local folders for the configuration file and the data volume and specifying the config file location in the command:

```
docker container run -d -P `
  --name prometheus `
  -v "C:\prometheus\data:C:\prometheus" `
  -v "C:\prometheus:C:\config" `
  dockeronwindows/ch11-prometheus '-config.file=/config/prometheus.yml'
```

Prometheus polls the all the configured metrics endpoints and stores the data. You can use Prometheus as the back-end for a rich UI component such as Grafana, building all your runtime KPIs into a single dashboard. For basic monitoring, the Prometheus server also provides a simple Web UI.

I can go to the IP address of the Prometheus server on port `9090`, and set up a graph view showing me the responses for my Web API, which gives me a different line for each request URL and response status code:

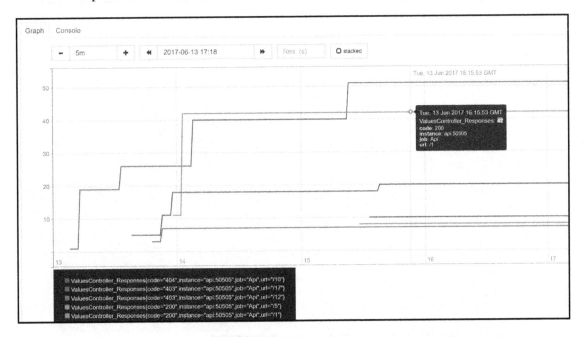

These are counters that increase for the life of the container, so the graphs will always go up. Prometheus has a rich set of functions so you can also graph the rate of change over time, aggregate metrics, and select projections over the data.

Other counters from the Prometheus `NuGet` package are snapshots such as the performance counter statistics. I can compare the memory usage of the Bonobo instance and the API by looking at the working set.

Using a stacked graph here shows that Bonobo is using more memory, but there's a sharp fall, which is probably after a .NET garbage collector run:

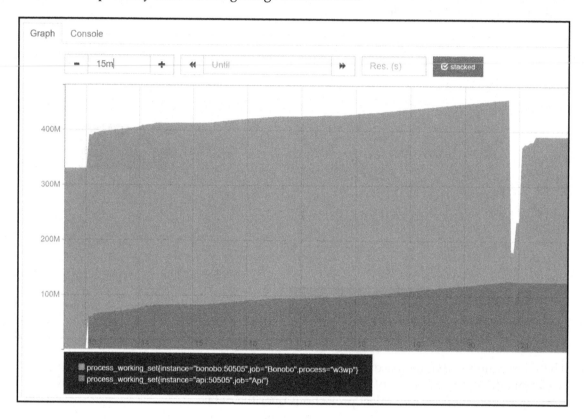

In chapter 8, *Administering and Monitoring Dockerized Solutions*, I demonstrated **Universal Control Plane (UCP)**, the **Containers-as-a-Service (CaaS)** platform in **Docker Enterprise Edition (Docker EE)**. The standard APIs to start and manage Docker containers lets this tool present a consolidated management and administration experience. The openness of the Docker platform lets open source tools take the same approach to rich, consolidated monitoring.

Prometheus is a good example of that. It runs as a lightweight server, which is well suited to running in a container. You add support for Prometheus to your application either by adding a metrics endpoint to your app, or by running a metrics exporter alongside your existing app.

You can add instrumentation to all your applications with very little effort and gain a detailed insight into what's happening in your solution. What's more, you can have the exact same monitoring facility in every environment, so in development and test, you can see the same metrics you use in production. This is very useful in tracking down issues when you're replicating bugs from other environments.

The bug fixing workflow in Docker

One of the biggest difficulties in fixing production defects is replicating them in your development environment. This is the first step in confirming that you have a bug and the starting point for drilling down to find the problem. It can also be the most time-consuming part of the problem.

Large .NET projects tend to have infrequent releases because the release process is complex, and a lot of manual testing is needed to verify the new features and check for any regressions. It's not unusual to have just three or four releases a year and for developers to find themselves having to support multiple versions of an application in different parts of the release process.

In this scenario, you may have version 1.0 in production, version 1.1 in **user acceptance testing (UAT)**, and version 1.2 in system testing. Bugs could be raised in any of these versions, which the development team needs to track down and fix while they're currently working on version 1.3 or even a major upgrade for 2.0.

Bug fixing before Docker

I've been in this position lots of times, having to context switch from the refactored 2.0 code base I'm working on back to the 1.1 code base that is due to be released. The context switch is expensive, but the process of setting up my development environment to recreate the 1.1 UAT environment is even more costly.

The release process may create a versioned MSI, but typically, you can't just run that in your development environment. The installer may be packaged with the configuration for a specific environment. It may have been compiled in release mode and packaged without PDB files, so there's no option to attach a debugger. And it may have prerequisites that I don't have available in development such as certificates or encryption keys or additional software components.

Instead, I need to recompile the 1.1 version from source. Hopefully, the release process has enough information for me to find the exact source code used to build the release, take a branch, and clone it locally (maybe the Git commit ID or the TFS change set is recorded in the built assemblies). Then the real problems start when I try to recreate another environment on my local development box.

The workflow looks a little like this, where there are lots of differences between my setup and the 1.1 environment:

- Compile the source locally. I'll build the app in Visual Studio, but the released version uses MSBuild scripts, which do a lot of extra things.
- Run the app locally. I'll be using IIS Express on Windows 10, but the release uses an MSI that deploys to IIS 8 on Windows Server 2012.
- My local SQL Server database is set up for the 2.0 schema I'm working on. The release has upgrade scripts from 1.0 to 1.1, but there are no downgrade scripts from 2.0 to 1.1, so I need to manually fix the local schema.
- I have stubs for any dependencies I can't run locally, such as third-party APIs. The release uses real application components.

Even if I can get the exact source code for version 1.1, my development environment is hugely divergent from the UAT environment. This is the best I can do, and it may take several hours of effort. To reduce this time, I could take shortcuts, like using my knowledge of the app to run version 1.1 against the 2.0 database schema, but taking shortcuts means my local environment is less like the target environment.

I can run the app in debug at this point and try to replicate the issue. If the bug is caused by a data problem or an environmental problem, then I won't be able to replicate it and it could have taken a whole day of effort to find that out. If I suspect the issue is to do with the setup of UAT, I can't verify that in my environment; I need to work with the Ops team to look at the UAT configuration.

But hopefully, I can reproduce the issue following the steps in the bug report. When I have the manual steps worked out, I can write a failing test that replicates the issue and be confident that I've fixed the problem when I change the code and the test runs green. There are differences between my environment and UAT, so it could be that my analysis is not correct and the fix won't fix UAT but I won't find that out until the next release.

How that fix does get released into the UAT environment is another problem. Ideally, the full CI and packaging process is already set up for the 1.1 branch, so I just push my changes and a new MSI comes out that is ready to be deployed. In the worst case, the CI runs only from the master branch, so I need to set up a new job on the fix branch and try to configure that job to be the same as it was for the last 1.1 release.

If any part of the toolchain has moved on between 1.1 and 2.0, then it makes every step of the process more difficult, from configuring the local environment, running the app, analyzing the problem, and pushing the fix.

Bug fixing with Docker

The process is much simpler with Docker. To replicate the UAT environment locally, I just need to run containers from the same images that are running in UAT. There will be a Docker compose or stack file describing the whole solution, which is versioned, so by deploying version 1.1, I get the exact same environment as UAT without having to build from the source.

I should be able to replicate the issue at this point and confirm whether it's a coding issue or something to do with data or the environment. If it's a configuration issue, then I should see the same problem as UAT, and I could test the fix with an updated compose file. If it's a coding issue, then I need to dig into the code.

At this point, I can clone the source from the version 1.1 tag and build the Docker images in the debug mode, but I don't spend time doing that until I'm pretty sure this is a problem in the app. If I'm using multi-stage builds with all versions pinned in the Dockerfile, the local build will produce an identical image to the one running in UAT but with the extra artifacts for debugging.

Now I can find the problem, write a test, and fix the bug. When the new integration test passes, it's executing against the same Dockerized solution I'll be deploying in UAT, so I can be very confident that the bug is fixed.

If there's no CI configured for the 1.1 branch, then setting it up should be straightforward because the build task will just need to run the `docker image build` or `docker-compose build` commands. If I want fast feedback, I can even push the locally built image to the registry and update the UAT environment to verify the fix while the CI setup is being configured.

The workflow with Docker is much cleaner and faster, but more importantly, there is far less risk. When you replicate the issue locally, you are using the exact same application components running on the exact same platform as the UAT environment. When you test your fix, you know it will work in UAT because you'll be deploying the same new artifacts.

The time you invest in dockerizing your application will be repaid by the time saved in supporting multiple versions of the app.

Summary

This chapter looked at troubleshooting applications running in containers, along with debugging and instrumentation. Docker is a new application platform, but applications in containers run as processes on the host, so they're still suitable targets for remote debugging and centralized monitoring.

Support for Docker is available in all the current versions of Visual Studio. Visual Studio 2017 has complete support, covering Linux and Windows containers. Visual Studio 2015 and Visual Studio Code currently have extensions that provide debugging for Linux containers, but you can easily add your own support for Windows containers.

In this chapter, I also introduced Prometheus, a lightweight instrumentation and monitoring component that you can run in a Windows Docker container. Prometheus stores the metrics it extracts from applications running on other containers. The standardized nature of containers makes monitoring solutions such as these very simple to configure.

The next chapter is the final chapter of the book. I'll end by sharing some approaches to get started with Docker in your own domain, including case studies where I have used Docker on Windows for existing projects.

12
Containerize What You Know - Guidance for Implementing Docker

In this book, I have used older .NET technologies for the sample applications to show you that Docker works just as well with them as it does with modern .NET Core apps. You can Dockerize a ten year old WebForms application and get many of the same benefits you get from running a greenfield ASP.NET Core **Model-View-Controller (MVC)** application in a container.

You've seen lots of examples of containerized applications and learned how to build, ship, and run production-grade apps with Docker. Now you're ready to start working with Docker on your own projects, and this chapter gives you advice on how to get started.

I'll cover some techniques and tools that will help you run a proof-of-concept project to move an application to Docker. I'll also walk you through some case studies to show how I've introduced Docker to existing projects:

- A small-scale .NET 2.0 WebForms app
- A database integration service in a **Windows Communication Foundation (WCF)** app
- A distributed IoT API app running in Azure

You'll see how to approach typical problems and how the move to Docker can help solve them.

Dockerizing what you know

When you move to a new application platform, you have to work with a new set of artifacts and new operational processes. If you currently use the Windows installer for deployment, your artifacts are Wix files and MSIs. Your deployment process is to copy the MSI to the target server, log on, and run the installer.

After the move to Docker, you will have Dockerfiles and images as the deployment artifacts. You push the image to a registry and run a container or update a service to deploy the app. The resources and activities are simpler in Docker, and they'll be consistent between projects, but there's still a learning curve when you start.

Containerizing an app that you know well is a great way to provide a solid basis to that learning experience. When you first run your app in a container, you may see errors or incorrect behavior but that will be in the domain of your own application. When you're tracking down the issue, you'll be dealing with an area you understand well, so although the platform is new, the problem should be easy to identify.

Selecting a simple Proof-of-Concept app

Docker is ideally suited to distributed applications, where each component runs in a lightweight container, making efficient use of a minimal set of hardware. You can choose a distributed application for your first Docker deployment, but a simpler application will be faster to migrate and will give you a higher chance of success.

A monolithic app is a good choice. It doesn't have to be a small code base, but the fewer integrations with other components it has, the more quickly you will have it running in Docker. An ASP.NET application that stores state in SQL Server is a straightforward option. You can expect to have a **Proof-of-Concept (PoC)** running in a day or two with a simple application.

Starting with a compiled application rather than the source code is a good way to prove that the app can be Dockerized without having to be changed. There are a few factors to consider when you're selecting your PoC application:

- **Statefulness**: If your target app stores the state in memory, you won't be able to scale the PoC by running multiple containers. Each container will have its own state, and you'll get inconsistent behavior as requests are handled by different containers. Consider stateless apps or apps that can use a shared state, such as using SQL Server as a session state provider for ASP.NET.

- **Configuration**: .NET apps typically use XML configuration files in `Web.config` or `app.config`. You can set up your PoC to use an existing config file as the base and then swap out any values that don't apply to the containerized environment. It is preferable to read config settings through Docker with environment variables and secrets, but staying with config files is easier for the PoC.

- **Resilience**: Older applications typically make the assumption of availability - the web app expects the database to be always available and doesn't handle failure conditions gracefully. If your app has no retry logic for external connections, your PoC will face an error if there are transient connection failures when containers are starting up.

- **Windows Authentication**: Containers aren't domain-joined. You can access **Active Directory** (**AD**) objects in containers if you create a Group Managed Service Account in AD, but that adds complexity. For the PoC , stick to simpler authentication schemes such as basic authentication.

None of these are major restrictions. You should be able to work on the basis of containerizing an existing app without changing code, but you need to be aware that the functionality may not be perfect at the PoC stage.

Generating an initial Dockerfile with Image2Docker

Image2Docker is an open source tool you can use to generate a Dockerfile for an existing application. It's a PowerShell module that you can run on the local machine, against a remote machine, or a Virtual Machine disk file (in Hyper-V `VHD` or `VHDX` format).

It's a very simple way to get started with Docker, you don't even need Docker installed on your machine to try it out and see what the Dockerfile would look like for your app. Image2Docker can work with different types of application (called **artifacts**), but the functionality is most mature for ASP.NET apps running on IIS.

On my development machine, I have an ASP.NET application deployed to **Internet Information Services (IIS)**. I can migrate that application to Docker by installing Image2Docker from the PowerShell gallery and importing the module to use it locally:

```
Install-Module Image2Docker
Import-Module Image2Docker
```

> PowerShell 5.0 is the minimum required version for `Image2Docker`, but the tool has no other dependencies.

I can run the `ConvertTo-Dockerfile` cmdlet, specifying the IIS artifact to build a Dockerfile that contains all the IIS websites on my machine:

```
ConvertTo-Dockerfile -Local -Artifact IIS -OutputPath C:\i2d\iis
```

This creates a directory at `C:\i2d\iis`, and inside the folder I'll have a Dockerfile and sub directories for each of the websites. `Image2Docker` copies the website content from the source to the output location. The Dockerfile uses the most relevant base image for the applications it finds `microsoft/iis`, `microsoft/aspnet` or `microsoft/aspnet:3.5`.

If there are multiple websites or web applications on the source, `Image2Docker` extracts them all and builds a single Dockerfile that duplicates the original IIS setup, so there will be multiple apps in the Docker image. That's not what I'm aiming for which I want a single app in my Docker image, so I can run with a parameter instead to extract a single website:

```
ConvertTo-Dockerfile -Local -Artifact IIS -ArtifactParam SampleApi -
OutputPath C:\i2d\api
```

The process is the same, but this time, `Image2Docker` extracts only a single application from the source, the one named in the `ArtifactParam` parameter. The Dockerfile contains the steps to deploy the application, and you can run `docker image build` to create the image and run the app.

This could be your first step in Dockerizing your application, and then you would run a container and check the functionality of the app. There may be additional setup needed, which `Image2Docker` doesn't do for you, so you'll likely be iterating on that generated Dockerfile, but the tool is a good way to get started.

> `Image2Docker` is an open source project. The source is on GitHub - use the short link `https://github.com/docker/communitytools-image2docker-win`. The repository has additional documentation, and you can see the roadmap of the tool in the issues list.

Engaging other stakeholders

A successful PoC should be possible in just a few days. The output of that will be a sample application that runs in Docker and a set of extra steps you need to productionize that PoC. If you're working in a DevOps environment where your team owns the delivery of your project, you can agree to make the investment to move to Docker for production.

For larger projects or larger teams, you'll need to engage with other stakeholders to take your PoC further. The type of conversations you have will depend on the structure of your organization, but there are some themes that focus on the improvements you get with Docker:

- The operations team often has friction in the handover from development when it's time to deploy the application. The Docker artifacts, Dockerfiles and Docker Compose files, are a central point where dev and ops can work together. There's no risk that the ops team will be given an upgrade they can't deploy because the upgrade will be a Docker image that's already been tried and tested.
- The security team in large companies often has to demonstrate provenance. They need to prove that the software running in production hasn't been tampered with and is actually running the code that's in SCM. This may be process-driven right now, but with image signing and Docker content trust, it can be explicitly proven. In some cases, security also need to demonstrate that a system will run only on certified hardware, and that's easy to do with secure labels and constraints in a Docker swarm.
- Product owners are often trying to balance large backlogs against long release schedules. Enterprise .NET projects are typically difficult to deploy - the upgrade process is slow, manual, and risky. There's a deployment phase and then a user testing phase, during which the application is offline to normal users. In contrast, deployments with Docker are fast, automated, and safe, which means you can deploy more frequently, adding features when they're ready instead of waiting months for the next scheduled release.
- The management team will have a focus on the product and the cost of running the product. Docker helps reduce infrastructure costs through more efficient use of compute resources. It helps reduce project costs by letting the team work more efficiently, removing the gaps between environments so deployments are consistent. It also helps increase product quality, as automated packaging and rolling updates mean you can deploy more often, adding features and fixing defects more quickly.

You can get started with Docker by running the **Community Edition (CE)** for your PoC, which you get with Docker for Windows on Windows 10 . Other stakeholders in your organization will want to understand the support available for applications running in containers. With Docker **Enterprise Edition** (EE) Basic, included in the Windows Server 2016 license cost, you have support from Microsoft and Docker, Inc. Operations and security teams may see a lot of benefit in Docker EE Advanced, which also gives you **Universal Control Plane (UCP)** and **Docker Trusted Registry (DTR)**.

The Dockerfiles and Docker images from your PoC will work in the same way on all these versions. Docker CE, Docker EE, and Docker EE Advanced all share the same underlying platform.

Case studies for implementing Docker

I'm going to finish by looking at three real-life case studies, where I have brought Docker into existing solutions or prepared a roadmap to bring Docker into a project. These are production scenarios, ranging from a small company project with tens of users to a large enterprise project with over a million users.

Case study 1 - an in-house WebForms app

Some years ago, I took on the support of a WebForms app for a vehicle hire company. The app was used by a team of about 30, and it was a small-scale deployment, they had one server hosting the database and one server running the web app. Although small, it was the core application for the business, and everything they did ran from this app.

The app had a very simple architecture: just one web application and a SQL Server database. Initially, I did a lot of work to improve the performance and quality of the application. After that, it became a caretaker role, where I would manage two or three releases a year, adding new features or fixing old bugs.

These releases were always more difficult and time consuming than they needed to be. The release usually consisted of:

- A Web Deploy package with the updated application
- A set of SQL scripts with schema and data changes
- A manual testing guide to verify the new features and check for regressions

The deployment was done outside office hours in order to give us a window of time to fix any problems we found. I would **Remote Desktop (RDP)** into their servers, copy the artifacts, and manually run the WebDeploy package and the SQL scripts. It was usually months between releases, so I'd rely on the documentation that I'd written to remind me of the steps. Then, I'd walk through the testing guide and check the main features. Sometimes, there were problems because I was missing a SQL script or a dependency for the web application, and I'd need to try and track down an issue I hadn't seen earlier.

Until recently, the application was running on Windows Server 2003. When the company wanted to upgrade Windows, I recommended the move to Windows Server 2016 Core and Docker. My suggestion was to use Docker to run the web application and leave SQL Server running natively on its own server, but use Docker as a distribution mechanism to deploy database upgrades.

The move to Docker was very simple. I used Image2Docker against the production server to produce an initial Dockerfile, and then I iterated on that by adding a health check and environment variables for configuration. I already had a SQL Server project in Visual Studio for the schema, so I added another Dockerfile to package the Dacpac with a deployment script for the database. It took only two days to finalize the Docker artifacts and have the new version running in a test environment. This was the architecture with Docker:

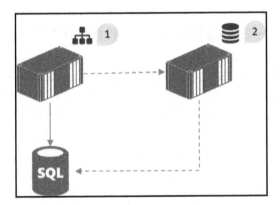

- **1**: The web application runs in a Windows Docker container. In production, it connects to a separate SQL Server instance. In non-production environments, it connects to a local SQL Server instance running in a container.
- **2**: The database is packaged into a Docker image based on SQL Server Express and deployed with the database schema in a Dacpac. In production, a task container is run from the image to deploy the schema to the existing database. In non-production environments, a background container is run to host the database.

Since then, deployments have been straightforward, and they always follow the same steps. We have a set of private repositories on Docker Cloud, where the versioned application and database images are stored. I configure my local Docker CLI to work against their Docker engine, and then I do the following:

- Stop the web application container
- Run a container from the new database image to upgrade SQL Server
- Use Docker Compose to update the web application to the new image

The biggest benefits from moving to Docker have been fast and reliable releases and reduced infrastructure requirements. The company is currently looking at replacing their current web server with two smaller servers, so they can run Docker in swarm mode and have zero downtime upgrades.

An additional benefit is the simplicity of the release process. Because the deployment is already tried and tested, using the same Docker images that are going to be used in production, there's no need to have someone who understands the app available to track down issues. The company's IT support folks do the releases now, and they can do that without my help.

Case study 2 - a database integration service

I worked on a big, complex web application for a financial company. It was an internal-facing app that managed very large volumes of trades. The frontend was in ASP.NET MVC, but most of the logic was in the service tier, written in WCF. The service tier was also a facade over many third-party apps, isolating the integration logic in the WCF layer.

Most of the third-party apps had XML web services or JSON REST APIs we could consume, but one of the older apps had no integration options. We used it only for reference data, so the facade was implemented as a database-level integration. The WCF service exposed nicely encapsulated endpoints, but the implementation connected directly to the external application database to provide the data.

Database integration is brittle because you have to rely on a private database schema instead of a public service contract, but sometimes there are no other options. In this case, the schema changed infrequently, and we could manage the disruption. Unfortunately, the release process was back-to-front. The Ops team would release new versions of database in production first because the app had support from the vendor in production only. When it was all working, they would replicate the release in the dev and test environments.

One release had a database schema change that broke our integration. Any features that used the reference data from the third-party app stopped working, and we had to get a fix out as quickly as possible. The fix was straightforward, but the WCF app was a large monolith and it needed a lot of regression testing before we could be confident this change didn't impact other areas. I was tasked with looking at Docker as a better way of managing the database dependency.

The proposal was straightforward. I didn't recommend moving the whole app to Docker - that was already on a longer-term roadmap - but just moving one service into Docker. The WCF endpoint for that the database app facade would run in Docker, isolated from the rest of the application. The web application was the only consumer of the service, so it would just be a case of changing the URL for the service in the consumer. The proposed architecture looked like this:

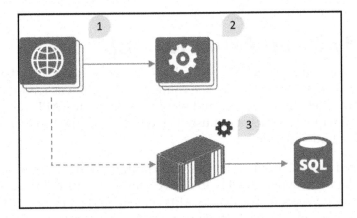

- **1**: The web application runs in IIS. The code is unchanged, but the configuration is updated to use the URL for the new integration component, running in a container
- **2**: The original WCF services continue to run in IIS but with the previous database integration component removed
- **3**: The new integration component uses the same WCF contract as earlier, but now it is hosted in a container, isolating access to the third-party application database

This approach has a lot of benefits:

- If the database schema changes, we only need to change the Dockerized service
- Service changes can be released without a full application release just by updating the Docker image
- It is a sandboxed introduction to Docker, so the dev and Ops teams can use it for evaluation

In this case, the most important benefit was the reduced amount of testing effort. For the full monolithic app, a release needs several weeks of testing. By breaking out the services into Docker containers, only the services that have changed need testing for the release. This drastically reduces the amount of time and effort, which allows more frequent releases, getting new features out to the business more quickly.

Case study 3 - an Azure IoT app

I was the API architect on a project delivering backend services consumed by a mobile application. There were two main APIs. The configuration API was read-only, the devices called it to check for updates to settings and software. The events API was write-only, the devices posted anonymous events about user behavior, which the product team used to design the next generation of devices.

The APIs supported over 1.5 million devices. The configuration APIs needed high availability; they had to respond quickly to device calls and scale to thousands of concurrent requests per second. The events APIs consumed data from the devices and pushed events to a message queue. Listening on the queue were two sets of handlers, one that stored all event data in Hadoop, for long-term analysis, and one that stored a subset of events to provide real-time dashboards.

All the components ran in Azure, and at the peak of the project, we were using cloud services, Event Hubs, SQL Azure, and HDInsight. The architecture looked like this:

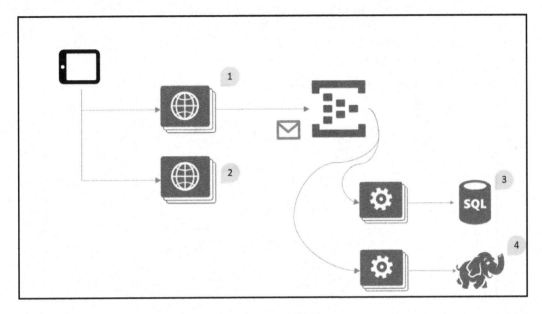

- **1**: The events API, hosted in a cloud service with multiple instances. Devices post events to the API, which does some preprocessing and posts them in batches to an Azure Event Hub.
- **2**: The Configuration API, also hosted in a Cloud Service with multiple instances. Devices connect to the API to check software updates and configuration settings.
- **3**: Real-time analytics data, used for a subset of key performance indicators. Stored in SQL Azure for fast access, as these are modest quantities of data.
- **4**: Batch analytics data, storing all the events posted by all devices. Stored in HDInsight, the managed Hadoop service on Azure for long-running Big Data queries.

This system was expensive to run, but it gave the product team a lot of information on how the devices were used, which they fed into the design process for the next generation. Everyone was happy, but then the product roadmap was canceled and there weren't going to be any more devices, so we had to cut running costs.

I had the job of reducing the Azure bill from $50K per month to under $1K per month. I could lose some of the reporting features, but the events API and configuration API had to stay highly available.

This happened before Docker was available on Windows, so my first revision of the architecture used Linux containers running on a Docker swarm in Azure. I replaced the analytics side of the system with Elasticsearch and Kibana and replaced the configuration API with static content served from Nginx. I left the custom .NET components running in cloud services for the events API feeding Azure Event Hubs with device data and the message handler pushing data to Elasticsearch:

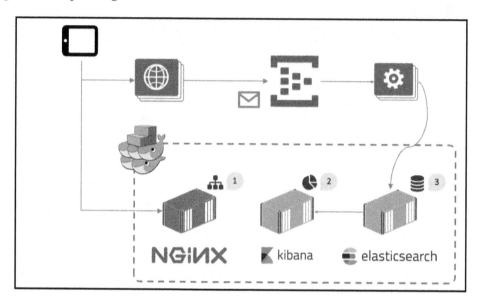

- **1**: The Configuration API, now running as a static website in Nginx. Configuration data is served as JSON payloads, maintaining the original API contract.
- **2**: Kibana used for real-time and historical analytics. By reducing the amount of data stored, we reduced the data storage requirements significantly, at the cost of losing detailed metrics
- **3**: Elasticsearch used to store incoming event data. A .NET Cloud service is still used to read from Event Hubs, but this version saves data in Elasticsearch

This first revision gave us the cost savings we needed, mainly by reducing the number of nodes needed for the APIs and the amount of data we stored from the devices. Instead of storing everything in Hadoop and real-time data in SQL Azure, I centralized on Elasticsearch and stored just a small subset of the data. Using Nginx to serve the configuration APIs, we lost the user-friendly feature the product team had in order to publish configuration updates, but we could run with far smaller compute resources.

I oversaw a second revision, when Windows Server 2016 launched and Docker on Windows was supported. I added Windows nodes to the existing Linux nodes in the Docker swarm and migrated the events API and message handlers over to Windows Docker containers. At this time, I also moved the messaging system over to NATS, running in a Linux container:

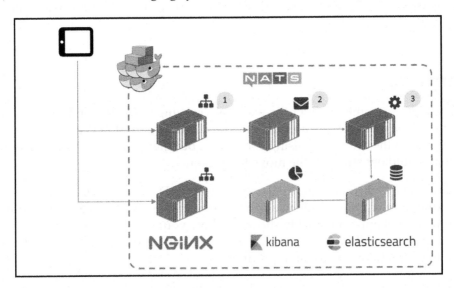

- **1**: The Events API is now hosted in a Docker container, the code hasn't changed; this is still an ASP.NET web API project, running in a Windows container.
- **2**: The messaging component is using NATS instead of Event Hubs. We lose the ability to store and reprocess messages, but the message queue now has the same availability as the Events API.
- **3**: The message handler reads from nats and saves data in Elasticsearch. The majority of the code is unchanged, but it now runs as a .NET console app in a Windows container.

This second revision further reduced costs and complexity:

- Every component is now running in Docker, so I can replicate the whole system in development
- All components are built with Dockerfiles and packaged as Docker images, so everything uses the same artifacts
- The whole solution has the same level of service, running efficiently on a single Docker swarm

In this case, the project is destined to wind down, and it will be easy to accommodate that with the new solution. Device usage is still recorded and shown with a Kibana dashboard. As fewer devices are used over time, the services need less compute, and we can remove nodes from the swarm. Ultimately, the project will run on minimal infrastructure, possibly just a two-node swarm, running on small VMs in Azure or it could move back into the company's data center.

Summary

Large and small companies all over the world are moving to Docker on Windows and Linux. Some of the main drivers are efficiency, security, and portability. Many new projects are designed from the ground up using containers, but there are many more existing projects that would benefit from the move to Docker.

In this chapter I've looked at migrating existing apps to Docker on Windows, recommending that you start with an application you know well. A short, time-boxed PoC for Dockerizing that app will quickly show you how your app looks in Docker. The outcome of that PoC will help you understand what you need to do next and who you need to involve to get that PoC moved into production.

I finished with some very different cases studies, showing you how you can introduce Docker in existing projects. In one case, I used Docker primarily for the packaging benefits in order to run a monolithic app without changing it, but to power clean upgrades for future releases. In another case, I took one component from a monolithic app and extracted it to run in a container, in order to reduce the testing burden for releases. And in the last case, I completely migrated an existing solution to Docker, making it cheaper to run, easier to maintain, and giving me the option to run it anywhere.

I hope this chapter has helped you think about how you can introduce Docker into your own projects, and I hope the rest of the book has shown you what you can do with Docker and why it's such an exciting technology. Thanks for reading, make sure to follow me on Twitter, and good luck in your journey with Docker on Windows.

Index

Lightning Source UK Ltd.
Milton Keynes UK
UKOW05f1803200917
309572UK00003B/11/P